Happiest YOU EVER

365 WAYS TO INVITE MORE

Love, Sex, Fun, Friendship, Fellowship, Community, and Career Satisfaction Into Your Life—EACH AND EVERY DAY!

Meera Lester, Carolyn Dean, MD, ND, and Susan B. Townsend

Aadamsmedia

Avon, Massachusetts

Published by Adams Media,
a division of F+W Media, Inc.
57 Littlefield Street,
Avon, MA 02322. U.S.A.
www.adamsmedia.com

Contains material adapted and abridged from *365 Ways to Look—and Feel—Younger*, by Meera Lester and Carolyn Dean, copyright © 2010 by F+W Media Inc., ISBN 10: 1-4405-0222-6, ISBN 13: 978-1-4405-0222-4; *The Everything® Guide to Chakra Healing*, by Heidi Spear, copyright © 2011 by F+W Media, Inc., ISBN 10: 1-4405-2584-6, ISBN 13: 978-1-4405-2584-1; *The Everything® Guide to Meditation for Healthy Living with CD*, by David B. Dillard-Wright and Ravinder Jerath, copyright © 2011 by F+W Media, Inc., ISBN 10: 1-4405-1088-1, ISBN 13: 978-1-4405-1088-5; *The Everything® Guide to Stress Management with CD*, by Melissa Roberts, copyright © 2011 by F+W Media, Inc., ISBN 10: 1-4405-1087-3, ISBN 13: 978-1-4405-1087-8; *365 Ways to Live Happy: Simple Ways to Find Joy Every Day* by Meera Lester, copyright © 2010 by F+W Media, Inc., ISBN 10: 1-6055-0028-3, ISBN 13: 978-1-6055-0028-7; *The Marriage Devotional: 365 Simple Ways to Celebrate Your Love* by Meera Lester, copyright © 2010 by F+W Media, Inc., ISBN 10: 1-4405-0224-2, ISBN 13: 978-1-4405-0224-8; *1001 Ways to Do Good* by Meera Lester, copyright © 2008 by F+W Media, ISBN 10: 1-5986-9474-X, ISBN 13: 978-1-5986-9474-1; *The Everything® Law of Attraction Book* by Meera Lester, copyright © 2008 by F+W Media, Inc., ISBN 10: 1-5986-9775-7, ISBN 13: 978-1-5986-9775-9; *Yes, We Can! 365 Ways to Make America a Better Place* by Paula Munier, copyright © 2009 by F+W Media, Inc., ISBN 10: 1-4405-0055-X, ISBN 13: 978-1-4405-0055-8; *The Everything® Great Sex Book* by Suzie Huemann and Susan Campbell, MD, copyright © 2004 by F+W Media, Inc., ISBN 10: 1-5806-2739-0; *The Everything® Easy Fitness Book, 2nd Edition* by Donna Raskin, copyright © 2007 by F+W Media, Inc., ISBN 10: 1-5936-7699-5; *The Everything® Get-a-Job Book, 2nd Edition* by Dawn Rosenberg McKay, copyright © 2007 by F+W Media, Inc., ISBN 10: 1-5986-9159-7; ISBN 13: 978-1-5986-9159-7; *The Everything® Dating Book, 2nd Edition* by Alison Blackman Dunham, copyright © 2006 by F+W Media, Inc., ISBN 10: 1-5933-7372-4; ISBN 13: 978-1-5933-7372-6; *The Everything® Guide to a Happy Marriage* by Stephen Martin, MFT and Victoria Costello, copyright © 2009 by F+W Media, Inc., ISBN 10: 1-6055-0134-4, ISBN 13: 978-1-6055-0134-5; *The Everything® Self-Esteem Book* by Robert M. Sherfield, copyright © 2004 by F+W Media, Inc., ISBN 10: 1-5806-2976-8, ISBN 13: 978-15806-2976-8; *The Everything® Personal Finance Book* by Peter J. Sander, MBA, copyright © 2003 by F+W Media, Inc., ISBN 10: 1-5806-2810-9, ISBN 13: 978-1-5806-2810-5, and *The Everything® Investing Book, 3rd Edition* by Michele Cagan, CPA, copyright © 2009 by F+W Media, Inc., ISBN 10: 1-5986-9829-X, ISBN 13: 978-1-5986-9829-9.

ISBN 10: 1-4405-3055-6
ISBN 13: 978-1-4405-3055-5
eISBN 10: 1-4405-3179-X
eISBN 13: 978-1-4405-3179-8

Printed in the United States of America.

10 9 8 7 6 5 4 3 2 1

Library of Congress Cataloging-in-Publication Data
is available from the publisher.

This book is available at quantity discounts for bulk purchases.
For information, please call 1-800-289-0963.

For my father and mother, Robert and Barbara Armstrong,
who taught me to find joy in the little things.

ACKNOWLEDGMENTS

I'd like to thank Paula Munier for her continued support and encouragement and for giving me this great project. I am very grateful to Jennifer Lawler for her thoughtful expertise and, as always, I would like to thank Matt Glazier for being helpful, patient, and a very good listener.

Finally, I would like to thank everyone at Adams Media who worked so hard to make this book possible.

INTRODUCTION

You probably picked up this book because you'd like to be happier in your life, but aren't sure exactly how to accomplish that. Unlike making cookies or learning to dance, you can't just follow a set of instructions and then expect to live happily ever after. As Eleanor Roosevelt said, "Happiness is not a goal; it is a by-product." What she meant is that you find happiness by doing things and being with people who make you happy, not by chasing after an ephemeral emotional state.

In the mid-'90s, there were 100 studies on sadness for every one study on happiness. The rapidly growing positive psychology movement has been quickly closing that gap, and studies by experts like University of Pennsylvania psychologist Martin E. P. Seligman, author of the book *Authentic Happiness,* are beginning to give us a clearer picture of why some people are happier than others. The leaders in the field have determined that the happiest people spend time in fulfilling relationships, they seek personal growth and intimacy, and they are engaged in absorbing activities—both recreational and career-related. They also possess characteristics associated with a rewarding spiritual life such as altruism, gratitude, and acceptance.

Since the 1930s, researchers in the Grant Study at Harvard have been following 268 men, trying to determine if there is a formula of some kind for a good life. Depression turned out to be a major drain on physical health. More broadly, pessimists seemed to suffer physically in comparison with optimists, perhaps because they're less likely to connect with others or care for themselves. Healthy behaviors cited in the study include selflessness, creativity, and successful relationships, while some of the negative behaviors include withdrawal, aggression, and isolation.

In short, the study demonstrated that happiness seems to be strongly connected to playing, working, and loving.

By focusing on strengthening seven key elements in your life, you will become a happier person. *Happiest You Ever* is structured in such a way that every week you'll spend time working on each of the seven elements. It contains a whole year of tips, tricks, and tried-and-true tactics covering every aspect of your life. Every week, you'll see how developing and implementing life skills in different areas of your life can bring you the happiness you've been craving.

- On Mondays, you'll examine your career.
- On Tuesdays, you'll concentrate on making a strong connection to your community.
- On Wednesdays, you'll focus on the friendships in your life.
- On Thursdays, you'll create greater satisfaction in your love life.
- On Fridays, you'll spend time with your family.
- On Saturday, you'll devote time to rest and relaxation, including outside hobbies and interests.
- On Sundays, you'll explore spirituality and fellowship.

This approach helps you create happiness in all areas of your life; no part is neglected. That doesn't mean you'll never be sad or deal with roadblocks again. It does mean that you will find ways to work through the challenges, with an increase of happiness as an added bonus. Take a year-long journey of happiness, and if you happen to bring some joy to others along the way, so much the better!

"When I grow up I want to be a little boy."

—Joseph Heller

Put Your Inner Child to Work

As you've grown older, you may have forgotten what it was like to be a child. In your struggle and determination to be mature and self-reliant, you may have locked yourself into a rigid way of thinking. This mindset precludes the "anything is possible" outlook found in children that allows them to explore the world around them with such wonder and joy. When you were a child, you probably had plenty of ideas about the kind of work you wanted to do and would enjoy doing and would be good at. Instead of dismissing those ideas as impractical or silly, consider that the younger you may have had some insight that the older you could use!

ASKING YOUR INNER CHILD FOR HELP

If you're currently unhappy or unfulfilled in your work situation, perhaps it's time to return to a child-like state of mind in which the sky is the limit. No one is saying you have to quit your job tomorrow, but allow yourself to explore the dreams you held as a child and ask yourself some important questions.

- What is it I really wanted to do with my life?
- What are the steps I would need to take?
- What is holding me back?

"Sure I'm for helping the elderly. I'm going to be old myself some day."

—Lillian Carter

Help Your Elderly Neighbor

The city has been suffering through a record snowfall, and one night, it occurs to you that you haven't seen your elderly neighbor for a couple of days. Chances are she's just fine, but there's also a possibility that she might need assistance. Even if you've only exchanged pleasantries, you shouldn't let that prevent you from dropping by.

Don't wait for the dramatic scenario above to connect with an older neighbor. Maybe you can perform a few simple errands or help around the house. Then again, she may just want someone to talk to. You won't know until you take the first step. That first step could very well take you on a journey full of rich rewards. You'll get a "helper's high" from all those endorphins. You'll decrease the sense of isolation—so prevalent in today's society—for both you and your neighbor. And you'll also be helping to build a stronger community.

LEND A HAND

Here are a few ways you can help out your neighbors—elderly, physically challenged, or otherwise:

- Be mindful of parking spots, particularly when you're entertaining and there are an influx of cars in the neighborhood.
- On trash day, volunteer to take your neighbors' garbage cans into their garage.
- Shovel, snow-blow, or salt your neighbor's driveway during and after a storm.
- Bring over a meal that can be defrosted and reheated if you know a neighbor's family member is ill. If you feel they're receptive and in need of company, offer to enjoy the meal with them.

"A true friend is someone who thinks that you are a good egg even though he knows that you are slightly cracked."

—Bernard Meltzer

Make Happy Friends

According to a study by James Fowler of the University of California—San Diego and Nicholas Christakis of Harvard University, each happy friend you have increases your happiness by an average of 9 percent, while each unhappy friend can decrease it by 7 percent. That's probably no surprise—we've all experienced having a good mood punctured by a negative friend. Cultivating friendships with people who are generally happy will have a measurable impact on your own happiness.

STAND BY YOUR FRIENDS

1. Of course, this doesn't mean you should abandon your friends when they're unhappy. If you know your best friend is signing her divorce papers on Friday afternoon, why not make plans to take her to dinner and a movie that evening? Those are the moments when she's going to need you the most. It's a situation like that that can test a friendship to its fullest.

2. The relationships that make it through are the ones we know are meant to last the rest of our lives. Hardships and trials can provide a wonderful opportunity for growth between two people. Standing by the people close to you and helping them work through their problems can increase their happiness and your own. It's a win-win situation for everyone.

"Somewhere there's someone who dreams of your smile
And finds in your presence that life is worthwhile
So when you are lonely, remember it's true:
Somebody, somewhere is thinking of you."

—Unknown

Define Your "A" List

If you want to find the right partner—and since being in a committed relationship is a factor in achieving happiness—it helps to have a sense of what you're looking for. Imagine your ideal partner. What qualities are most important to you? Consider things like kindness, confidence, empathy, good manners, fidelity, charisma, and, yes, even appearance. If you already have someone in your life, this list can be a great way of reminding yourself what attracted you to your partner in the first place. It's important to remember what makes that person so special to you.

PUT IT IN WRITING

1. Once you've imagined all the qualities you want in an ideal partner, whittle down your list to only the most crucial qualities, without which that person wouldn't make a good fit for you. Write these qualities down. This is your "A" list. As you decide which characteristics are mandatory, make a "B" list with the qualities you'd like your ideal partner to have but that aren't absolutely necessary to your happiness.

2. Next, for each of those "A" list qualities, write down precisely what you mean. If a sense of humor is important to you, what kind of humor—sarcasm or slapstick; clean jokes or racy ones? Where does your idea of confidence end and arrogance begin? Is it possible for someone to have so much charisma that he won't give you an equal share of his time? In other words, define your terms. Though the partner you eventually choose may not have every quality on your "A" list, having a clear idea of what you're looking for can help you make a good selection.

"The whole family can begin with the end in mind,
a common purpose, a common vision."

—Stephen Covey

Create a Mission Statement

To bring your family together with a common goal and give everyone a feeling of purpose and belonging, all you'll need is a pen and some paper. If you have a dry-erase board and some markers, that's even better. Gather everyone in the family together and explain that you're going to create a mission statement—a written declaration that expresses the intentions, purpose, and priorities of the family.

Ask each person to suggest words to describe your family. What kind of behavior is acceptable and unacceptable in your home? What are your family's goals? What are your priorities? For example, "The Turner family treats each other with respect." Agree on the mission statement, then print it out, have everyone sign it, and post it prominently. Revise as your family grows.

DARE TO DREAM: WRITE A FAMILY VISION STATEMENT

If your family enjoyed creating a mission statement, they'll probably benefit from making a vision statement. Your mission statement answered the question, "Why does our family exist?" Your vision statement will look into the future and answer the questions, "Where will our family be in five years? What will we have accomplished?" Follow the same format that you did for creating your mission statement, and use the following formula to write your vision statement: "Five years from now, our family will _____ by _____."

"I have a farm and I love it there. There's really nothing to do, but even watching the chickens, it's fun."

—Salma Hayek

Visit a Farm

You don't have to spend a month in the wilderness to get back to nature. Even a day trip to a local farm can put you back in touch with the good bounty of Mother Nature. Many farms are now offering tours of their facilities and a chance to buy the fruits of their labors. From fresh black-berries in the summer to crisp apples in the fall, you can spend some delicious time outside indulging in fresh produce—and still have lots to take home with you.

1. Have you ever wondered where the cream in your coffee comes from? Or stared at the eggs in the grocery store and wished you could try one straight from the farm? Or just hankered from some down-home homemade ice cream? Try visiting a dairy farm.
2. Many of the foods you enjoy daily can be traced to their source within an hour's drive, providing you with better nutrition, new insight, immense enjoyment, and wonderful stories to share with your friends. With a little imagination, you can find the perfect break from your mind-numbing routine and return to work as fresh as the lettuce you brought home.

KEEP CHICKENS

Many Americans—from the Kardashians to city dwellers—are keeping chickens. In fact, the commercial hatcheries that supply baby chicks report a 7 percent increase in business since the recession. Whether you raise chickens for the fresh eggs for your own breakfast, or for sale to your neighbors, or both, keeping chickens is an increasingly popular way to put food on the American table.

*"A habit of devout fellowship with God is the spring
of all our life, and the strength of it."*

—Henry Edward Manning

Connect to Your Creator

If you wake up Sunday morning, eager to attend your regular religious services, but you can't go because of work commitments or another problem, such as a car that won't start, you can still cultivate a sense of fellowship in your life. Even though you're not going to spend Sunday with your fellow believers, you're not going to be on your own.

You'll have abundant opportunities throughout the day to renew your spiritual side by renewing your connection to your Creator. Focus on appreciation and humility throughout the day, and you will begin to realize that it's the same feeling you often experience at the religious services you missed that morning. You can never replace the fellowship you enjoy on Sunday mornings with your friends and loved ones, but you can always take some time to strengthen your connection to your Creator.

GREET THE MORNING

Before you reach for your phone to check your e-mail and messages, take a few minutes to breathe and enjoy the morning.

1. Take some time to relax, breathe deeply, and let the beautiful morning envelop you.
2. Can you hear any birds singing? Is your loved one lying peacefully next to you? Feel gratitude for those things.
3. As the day goes on, remember to pause and repeat the process of breathing and expressing gratitude for the world in which you live.

"I claim Dickens as a mentor. He's my teacher.
He's one of my driving forces."

—Anne Rice

Choose a Mentor

Whether you work for yourself or for a large corporation, choosing a mentor is something you should consider. A mentor can be a valuable source of wisdom and experience and provide you with opportunities to network with other individuals in your field. Pick someone you respect and ask her to mentor you. Check with your HR department and see if the company has formal mentoring available, and if you are self-employed, look for a successful, experienced person in your field. Most people will be pleased and flattered to pass along advice or act as a sounding board with ideas you have. But if someone declines your request, have a backup list ready so you can ask someone else.

MEET YOUR MENTOR

1. Make arrangements to meet with your new mentor for the first time. Remember to establish ground rules that will create a valuable and enjoyable relationship for both of you. Make sure that both of you agree to and understand the limits in terms of time, contact, and extent of personal involvement.

2. Create a schedule for regular meetings, which will require setting an hour or so aside each week.

3. If it makes either of you more comfortable, you might want to put these details in writing.

4. If your business relationship leads to a discovery of common interests, you might want to take your affiliation "outside the office." For example, you might both enjoy football or French cooking. And remember that all successful relationships work both ways. Your mentor may be more experienced and successful than you are, but he or she still needs support, encouragement, and someone to listen just like everyone else.

WEEK TWO

"The best path through life is the highway."

—Henri Frédéric Amiel

Adopt a Highway

Connecting with your community can increase your happiness. One way to care about your community is to help clean it up! Have you ever noticed a stretch of road that struck you as particularly beautiful? It probably looks that way because a group of dedicated volunteers has chosen to adopt it and made a commitment to keep it clean. You probably know a piece of road that deserves equal attention. This is your opportunity to do your part and get others involved as well.

The benefits are not just limited to a cleaner highway for everyone to enjoy. If so desired, your group of volunteers can create their own identity with a name and logo, which can be placed on a highway sign for the world to see.

GETTING STARTED

First, you'll need a group of like-minded people. Consider asking members of a hobby group you belong to, your church, or your neighborhood association.

1. Then contact the "Adopt a Highway" coordinator at your state's department of transportation.
2. Most of the equipment will be provided for you, and you'll even be instructed in safety procedures.
3. You'll be asked to adopt a stretch of highway for a predetermined length of time and agree to pick up trash three to four times a year.

"It is the friends you can call up at 4 A.M. that matter."

—Marlene Dietrich

Phone a Friend

With all the social networking tools available today, personal phone calls appear to have become a thing of the past. Perhaps we believe we just don't have the time for polite conversation. No matter how busy we are, we should always make time for the things in life that are important to us.

Make a list of the most important people in your life. This list could include persons from your past with whom you've lost touch, but it could also include people you see every day, but never have the time for more than a "hello." Set aside ten minutes each day and call one person on the list until you've phoned everyone.

MAKE A PHONE CALL COMMITMENT

1. Why not make a commitment to call one or two friends or family members each and every day? There doesn't need to be any purpose for the call. People we care about are always pleased to hear from us, even if there isn't anything pressing to talk about. It's always nice to hear a friendly voice on the phone. It lets us know the people we care about are thinking of us, too!

2. The calls may seem awkward at first. After all, you're probably out of the habit of "just talking" without a goal in mind. You may want to keep the calls short to begin with. Perhaps start by saying, "I was just thinking of you and I thought I'd call to see how you are." Before long, you'll be looking forward to those calls as a needed distraction from your busy day.

"I love thee to the depth and breadth and height my soul can reach."

—Elizabeth Barrett Browning

Leave a Note under Your Lover's Pillow

Write your significant other a love note and tuck it under his or her pillow. Even if you're not around when your partner finds your love letter, rest assured you'll have made your partner's day.

If your partner is traveling out of town, sneak an "I love you" or "I miss you" note into his or her suitcase. When your lover discovers your little gift while unpacking, it will make him or her feel loved and excited to get back home to see you!

DO YOUR RESEARCH

Make your love note special by going beyond "I love you."

- Make a list of your partner's qualities that you love the most.
- Include a snapshot of the two of you doing something fun or meaningful.
- Research love poetry (like the Browning quote above) and share it with your partner.

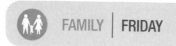 FAMILY | FRIDAY

"In the childhood memories of every good cook, there's a large kitchen, a warm stove, a simmering pot and a mom."

—Barbara Costikyan

Cooking with the Kids

If you have children, your kitchen is probably the busiest room in the house, especially if you're trying to prepare a meal. There's nothing kids like better than to gather around the counter or the table, asking for a taste, wanting to help, and peppering you with questions. Why not encourage and nurture their interest and cook something with them?

Make sure your project is age-appropriate; the child's safety should be your first priority. For very small children, making a simple salad might be a good choice. For older children, pick one of their favorites— perhaps spaghetti. As you and your kids grow more confident in your skills, you can move on to more complicated and varied recipes. But remember, this project isn't about the menu. It's about instilling confidence in your child and spending time together.

SPREAD THE LOVE

1. Your children will probably enjoy sharing the fruits of their labors by sharing the results with friends, family, even teachers at school. You can encourage their love of cooking by letting them hear compliments from others.

2. Perhaps you can even find an old family recipe to share with friends and your community. Write up the recipe on cards and include it with a gift of food.

3. And if you don't have children of your own, don't hesitate to "borrow" a child and began to build skills that will last him or her a lifetime.

"I think cinema, movies, and magic have always been closely associated. The very earliest people who made film were magicians."

—Francis Ford Coppola

Watch a Movie

Most of us love to go to the movies. If you're one who does, it's probably something you plan for in advance. You may go online, check show times, read the reviews, and phone your friends to find company for your outing. There's something to be said for just going by impulse—heading to a movie theater and deciding then and there to check out a particular movie you've been wanting to see.

GO SOLO

1. It's nice to have a companion, but that doesn't have to be a deal-breaker. There can be something refreshing about taking in a movie alone on the spur of the moment. You don't have to make a regular routine of it, but you might be surprised by how relaxing it can be to sit back and take pleasure in a movie on your own. You just might want to do it again someday. There are certain activities we associate with a group of friends or family, but some of them can work beautifully as a means of solo relaxation.

2. You probably have a mental list of numerous activities you'd like to try or like to do again if given the chance. Perhaps you haven't found the time, but maybe you haven't pursued these pastimes because you didn't have a companion. There's no reason you can't do many, if not all, of the items on your list by yourself. Make a written activity wish list and promise yourself to do at least one thing a week, even if it's on your own.

"Just as a candle cannot burn without fire, men cannot live without a spiritual life."

—Buddha

Take a Sacred Labyrinth Walk

The purpose of a labyrinth walk is to provide an opportunity for you to clear your mind by focusing on a single task. You start at one point in the labyrinth and walk until you reach the center.

This practice has been in use for thousands of years and is meant to give people a way to reach their own spiritual center. Walking the labyrinth can mean any number of things to any number of individuals. It's not specifically associated with any particular denomination of faith.

START YOUR SPIRITUAL WALK

The walk exists as a way for you to do away with the distractions that run through your everyday life. You simply have to open your mind to the possibility of what walking a labyrinth can do for you, but you must want to find your spiritual center. A labyrinth walk can be a perfect place to start on such a journey.

- It's okay if you've never heard of a sacred labyrinth walk or what it might entail. One website, *www.sacredwalk.com,* offers a basic description and links to literature, and it's probably your best place to start.
- When it comes to finding a labyrinth walk in your area, Google is the way to go. It should be able to point you in the direction of one nearest to you.

*"Obstacles are those frightful things you see
when you take your eyes off your goal."*

—Henry Ford

Keep Your Eyes on the Prize

What is your ultimate career goal? Once you figure out your goal and why you want to achieve it, then it will be much easier to determine your role or purpose in the business world. Do you want to earn a lot of money, be the CEO of a company, own your own business, or travel around the world during your career? Once you've discovered the answer, you need to follow up with some even more important questions. Why do you want to make a lot of money? Is it to support your family, is it so that you no longer have to work? Why do you want to travel, or better yet, why wouldn't you want to travel in your career?

PICTURE SUCCESS

Once you've decided on your ultimate career goal, put it on paper—as pictures, not words.

1. Find a visual symbol of your ultimate goal. If your goal is to travel extensively while working, you could either find a picture from a magazine such as *National Geographic Travel* or a scenic postcard from a place you've always wanted to see. If your dream is to be the president of a large corporation, choose a company that you admire and respect, and find a picture of their logo or their headquarters.
2. Display your picture or symbol in a location where you can see it often. Make it easy for yourself to keep your eyes on the prize!

WEEK THREE

"One of the greatest things drama can do, at its best, is to redefine the words we use every day such as love, home, family, loyalty and envy. Tragedy need not be a downer."

—Ben Kingsley

Take In a High School Play

It may have been a while since you were in high school, but a lot of things haven't changed very much. Cafeteria food still leaves a lot to be desired, half the lockers are still jammed, and finding a date for the homecoming dance can still be a demoralizing task. One thing that definitely hasn't changed is the fact that high schools often raise money through the production of plays and similar forms of entertainment. They promote their endeavors through the local paper, community bulletin boards, and especially on the large reader board standing in front of the school.

Show your support by attending a high school play. It doesn't have to be Broadway for the show to be a pleasurable one. The kids don't have to be professionally trained Shakespearean actors to give a heartfelt performance. The important thing is that this is their Broadway, and by encouraging their passion, you might be nurturing a future star.

FIND OUT HOW YOU CAN HELP

Phone your local high school and ask about coming events, including talent shows, musical productions, and plays. Ask if you can help with any of the details of putting on the shows.

1. If you have production experience, offer to help coordinate the show. If you're a musician, offer to play the piano for the choir.
2. Promote the event(s) throughout the community in any way you can. Sell tickets, post fliers, e-mail your friends and family.
3. Offer to do the jobs no one really wants to do but that have to be done—collect tickets at the door, show attendees to their seats, clean up afterward.

"The greatest gift we can give one another is rapt attention to one another's existence."

—Sue Atchley Ebaugh

Give Random Gifts

Why should you wait until a birthday or a holiday to get your friend a gift? Sometimes it's nice to be reminded that someone was thinking of you without some kind of reason behind it. A gift for no particular reason can remind your friend that you're just glad to know them. That sentiment can be as powerful as a thoughtful gift on their birthday or during the holidays.

GIFT-GIVING POINTERS

1. The gift doesn't have to be expensive, and it certainly doesn't have to be complicated or elaborate. You might be walking through a store, your mind running in a hundred different directions, when you happen to notice some small item a special friend might like.

2. When you present the gift, make sure your friend understands its intent. You don't want her to think she's suddenly indebted to you in some way. Just tell her it was something that made you think of her, and that you wanted her to have it. Her surprise at being remembered in such a way will be repayment enough, and when she opens her gift, the reward is even greater.

"Make love when you can. It's good for you."

—Kurt Vonnegut Jr.

Sex: It Does a Body Good

If you're doing it right, sex feels amazing. Orgasms release the cuddle hormone oxytocin and feel-good endorphins, which help make you feel happier and emotionally closer to your partner. They also temporarily decrease feelings of pain by more than 50 percent. Oh, and they render the "I have a headache" excuse null and void, because orgasms can actually make your headache or migraine go away.

Having sex can also be a good aerobic workout, depending on how creative you are with your positions and how much you get into it. Even if you aren't having vigorous sex, making love three times or more a week can decrease your chance of a heart attack or stroke by up to 50 percent, improve your ability to sleep, and lessen your chance (if you're a guy) of getting prostate cancer. Plus, you'll live longer! A longevity study by Duke University and another by a British organization revealed a strong correlation between patients who lived a long life and patients who enjoyed sex and had it frequently.

JUST SAY YES

Sex can make you feel wonderful, too! The next time your partner makes advances and you're about to say no because you're cranky, sore, or on your way to the gym, change that no into a yes and see what happens. Making love can lift your mood, ease your aches and pains, and give you the workout you wanted right in your own home!

"Vacation: a period of travel and relaxation when you take twice the clothes and half the money you need."

—Author Unknown

Start a Vacation Jar

You'd like the family's next getaway to be terrific, but you're worried about money. You know the family has to cut back on some expenses, but you're not sure how to go about it. This could be the perfect chance for the entire family to come up with a plan to finance the trip and then stick to it.

Talk to your family about ways each person can contribute to a vacation fund. For Mom and Dad, it might be giving up that daily cappuccino on the way to work. For the teenagers, it could be missing the Saturday night trip to the movies every second week. Put the money in a jar so you can see it accumulate. Not only will your family have the opportunity to work together for a common goal, they may just well have the best vacation ever!

MAKE YOUR OWN FAMILY VACATION JAR

- You can purchase large, decorative jars online, or perhaps you know someone with a large family who has an empty mayonnaise or peanut butter jar you can use.
- Collect some pictures from magazines or travel brochures of places your family wants to visit and decorate your jar.
- Print off some words to describe your vacation—fun, exciting, adventure—and add these to your jar.

"Technology . . . is a queer thing. It brings you great gifts with one hand, and it stabs you in the back with the other."

—C. P. Snow

Shut Off Your Smart Phone

It might be difficult to shut off your smart phone, iPad, computer, and television, but it's not impossible. You can find some time in your day to turn everything off. If you think you can only manage an hour to start, that's fine.

Sooner rather than later you're going to be aware of all that silence. It's not as bad as you might have thought, is it? Look out the window if you're still not sure. The world is most likely still standing in one piece. Avoid turning any of your electronic devices on for at least an hour. If you feel like going for more, then feel free to do so. All you need to do is sit back and stare out the window, stare at the ceiling or even sit on the porch and stare out at the backyard. You can spend some time with a book if you want, but it might be better if you just leave everything behind for a little while. When was the last time you relaxed by literally doing nothing more than being alone with your thoughts? That silence can be intimidating at first, but it can quickly become invaluable.

UNPLUG WITH YOUR MATE

1. Most couples need a respite when their lives feel overwhelmingly full and chaotic. Unplug from as much sensory input as possible. Turn off all the electronics—that includes computers, digital assistants, cell phones, radios, and televisions. You can both let go and empty yourselves of the sensory overload your bodies and minds have accumulated and begin to soak up peace.

2. After a day of unplugging, light candles, which have been used for centuries to beckon peace and to call forth a sense of the sacred. Sit in comfortable chairs and meditate together for a while or just sit and share a glass of wine or sparkling apple cider. Be still and enjoy each other's presence in that moment.

"At every crisis in one's life, it is absolute salvation
to have some sympathetic friend to whom you can
think aloud without restraint or misgiving."

—Woodrow Wilson

Prepare for a Crisis

A crisis is like a sucker punch to the stomach. It comes out of nowhere, knocks you off your feet, and leaves you breathless and baffled. But you don't have to sit back and wait to be overwhelmed by the next crisis that comes your way. Most companies and organizations have a crisis-management plan in place, and you, too, can develop a few techniques to help you feel prepared. Knowing what will get you through the next minute and the minute after that can be as helpful as having an escape plan for the unlikely event that your house catches on fire.

MAKE A CRISIS PLAN

Think about what you would need to be grounded and focused if a crisis were to show up in your life five minutes from now. What could instantly calm you and help you deal with a rise in possibly negative emotions? Would a whiff of sandalwood help? Would fingering your prayer beads work best, or finding a place of absolute silence where you could think and pray?

1. Consider various possible scenarios, such as a medical emergency, a house fire, a flood. What would you need in those situations? For example, would it make sense to start building an emergency fund now to help deal with a crisis? If you keep all of your important documents at home, would it make sense to keep a backup copy somewhere else? Write these steps down.
2. Implement the steps of your plan that you need to do right now, such as arranging to discuss a will with your lawyer.

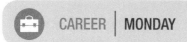

"We spend January 1 walking through our lives, room by room, drawing up a list of work to be done, cracks to be patched. Maybe this year, to balance the list, we ought to walk through the rooms of our lives . . . not looking for flaws, but for potential."

—Ellen Goodman

Make a List (and Check It Twice!)

Perhaps you're someone who already loves to make lists, but if you think lists are useless, then it's time to learn to make one work for you. Use lists to inspire you, to help you remember, and to prevent you from putting things off. If you're feeling overwhelmed, use a list to help you focus your mind and relieve some of that stress.

WHERE TO BEGIN

You can get through anything with an organized, prioritized list—step by step!

1. Start by making a list of all the tasks you need to complete. Don't worry about placing them in any particular order.
2. Go through your list and note your most important tasks. Order everything on it according to priority.
3. If you are faced with a large task, make a list of the steps needed to accomplish the work, and then prioritize these steps as you did with your original list.

"God Almighty first planted a garden. And indeed,
it is the purest of human pleasures."

—Francis Bacon

Build a Community Garden

If you long for the taste of homegrown vegetables, you might want to start a community garden. Long before you are steaming fresh green beans or enjoying corn on the cob, you will have enjoyed the opportunity to work with your neighbors in the fresh air and sunshine, create something beautiful, and build lasting relationships through achieving a common goal.

This can be a daunting task for just one person, so you're going to need an enthusiastic and like-minded group. You can work with friends, neighbors, or a local organization. Prospective gardeners can be found by placing an ad in a local paper, putting a notice up in an online forum or mailing list (don't forget Facebook!) or even visiting a nearby gardening center.

PLAN BEFORE YOU START

1. There are many ways to get started, but you'll need a plan before you dig the first hole. You'll need to address such obvious questions as where to find the land.
2. You'll also need to consider more minor issues like insurance and troubleshooting.
3. Then phone a few friends or neighbors to gauge and generate interest in your project.

"We secure our friends not by accepting favors but by doing them."

—Thucydides

Help Your Friends Take a Break

Of course, you're happy for your friends when they finally get a chance to go on vacation. Most of us tend to work too hard most of the time, and it's rare that we take time for ourselves. Some people can't even manage to get away once a year, so the opportunity should be taken when it comes. You can help your friends by taking a worry or two off their minds. If you know friends who don't have a planned vacation, but still need a well-deserved break, give them a call and offer to take care of things for them if they decide to take that break. Your offer may motivate them to get away for the weekend they need so much.

OFFER HOUSE SITTING OR OTHER NECESSARY SERVICES
Give specific suggestions as to how you can help your friends instead of a generic, "Give me a call if I can do anything for you." Who knows? They might pick up a souvenir for you from wherever they happen to go.

1. Offer to look after your friends' homes while they're away.
2. Perhaps they have a dog or cat that needs to be fed and walked every day. If you offer to take care of that, you might save your friend the trouble of having to find and pay for a kennel.
3. They don't need to have a pet for you to lend a hand. Your help could be in the form of watering their plants, getting their mail, or doing any other small tasks that will allow them to breathe a little easier while they're away.

"Electric-flesh arrows . . . traversing the body. A rainbow of color strikes the eyelids. A foam of music falls over the ears. It is the gong of the orgasm."

—Anaïs Nin

Boost Your Self-Esteem with Orgasms

Even before the scientists step in, it's easy to believe that having orgasms can make you feel good about yourself. Orgasms are intensely pleasurable, and you can't help but be impressed that your body is able to produce such sensations. If you're giving yourself an orgasm, your confidence should feel that much higher.

Beyond that, science shows that having orgasms can actually improve your self-esteem because of the chemicals they release. During orgasm, blood flows into the prefrontal cortex of the right side of the brain. This part of your brain is responsible for decision making and personality expression, and when stimulated by the orgasm, it makes the body feel a profound sense of gratification.

EXPERIENCE THE OTHER BENEFITS OF ORGASM

Gratitude isn't the only benefit of orgasm! You'll feel better after an orgasm for a multitude of reasons.

1. Orgasms also can reduce the effects of depression, because they release endorphins, hormones that improve mood.
2. To top all of that off, the German sex researcher Werner Habermehl believes that the more sex you have, the more intelligent you become, because adrenaline and cortisol are released during lovemaking.
3. So the next time you've got the body image blues or your self-esteem is in a slump, don't reach for the jelly doughnuts or sit there feeling sad. Try having an orgasm—either on your own or with someone you love—and lift your spirits the natural way!

"The other thing is quality of life; if you have a place where you can go and have a picnic with your family, it doesn't matter if it's a recession or not, you can include that in your quality of life."

—Jim Fowler

Pack the Picnic Basket

When's the last time your family went on a picnic? If you can't remember, or if the answer is never, then you're missing out on a wonderful experience that can bring everyone together. Summer is the usual time for picnics, but you can certainly plan one during spring or fall if you keep an eye on the weather report and make sure everyone dresses appropriately.

PLAN THE PERFECT PICNIC

Involve everyone in the family from the start. The first step is to choose a date for your picnic. Then you need to decide where to go. The local park will do just fine, but a simple online search might give you some suggestions for possible locations.

1. Get everyone's input on the menu. You can stick with traditional favorites or indulge your adventurous side and try something new. Find some different picnic recipes on recipe websites. Most of the big food companies have some great recipe ideas on their websites.
2. You'll need a basket for the nonperishable items and a cooler for your drinks and for perishable foods, such as those made with mayonnaise.
3. Finally, you should confirm the guest list. Encourage everyone in the family to come. Older children might be reluctant, so try to be firm without being demanding. You might even want to include an older relative or someone else in your extended family.

"To dare is to lose one's footing momentarily.
To not dare is to lose oneself."

—Soren Kierkegaard

A Map and a Few Darts

No doubt you've seen it in the movies. Somebody wants to go on vacation and visit some part of the country they've never been to before. Rather than sit around trying to figure it out, they put up a map of the country, close their eyes, throw a dart towards the map and commit themselves to going wherever the dart takes them. It's more than just a cliché. It's taking a big chance. What if it doesn't work out? What if it's a place you've been to before? What if it doesn't seem like your kind of place?

Sometimes to get at a chance to truly relax, we need to take some chances and open ourselves to the ability to be surprised. If you've ever experienced the thrill of the open-road with nothing but adventure and possibility stretched out in front of you, that old cliché of the map and dart can be what finally moves you from just thinking about it to actually doing it. If you feel like you're trapped in a rut, then you need to think of something that's going to get you out of that rut—and fast. It might have to be something that truly lights a fire under you. So get out that map and a few darts, and fire away!

TRY A TRAVEL BLOG

If you're longing for adventure, but you're not quite ready for the map and dart routine, check out *www.travelpod.com* to share in thousands of travel experiences from hundreds of countries. Enjoy photos and videos and enjoyable, informative stories while making your own decision on where to travel.

*"A man has to live with himself, and he should see
to it that he always has good company."*

—Charles Hughes

Live with Integrity

Integrity is about living a life that is beyond reproach—regardless of whether the legal system is involved. Integrity, according to author Robert Grudin, also involves continuity. It is not something that you profess one day and abandon the next. Integrity is about doing what is right through thick and thin, day in and day out, year after year.

An integrity plan is your personal mission statement. It is the statement by which you plan to live, act, treat others, and interact in the world. Having an integrity plan for your life is a declaration that guides you when things get dark and confusing.

CREATE AN INTEGRITY PLAN

You can begin to develop your plan by making a list of the things that you value in your life. Your list may include things such as:

- Truth
- Honesty
- Fairness
- Spirituality
- Friends

After you have completed your list, you can begin to create a statement that incorporates your ideas for moral living, the things you value, and what you plan to do to protect your value system. It will have a forceful action verb to give the statement power, it will have objectives that guide you, and you will symbolically sign your name to this statement. An integrity statement might read something like this:

"I believe in truth and fairness. In my actions, I will not do any deed that will jeopardize my integrity or the integrity of my friends. I will never compromise truth and fairness for personal or professional gain."

*"If a cluttered desk is the sign of a cluttered mind,
what is the significance of a clean desk?"*

—Laurence J. Peter

Keep It Clean

Do you arrive at work each morning, survey your work area with a sinking heart and vow to clean your desk space—tomorrow? If the top of your desk is beginning to look like a war zone, then it's time to deal with the problem.

Make a trip to an office supply store, where there is a vast assortment of desk organizers available. You might want to get a "take action" tray, a place where you can place items that need your immediate attention. Some people use an accordion folder marked with days of the week to organize work that can be dealt with at a later time. Be creative and find out what works for you.

PUT EVERYTHING IN ITS PLACE

1. To get started, you'll need three containers. The first one is for the vital things you want to keep. Container two is for the things you want to throw away, and the third container is for things you can either store, take home, or give away.
2. Next, remove everything from your desk except the computer, phone, and other "permanent" fixtures.
3. Then evaluate and sort each item. With each piece, ask yourself, "Why am I keeping this?" You are not allowed to put anything back on your desk.
4. Once you have sorted the items from your desk, deal with each pile: throw away the things you don't need to keep, store/take home/give away the items in the store/take home/give away pile, return the items you need to keep on your desk to your desk.
5. If you don't want your desk to quickly return to its previous state of chaos, remember to take action on every single article that arrives at your desk. Keep it, throw it out, or move it away from your work space.

WEEK FIVE

"Dogs are not our whole life, but they make our lives whole."

—Roger Caras

Visit the Dog Park

You're not the only one who's getting tired of the same old walk around the block. Chances are your dog is, too. Dog owners all over the country have decided to change things up a bit, and they've created parks specifically designed for people and their dogs to meet and interact. These parks offer a variety of dog-friendly amenities including off-leash areas, fencing, water, and parking, often in a lush, green setting. Dogs are given the chance to socialize in a safe environment while owners enjoy the company of other dog lovers.

A quick search online will provide a wealth of information and even local listings. There are even online groups who organize visits to these parks. What if you can't find a dog park in your area? Websites such as *www.dogpark.com* provide the information you need to get started on creating one. Don't be surprised if someone else has already gotten the ball rolling, but there's no reason why you can't pitch in, too. A good dog park can be endlessly beneficial to a community. Your dog will thank you, too.

BE A VOLUNTEER DOG WALKER

If you don't own a dog, you can still enjoy spending time with a four-legged friend. Contact your local animal shelter and offer your services as a dog walker. You can help give homeless dogs the exercise, affection, and socialization they need to remain healthy, happy, and adoptable.

"That's the object of going to a gym, having fun."

—Joe Gold

Support Your Friends' Exercise Goals

When your friends tell you that they're going to start an exercise program, you congratulate their resolve and tell them they're doing the right thing. You mean every word of that, but your support doesn't have to start and finish with mere words. Chances are you've been meaning to get more exercise yourself, so why not take advantage of an opportunity to do so and cheer on your friend at the same time? People who work out together are more likely to stick to the program. Not only will your body benefit from the exercise, but so will your friendship!

MAKE THE MOST OF YOUR TEAM EFFORT

If you have a friend who has been talking about getting in shape and shedding a few pounds, give her a call and see if she'd like to team up with you at a local fitness center. You don't have to wait for your friends to come to you. Consider these additional benefits:

1. Some gyms have special rates when more than one person signs up at the same time. Together, you can set goals and help one another reach those goals. Picking up a new exercise regime can be a difficult undertaking, especially for anyone who's never done it before. The more help we can get with maintaining discipline and a schedule, the more likely the whole venture is going to succeed.
2. Your friend will also enjoy the opportunity to reciprocate the favor of supporting your desire to trim a few pounds and get in better shape. When you have a familiar face and some good conversation to keep you busy, it doesn't really seem like work anymore. It can quickly become one of the most enjoyable parts of your day.

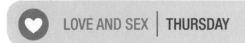

"The eyes are the mirror of the soul."

—Yiddish proverb

Look into Your Lover's Eyes

They say the eyes are the windows into the soul. That is very romantic, but for some people it can be very frightening. Looking and holding another person's gaze can make you feel very vulnerable, especially in a new relationship or in one that has caused a lot of hurt. But it can also be a way to connect or reconnect with your partner.

True intimacy can be tricky to discover and even more difficult to maintain, but it's worth it. So take a good, long look into your partner's eyes. You'll be strengthening your relationship and giving it a much better chance of going the distance!

SCHEDULE A LOVING LOOK

Don't let those long, loving looks become a matter of chance. Make a specific effort to look lovingly at your partner. To engage in this exercise, sit across from your partner and look into each other's eyes for five to ten minutes (set a timer, if necessary). Try to resist the need to be silly and instead notice the look in your lover's eyes and the emotions you feel. When the physical part of the exercise is complete, share what thoughts arose for you.

"Good sayings are like pearls strung together."

—Chinese proverb

Give a Little Inspiration

Everyone in your family faces different and daunting challenges each and every day. Why not send your loved ones off to work and school with something extra? Start their day with an inspiring quotation—something to replay in their minds throughout the day and energize and encourage them. An inspirational quotation can bring some positivity to their world, a place that's often filled with pessimism and doubt.

At the end of the day, initiate a discussion about the quotation. You can ask everyone what the quotation means to them and whether or not they remembered it as they went through their day. Conversations like this will guide you in making subsequent choices for your quotation. Don't be discouraged if your experiment is not an obvious or immediate success, and don't forget to pick a new quotation for tomorrow.

FIND INSPIRATION ONLINE

So where do you find appropriate quotes to share with your loved ones? There are many websites where you can find quotes on every subject and for every occasion.

1. Take some time to visit a few sites.
2. Make some notes or print off quotes that you find particularly appealing.
3. For your first quote, start simple with something short and easy to remember.
4. Write it on a piece of paper and stick it on the fridge, tape it to the back door, or slip a copy into everyone's pocket—in short, make it obvious and accessible to read throughout the day so you can all become inspired.

"Music is enough for a lifetime, but a lifetime is not enough for music."

—Sergei Rachmaninoff

Read a Good Book and Listen to Good Music

Chances are those shows on your DVR can wait for another hour or even until another evening. The next time you feel like relaxing after a long day, pick up your music player and that book you've been meaning to finish or start. Grab your favorite chair in the house, sit back, get a playlist going that's guaranteed to unwind your frazzled mind, and sink into whatever it is you're reading.

LOSE YOURSELF IN A BOOK

1. Many leisurely activities make us conscious of the time. Losing yourself in a good book and some of your favorite music can eliminate that awareness altogether. The combination of great music and literature that pulls you in can have that effect on you immediately. You're too busy enjoying these things working together to think about the troubles of the day or the worries of tomorrow. You've submerged yourself completely in something that is out of this world.

2. You may enjoy the experience so much that when you finally decide to take a break, you'll discover that you weren't even aware of the time as it moved past you. All that concerned you was the music in your ears and the book in your lap. Relaxing doesn't get any easier.

3. If you're not sure what to read, do a Google search using the search terms "recommended reading" or "reading lists," and you'll be overwhelmed with hundreds of recommended and notable books from libraries, bookstores, and national book and educational councils. If you find something that intrigues you, go to an online bookstore such as Amazon.com for further information and customer reviews.

"Inhale, and God approaches you. Hold the inhalation, and God remains with you. Exhale, and you approach God. Hold the exhalation, and surrender to God."

—Tirumalai Krishnamacharya

Breathe a Sigh of Relief

You've dealt with crisis. When it concluded, did you breathe a deep sigh of relief? Whether the crisis you faced took hours, days, weeks, or months to resolve, it probably wasn't something that inspired happiness. But take a lesson from that experience: If you feel stressed, tense, unhappy, take a deep breath and release the worry.

Seek out that special place inside yourself where you can feel peace and joy at the miracle of being alive and out of harm's way. Breathe deeply. Remain quiet, sink into awareness of your inward and outward breathing cycles, and allow your mind to dive deeply into the space between the breaths. That is a very potent place of stillness and calm. There you experience yourself in a whole new way, beyond body and even the consciousness of your mind. As the breath slows, thinking slows as well. You will experience peace.

FOCUS ON GRATITUDE

1. Breathe deeply and draw into your body the subtle energy of the earth, sun, and wind. Imagine each breath you inhale as positive or light energy and each breath exhaled as negative or dark energy.
2. Take pleasure in the miraculous processes of life going on throughout your body and express your overwhelming gratitude to your Creator.

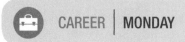

CAREER | MONDAY

"There are always three speeches, for every one you actually gave. The one you practiced, the one you gave, and the one you wish you gave."

—Dale Carnegie

Make a Toast

If you're someone who steers clear of speech making, maybe it's time to overcome your anxieties and insecurities. Improving your communication skills by learning to present a well-organized and thoughtful speech is a proven way to jump-start a career. A simple search online will provide you with numerous articles written on speech making. For example, *www.public-speaking.org* has more than 100 articles on public speaking.

If attending a learn-by-doing workshop appeals to you, you'll want to check out *www.toastmasters.org*. Since 1924, Toastmasters International has helped over four million people develop better communication and leadership skills. Meetings are held at various times during the day in communities and corporations all over the world.

OVERCOME YOUR FEAR

It is estimated that three out of four people suffer from a fear of public speaking. If you have speech anxiety, something that will help is practice, practice, and more practice.

1. Practice your speech alone. Read it out loud.
2. Practice in front of a mirror to see how you look while speaking, and then read your speech out loud while standing in a corner to get an idea of how you sound.
3. Rehearse your speech using a tape or video recorder.
4. Get further practice in front of an audience, even if it's only one person.

WEEK SIX

*"Let's face it, a nice creamy chocolate cake does
a lot for a lot of people; it does for me."*

—Audrey Hepburn

Hold a Bake Sale

There's a reason why the bake sale has been a fundraising staple for decades now. It remains a fantastic way to get people involved, to do something for a cause and to have a delicious reward for all that hard work. The reasons can be varied, but the end result is almost always the same. By going to this familiar favorite, you create a reason for anyone in your community to get involved with only a minimum of time and effort.

It doesn't have to be elaborate. No one is expecting gourmet cakes and cookies, but you would be surprised at how much people love a homemade carrot cake or fresh chocolate chip cookies with a nice glass of milk. You might also be surprised at how many people are always looking for an excuse to do a little baking. The part that won't be a surprise is how quickly and easily such an endeavor can bring people together.

FIND A CAUSE

If you're convinced a bake sale could bring members of your community together, but you don't have a cause, don't let that stop you! Find a cause to support.

1. Look around at what your community needs. Perhaps your school needs new band uniforms. Or maybe your church would like to visit an amusement park in the spring. Or perhaps the soccer team could use some extra money.
2. Or visit *www.strength.org* and find out how you can help feed the nation's hungry children. Many well-known companies in the food industry have joined together in a national campaign that mobilizes Americans to end childhood hunger by holding bake sales in their communities.

"A good traveler has no fixed plans, and is not intent on arriving."

—Lao Tzu

Take a Road Trip

You love to get away, but your wallet is a little thin. Your dreams of visiting exotic locales doesn't necessarily mean you have to hop on a plane and fly halfway across the world. Unless you travel the country for a living, there's a good chance you haven't even come close to seeing all there is to see in your own geographic backyard. There could be wonders just waiting for you across the state line. Those thoughts can elicit a craving for a road trip.

HEED THE CALL OF ADVENTURE

A good road trip can be about going it alone, but you can have an even better time when you bring a friend along.

1. You may have already discussed the idea with one of your buddies. Call your friend and see if she's still up for it.
2. You can come up with a detailed plan of where you're going, where you'll stop as you go, and the places where you want to stay.
3. Or you can just throw a couple of bags in the trunk and hit the road with no plans more elaborate than getting away from the familiar as soon as possible.
4. You can even bring a third or fourth friend to make it really interesting. The more voices you bring to the adventure, the greater your chances for that adventure being exactly the kind of unpredictable, exciting journey you might need to finally unwind and enjoy yourself.

*"To be overcome by the fragrance of flowers
is a delectable form of defeat."*

—Beverley Nichols

Try Some Scents-uous Surroundings

Having a great-smelling bedroom will help make the average bedroom feel more like a love nest. All of us have certain scents that turn us off and those that turn us on, but you won't know what aromas your partner likes until you've known him or her for a while. So until you learn that your partner goes wild at the scent of leather, fresh-cut grass, or honeysuckle, hedge your bets and try some scents that have been given the green light for most men and women. Cinnamon buns, strawberries, and pumpkin pie are said to send more blood flow to the penis, whereas a woman can turned on subconsciously by the scent of licorice. For both sexes, vanilla, lavender, peppermint, banana bread, cucumber, jasmine, orange, and musk can get the juices flowing.

PICK YOUR METHOD

To bring these scents into your home, choose among a variety of options, depending on your personal preference:

- Scented candles. When lit, these can also cast a flattering romantic glow around the room.
- Diffusers. Once you set one of these out, it works continuously to provide a pleasant aroma—no extra work required.
- Essential oils. Put a few drops of an essential oil or fragrance oil onto your pillow or cotton sheets for a simple, yet potent, invitation to enjoy.

Just remember to start small so your bedroom doesn't end up smelling like the perfume section of a department store.

*"Music expresses that which cannot be put into
words and cannot remain silent."*

—Victor Hugo

Celebrate with Music

Music is an integral part of our lives. It forms part of our earliest memories and holds an undeniable power over us all. It can change our attitude and transport us back in time. As a family, share your love of music with each other. Pick a date for a music night and talk about what you like to listen to, what your children like to listen to, and why. Then play a few songs that each family member likes.

HOST THE EVENT

Once you've picked the date for your music night, establish a few ground rules on the subject of quiet, respectful listening and polite open-minded discussion. No one should feel attacked for their musical choices; the idea is to use music night to gain greater understanding and appreciation of each other.

1. Ask everyone to gather their favorite songs: MP3 players, CDs, tapes, vinyls, 8-tracks, or even sheet music and a piano if one is available.
2. Roll a pair of dice to see who goes first, and then everyone listens to a full song of that person's choosing. He or she can introduce the song with reasons for choosing it, and the rest of the family can discuss the piece when it's over.
3. Don't forget to add to the party atmosphere with some favorite snacks and drinks, and if the urge hits you, make some room and get up and dance. You have a lot to celebrate!

"I hope you love birds too. It is economical. It saves going to heaven."

—Emily Dickinson

Start Bird-Watching

Bird-watching doesn't necessarily involve a lot of time and work. All you have to do is walk by the window and happen to notice your feathered visitors. You can watch and enjoy them for a moment, and then move on with your day. What matters is that you took a moment to let your mind move towards something more pleasant. Relaxing for even a few minutes can be a wonderful shot in the arm to a dreary day. If you want to find some binoculars, pull up a chair, and get more out of the experience, there's nothing wrong with that, too.

BUILD A BIRDHOUSE

A flock of birds enjoying the food and shelter you've left out for them is a soothing sight. By building a bird feeder or birdhouse for your backyard, you're not just providing food and a place to rest for any of the birds who happen to populate your area, you're also giving yourself the marvelous gift of being able to look out from your house or even just outside your door to watch a beautiful snapshot of nature in action.

- If you're the kind of person who likes working with your hands, you're welcome to build your choice of house or feeder.
- But there's nothing wrong with buying something to draw those birds to your property. It could be elaborate enough to function as a nest or as simple as a small feeder.

"When you hold resentment toward another, you are bound to that person or condition by an emotional link that is stronger than steel. Forgiveness is the only way to dissolve that link and get free."

—Catherine Ponder

Let Go of Anger

Holding on to anger, resentment, and hostility hurts you psychologically, emotionally, and physically. Don't give over your power to have positivity in your life just to harbor a grudge. You need to find a way to move past it. Don't let another day go by without spending some time intentionally releasing any anger or annoyance you feel about others.

FORGIVE, BLESS, AND RELEASE

If you are holding on to anger or hurt instead of forgiving the person who violated you, you are limiting your capacity to feel good. Many great religious and spiritual traditions address the issue of forgiveness, reminding us that at our sacred center or core, we are inherently happy. When we hang on to resentment, pain, or anger from the past and recall it in the future, we hurt ourselves. Some yoga teachers have even suggested a connection between a tendency to hold on to resentment and bitterness and the development of heart problems. Don't close down your heart and your feelings. Overcome those negative emotions.

1. Whenever you slip into a place of pain and sadness, say a blessing for yourself.
2. Then say a blessing for the person who hurt you. Tell her (in your heart, if not out loud) that you will no longer take her or the memory of that incident any further into your life.
3. Then intentionally release the anger and hurt. Say an affirmation such as, "I release the anger I feel over this hurt."

Forgive, bless, and release. That's the way to keep your heart and mind open.

"Build up your weaknesses until they become your strong points."

—Knute Rockne

Evaluate What May Be Holding You Back

At times, you need to evaluate where you've gone wrong so you can fix the problem and get back on track. If it's been some time since you've been promoted or received a raise or if your career hasn't developed in the way you want, take a hard look at what you're doing—or not doing—that's holding you back. The reason you haven't advanced may have nothing to do with you—for example, the economy may be in a slump—but if your actions or inactions have held you back, it's important to take the necessary steps to fix these trouble spots so you can improve your earning potential and also provide yourself with greater job security. The good feelings that come from making positive changes in your career can filter into other areas of your life, and your self-esteem should get a healthy boost.

LOOK FOR TWO REASONS

1. There's no need to overwhelm or depress yourself with a litany of your shortcomings. Make a list of two, and only two, reasons why you believe you haven't moved forward in your career. You might want to take a look at what the new hires are bringing to the table and ask yourself if you have, at the very least, the skills they're walking in with.

2. Then, for each reason, think of two things you can do to transform your liabilities into assets. For example, if you believe you need to improve your time management skills, you might list getting to work ten minutes early and using a day planner as two ways to improve this area of your career. If you want to move on to more reasons later, that's fine, but remember to start with just two. It can be amazing what just two can do!

> *"You give but little when you give of your possessions. It is when you give of yourself that you truly give."*
>
> —Kahlil Gibran

Give a Bowl of Soup and a Smile

Volunteering at a soup kitchen is always one of the most popular New Year's resolutions. It's an admirable pledge, but why wait? If there's a soup kitchen in your community, chances are that it runs year-round, and it probably needs volunteers all the time—not just on major holidays. In most cases, volunteers make it financially possible for places like soup kitchens to exist. It's always a good time to lend a helping hand.

GET MORE THAN YOU GIVE

Helping feed the hungry requires a lot less of your time and energy than you might think. Even if you only sign up for a couple of hours on the weekend, the rewards of such a minor contribution can be profound. You will be contributing to something greater than yourself and be left with the knowledge that your small act has made a world of difference.

1. Go to *www.dosomething.org* and use their volunteer database or search the phone book to find a soup kitchen near you. Get in touch with the organization and find out what they need.
2. If your local soup kitchen isn't looking for volunteers at the moment, try a retirement home in your area.

*"Whoever wishes to keep a secret must hide
the fact that he possesses one."*

—Johann Wolfgang von Goethe

Keep One Another's Secrets

Relationship experts say that intimacy is strengthened and bonds deepened when couples regard keeping each other's secrets as a sacred trust. Safeguard the confidences that your friend shares with you. Keeping your word to your friend makes possible the revealing of vulnerabilities, fears, aspirations, and dreams. A secret can be a wonderful development, such as an upcoming promotion that your friend wants to keep under wraps, or it can be a dark and painful experience or psychological wound that you carry from your past.

SHARE A SECRET

1. When people understand that they can always count on their friends to support and love them and keep private the secrets they share, the friendship is strengthened. Affection is deepened. Such an intimate sharing serves as a safety valve for both of you. What is not possible or advisable to tell others, you know you can tell your friend.

2. Think of a secret from your childhood that you would like to share with your friend. It could be that crush you had on your eighth-grade biology teacher or how you slipped away from your Aunt Tillie's ninetieth birthday bash to play games with a friend at the local video arcade.

"Music melts all the separate parts of our bodies together."

—Anaïs Nin

Let Music Put You in the Mood

If your lover is musically inclined, the two of you could spend time going through each other's music collection and finding songs that get you in a romantic or sexual mood or ones that you think it would be fun to make out or have sex to. You'll learn a lot about each other and what gets each of you in the mood as you share your songs, and you might even find a favorite new band or two.

MAKE A SEXY PLAYLIST

Making a sensual playlist can be a lot of fun. You could even make it into a date!

- Whether you choose to take on this project as a couple or compile songs on your own, it makes sense to make more than one playlist.
- Your sexual mood can change, so while one night you're going to want to have slow and intimate sex, on another night you might just want to tear your lover's clothes off.
- And if you like listening to music while making love, you're not going to want to have the same soundtrack for both of those nights.

"Feelings of worth can flourish only in an atmosphere where individual differences are appreciated, mistakes are tolerated, communication is open, and rules are flexible—the kind of atmosphere that is found in a nurturing family."

—Virginia Satir

Overcoming the Obstacles

It's a fact of life: Every family has its share of disagreement, but you may not know about a problem until it has erupted into a full-scale war. To prevent this, be sure that clear and frequent communication is a priority in your family, whether between marriage partners, siblings, or parents and children. It also means being willing to listen and accept criticism, whether you're a child or an adult.

HOLD A REGULAR FAMILY MEETING

You can help prevent this from happening by making a decision to hold a regular family meeting. A meeting like this can only work if the whole family is present, so the biggest challenge you may face is coordinating everyone's schedule and motivating them to attend. Serve a special meal or dessert as an enticement, rent a much-anticipated movie or play a favorite game.

1. Remind everyone to listen politely. Start with a topic that will create an upbeat mood. Ask everyone to think of something positive about the family. Follow this by asking each family member to share something that bothers them.

2. Listen carefully to the feelings expressed and ask open-ended questions. Invite participants to brainstorm solutions to the problems presented.

3. End your meeting on a positive note by asking everyone about their plans for the coming week. You'll have the perfect opportunity to hear about tests, appointments, and special projects.

"Cooking is like love. It should be entered into with abandon or not at all."

—Harriet Van Horne

Cook at Home

Cooking is considered one of the ultimate forms of relaxation by a great many people. It puts the world behind us by putting us into a rhythm of following the directions, sticking to a precise schedule, and anticipating the delicious meal to come. Even if you're too busy to cook every night, try to set aside one night a week for some kitchen time.

STIR UP AN OLD FAVORITE

Most of us love to try new dishes and eat at new restaurants to avoid getting bogged down with the same old thing night in and night out. But sometimes that results in forgetting our old favorites. There's no reason why you can't change up your schedule a bit by resolving to cook your favorite dish once in a while. You can try the idea once a month or even once a week.

Your recipe can be for anything you want from any period in your life. Perhaps you're longing for a plate of the one-of-a-kind macaroni your mother used to make. Experimentation in the kitchen can be wonderful, but it doesn't have to be a new thing each and every night. The old favorites are just that for a reason.

"The path of spiritual growth is a path of lifelong learning."

—M. Scott Peck

Find Answers in Your Spiritual Beliefs

When your heart is heavy because you cannot figure out the best solution to a relationship problem, turn to your spiritual beliefs. It's been said that every problem has an answer, and often the right answer is the simplest and the one most overlooked. Consider the teachings of Norman Vincent Peale. He was the author of *The Power of Positive Thinking*, a popular self-help guide first published in 1952, and advocated that people trust that God's higher power was always with them. He observed that when they affirmed, visualized, and believed that God's power was at work in their lives, they energized their belief, actualized that power, and achieved astonishing results.

PUT FAITH INTO PRACTICE

Attend your favorite house of worship, be it a synagogue, church, temple, mosque, meeting house, or other type of place where you can find the answers you seek in an environment that provides a spiritual vibe. Then try the following three steps:

1. Think about the problem and give it over to a higher power, according to what you believe.
2. Ask for the answer to come to you as inspiration.
3. Then stop analyzing and let it go. Expect the answer to reveal itself.

"You may make mistakes, but you are not a failure until you start blaming someone else."

—Mary Pickford

Make Good on Your Mistakes

If you've made a work-related mistake recently, an error no one is aware of yet, then act upon it immediately. No one likes to make mistakes, but when you've messed up at work, admit it to your boss right away. Though you might be afraid of taking the heat, accepting blame before your boss (or client) realizes what's happened makes you look trustworthy and confident.

Unless you've committed a major transgression, your superiors are more likely to remember that you had the guts to come forward about your mistake than they are to remember what you did wrong. And that can pay off for you in a big way in the long run.

WEEK EIGHT

WRITE A LETTER

To initiate this exercise, you're going to write yourself a letter. Imagine that you are talking to your boss or client and write down exactly what you would say.

1. Explain why things went wrong and how you'll work to ensure that it won't happen again in the future.
2. Read your letter out loud and make any changes as you see fit. Read it aloud again, and continue to edit until you are happy with the end result.
3. Read your letter over once or twice to give yourself a shot of confidence, take a deep breath, and do it! Situations like this are rarely as unpleasant as we imagine they are going to be.

"Wherever there is a human being, there is an opportunity for kindness."

—Seneca

Give to Your Local Food Bank

Nearly one in four children in this country is hungry. Donating to a food bank is a wonderful way for you to do your part to help solve this problem. Every community has a food bank. Visit *www.feedingamerica.org* to find one near you. The nation's recent economic instability as well as the growing number of low-income families who depend on food banks as a source of assistance has made it increasingly important to support your local food bank.

ORGANIZE A FOOD DRIVE

Since you're doing this for the community, it makes perfect sense to involve the community.

1. Organizing a mass donation for your local food bank is a simple, direct, and rewarding way to get as many other people involved as possible. It goes without saying that you are not the only one in your neighborhood who would be willing to work on this project.
2. Print and post or hand out some fliers or create a Facebook group to organize a group of like-minded individuals, and the results may impress you. A small group of committed people can easily accumulate a generous donation.
3. Approach the manager of your local grocery and ask if you can collect donations in his store. People are inclined to donate when they have the convenience of buying and donating at their fingertips.

"Only your real friends will tell you when your face is dirty."

—Sicilian proverb

Treasure Your Best Friend

Learn how to cherish your best friend. If she is angry, frustrated, or distressed, patiently listen to her venting. If her feet hurt from walking all day at the industry trade show, offer to join her at the nail salon for a pedicure. Any time your best friend feels overwhelmed, ask what you can do to lighten the load. Best friends give mutual support when it's needed. They listen to and hear not only what you say, but also what you don't say.

SHOW YOUR FRIEND YOUR LOVE

Here are a few more ways to be a better best friend:

- Be loyal.
- Be honest.
- Make your friendship a high priority.
- Let go of expectations.
- Defend your friend if and when it becomes necessary.
- Actively listen to what your friend tells you, repeating back the words to be certain of the message.
- Be trustworthy.
- Be available when your friend needs you.
- Protect your friend's confidences as you do your own secrets.
- Praise your friend when she does something to deserve recognition.
- Present your friend with a friendship card on the first Sunday in August, National Friendship Day. Give her a big balloon on which you use a felt pen to write a heartfelt or silly message.

"I love lingerie and feminine things. It makes me feel nice to look good and turn somebody on by doing so. It's an incredible rush. And when it turns a man on—fantastic. But no matter what, I'm getting off."

—Lorri Bagley

Buy Something Sexy

If you want to turn your lover on, go buy some sexy lingerie. For men, this could be a hot new pair of boxer briefs or something more Speedo-like. It depends on what turns your partner on. For women, the options are vast. There's silky sleepwear or a corset and lacy garter belt. Or the teddy. Or a tempting push-up bra and matching sheer panties. Or just a sexy thong and a pair of heart-shaped pasties.

The next time you want to heat things up, dress in a pretty, naughty slim-to-nothing that will fire his imagination and put him in the mood for love. Think of yourself as a present. Once you've titillated him into a feverish desire to possess you, he gets to unwrap his present from layers of lace and satin and ribbon.

TRY A SEXY STRIPTEASE

You may not feel like a runway model, but your lover will certainly enjoy it if you pretend you are.

1. While your partner is doing the dishes or relaxing on the couch or in the bedroom, go into another room and slip on your sexy outfit. Do up your hair and your makeup. Then come out and watch his jaw drop.
2. Model your new outfit for him, but don't let him touch just yet!
3. If the moment feels right, start doing a little striptease for your partner with or without music. The key to a sexy striptease is confidence and going slow enough to tease your partner. So, even if you're feeling nervous, don't rush.
4. Once you and your partner are completely turned on, finish what you started!

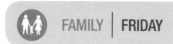
"Your children need your presence more than your presents."

—Jesse Jackson

Strengthen Your Bond with Your Children

It's easy to get caught up in the demands of a busy life and forget what's really important. Not only do you need to strengthen and nurture your bond with your partner, you need to do it with your children as well. In addition to spending time together as a family, make sure you have plenty of opportunities to interact individually with each of your children.

MAKE A DATE—WITH YOUR KIDS!

Couples trying to find critical time for each other often set up a date night as a way to keep their relationship healthy and interesting. How about making a regular date with each of your children? It's a terrific—and tangible—way to show them how important they are.

1. It shouldn't be hard to come up with an idea for a date night if you consider the age of the child and his or her particular interest. Make sure you choose something your child wants to do; otherwise your date could turn into just another boring session of running around and doing errands.

2. Be creative and definitely do some thinking "outside the box." For example, if your older child enjoys cooking, consider signing up for a cooking class at the local college. Or your five-year-old fashionista would probably be thrilled with a trip to her favorite store to find that special outfit.

3. Make sure you allow some time for communicating during your date. Ask lots of open-ended questions, and be prepared to answer a few questions yourself. Be sure to discuss the details of your next date or any other topic your child may want to pursue. But most of all, enjoy yourself!

"I love fishing. You put that line in the water and you don't know what's on the other end. Your imagination is under there."

—Robert Altman

Share a Hobby

Every hobby isn't going to work for everybody. What makes one person relax can be sheer boredom for another. There's nothing wrong with knowing something isn't for you. The problem is with making up your mind about something before you give it a try. Consider trying a hobby your partner or children enjoy even if you've previously dismissed it. You might surprise yourself!

TAKE UP FISHING

People often make up their minds about fishing before giving it a try. They eliminate it as a possible activity before they even pick up a pole.

1. You'll never know until you give it a try. You can always bring someone who knows a little more about it, or you can go to a sporting goods store for the supplies you need and find the nearest fishing hole.

2. Discover for yourself if fishing is as peaceful and soothing as many claim it is. For millions of enthusiasts, catching the actual fish is almost secondary. For them, fishing is about being out in nature, surrounded by calming sounds and beautiful sights.

3. You don't have to own an expensive boat and sophisticated supplies. All you need to get started is some bait and a fishing lure. If the notion of silence followed by more silence appeals to you, fishing may be worth considering.

4. Check out *www.takemefishing.org* or *www.activeangler.com* to give you some inspiration, answer some of the questions you might have, and to help you make a list of the supplies you're going to need.

"One of the things I learned the hard way was that it doesn't pay to get discouraged. Keeping busy and making optimism a way of life can restore your faith in yourself."

—Lucille Ball

Give Yourself the Gift of Optimism

Optimism does not mean that you are constantly and eternally happy; it simply means that you have an outlook on life that is generally upbeat and positive. It means that you know and value hope. Optimists believe that their actions matter. They do not profess to be able to *change* the world, but they do profess to *matter* in the world. Optimism is all about an outlook. It is less about how you are treated and more about how you treat.

Optimists find joy in small things. They enjoy sunsets, a good conversation with a close friend, and life in general. They are more concerned with having many small joys rather than having one huge joy. When you give yourself the gift of optimism, you will see your spiritual nature flourish and prosper.

ENJOY AN ENTIRE DAY OF OPTIMISM

List at least three positive, optimistic, hopeful statements for each item on this list.

- Your career
- Your spouse/partner
- Your best friend
- Your worst foe
- Your abilities
- Your faith
- Your livelihood
- Your mental well-being
- Your physical well-being
- Your finances
- Your opportunities

Now, for a full twenty-four hours, think positive thoughts! Then try it for two days, a week, a month.

"Better three hours too soon than a minute too late."

—William Shakespeare

Be on Time and Be Prepared!

If you want to get on the wrong side of your boss and coworkers, make a habit of showing up late and unprepared for meetings. Most people believe they've already lost precious minutes by being stuck in a meeting, and if you wander in late with nothing to add, you can be sure you'll be getting the cold shoulder—or worse.

If you take all of your meetings seriously and show up to each on time and with ideas that you researched in advance, not only will you impress your coworkers, you'll also win points with your boss. Though your boss and coworkers might not want to use the ideas you present, you'll at least prove to them that you're a confident, creative thinker, that you're dedicated to your work, and that you're a team player. These are the kinds of strong qualities supervisors look for when they're considering who to promote and who deserves a raise.

WEEK NINE

TAKE ADVANTAGE OF SOME ASSISTANCE

If you need some help making it to your meetings on time, take advantage of technology to help you remember.

1. Use your cell phone or smart phone. You can set appointments and reminders using the alarm or ring tone.
2. Make a point of giving yourself some extra time. This will give you an opportunity to review your resources.
3. Use a software program or a smart phone application to make a checklist of must-have materials for your meeting so that nothing gets left behind.

"It takes a village to raise a child."

—African proverb

Seek Helpful Tips from Other Parents

If you don't always know the ideal way to handle a child-rearing situation, parenting can become stressful. Getting insights from other parents is often helpful. In her book, *It Takes a Village*, former First Lady Hillary Rodham Clinton advocates for children to be brought up not only by their parents, but rather by many other people in our interdependent world. Read or review it. Then make it a point to have coffee with another couple who are parenting children about the age of your child. Talk with them about the positives and negatives of parenting in today's American society.

FIND OTHER PARENTS

Where do you find this support? Look around you—you'll see other parents everywhere and, with a little bit of effort, can connect with them in rewarding ways.

1. In your "village" (or neighborhood or community), you will meet other parents at the park, in the baby-food aisle at the market, in the pediatrician's office and dentist's waiting room, at your house of worship, on the soccer field, at PTA meetings, and a host of other places.

2. Take the opportunity to form friendships with them. Ask them how they have dealt with particular parenting or family issues that you and your spouse might be facing.

3. Question them about how they intend to raise resilient, well-adjusted children. Gain from their experiential, real-world knowledge. Above all else, be patient. Remember that time changes everything, and even if times are tough, better days are ahead.

"A good friend is a connection to life—a tie to the past, a road to the future, the key to sanity in a totally insane world."

—Lois Wyse

Don't Forget Your Friends

It's a great thing to have someone new in your life. The dating scene can be a rough ocean to travel, and the relief and joy of finding someone can have a tremendous impact on so many facets of your life. One area it shouldn't affect is your relationships with your closest friends.

There's no doubt that they're thrilled for you. These were the same people who were there for you when things didn't seem quite as wonderful. The true friends will continue to be just that after that new relationship has begun. But sometimes we can forget them. The shine of a new relationship can override just about everything else around us. One of the things that can suffer the most is friendships. If we're not careful to remember the other people who matter to us we can find ourselves with someone who feels neglected and forgotten.

MAKE A DATE NIGHT JUST FOR FRIENDS

Avoid forgetting your friends. Going out with your significant other is important, but it doesn't have to be every single night.

1. Consider switching things up a bit and inviting your best friend or friends out for a night on the town instead.
2. Chances are that your mate has significant friendships that may have been neglected since the two of you started your relationship. Why not suggest setting aside one night of the week when you part ways as a couple and seek out your own friends for some fun and relaxation?

> *"There are times not to flirt. When you're sick. When you're with children. When you're on the witness stand."*

—Joyce Jillson

Engage in the Fine Art of Flirting

Get out there and flirt with someone today. If you're in a relationship, flirt with your partner; if you're single, flirt with someone cute you see. If you start innocently, most people will flirt back, and that can be a huge confidence booster. Flirting, which is usually done with the intention of sparking a romantic or sexual interest in the other person, can take many forms.

You can flirt just by starting a conversation with someone. As you continue to talk, keep eye contact (but don't stare), smile, and laugh when the person says something funny or cute. If you feel a connection, you can brush the person's shoulder or touch him or her in a playful way. If you keep it going and the flirting is mutual, it might even lead to something more.

NOTICE WHEN SOMEONE IS FLIRTING WITH YOU

Look for these signs that someone is flirting with you—then return the favor! Someone is flirting with you when he or she:

- Mimics your body movements
- Smiles and makes eye contact with you
- Keeps walking by you
- Plays with his or her hair
- Acts intentionally coy or shy
- Touches you when you're talking

"To observe people in conflict is a necessary part of a child's education. It helps him to understand and accept his own occasional hostilities and to realize that differing opinions need not imply an absence of love."

—Milton R. Sapirstein

Coping with Conflict

No one is born knowing how to deal with conflict, but coping with this common, yet powerful, issue is a critical skill. As with so many other things, your children look to you and your partner to both model and teach them effective ways to deal with conflict. You don't need to hide conflict from your children; you just need to model good approaches to it. Let disagreements be an opportunity to set an example for your children.

ROLE-PLAY CONFLICT RESOLUTION

You don't have to wait for a problem to actually occur before you begin to help your family learn some valuable skills.

1. Gather the family together and tell everyone that you're going to do some role playing. Select two people and ask them to imagine themselves in conflict.
2. Suggest several possible scenarios. You can even pose as one of the actors to get things started. When the conflict becomes obvious, bring the role playing to an end.
3. Ask the two actors how the conflict made them feel, and introduce the idea that honest and respectful communication is the first step to resolving conflict.
4. Next, go around the group and ask each person to suggest a possible solution to the conflict. Remind everyone to avoid passing judgment or assigning blame.
5. Select someone to write each solution down. Get as many solutions as possible, and then read the list aloud. Go around the group again, and ask everyone for feedback.
6. End the exercise on a positive note by thanking everyone for their participation and congratulating your actors on a great performance!

"A story should have a beginning, a middle, and an end . . . but not necessarily in that order."

—Jean-Luc Godard

Write a Novel

Every year marks National Novel Writing Month, or NaNoWriMo—a project for aspiring writers, veterans of the craft, or anyone who wants to give writing a try. You can find the website at *www.nanowrimo.org.* The premise is to write a 50,000-word novel in one month. It sounds like a huge amount of pressure to be creative, but if you go to the website, you'll realize that it's a pretty casual affair. Nobody's going to twist your arm to write that novel. Pride and money are not on the line. The idea behind the site is to celebrate the wonderful world of writing and to engage your creative side. It's an exercise that exists for the joy of craft. Some people find that to be the best therapy there is.

DEVELOP A WRITING HABIT

You don't have to wait until November to play around with the idea of a novel. You don't even have to write a novel.

Take an hour or two every night or every other night to sit down at your desk or at your laptop and write. Don't think about it. Don't let your brain swell with visions of glory or the stress of coming up with something everyone is going to like. Let go of those notions and get lost in the pleasure of writing something. It can be a poem, a short story, a screenplay, a novel or anything that gets the keys clicking.

"Life is a shipwreck but we must not forget to sing in the lifeboats."

—Voltaire

Create a Mantra

Using a mantra may strike you as rather strange at first, but an important step on the path to spiritual growth is your willingness to try new approaches. So come up with a mantra that will help you feel connected to a higher purpose.

A good mantra is something you can use at any time of the day. It can reaffirm your goals and remind you of what's pushing you to succeed in life. It can also maintain your spiritual center and establish the core values that dictate your thoughts, your actions and, indeed, your entire life. That's quite a bit of ground for a few simple words that you've come up with yourself.

TRY THIS SIMPLE MANTRA YOGA EXERCISE

- Choose a single word or expression, limiting it to about five syllables (for example, "nightingale").
- Recite the word very slowly for about one minute. Draw out every possible sound from the word, and vibrate those sounds. In this example, the *n*'s and the *l* offer good possibilities for humming the sounds.
- Recite the word for another minute, picking up the pace. Repeat this three more times, each time speeding up the recitation.
- When you're finished, the word will have evoked sounds, thoughts, and feelings you did not have when you started.

"Surround yourself with the best people you can find, delegate authority, and don't interfere as long as the policy you've decided upon is being carried out."

—Ronald Reagan

Learn to Delegate

When you're working on a large project, do you try to take everything on all by yourself or do you try to divide the tasks among your coworkers? If you're the type to put in long hours to complete a project that would be better served by multiple brains and hands, it's time to learn how to delegate if you want to be an effective manager. For instance, the editor of a magazine isn't expected to write, edit, and design the entire magazine herself.

Are there parts of a project you're overseeing that another colleague is more qualified to deal with? If so, assign it to that person.

WEEK TEN

BREAK IT DOWN

If you're not currently working on anything big or complex enough for you to delegate parts of it to your coworkers, you still should be able to visualize yourself delegating tasks effectively. The following exercise will help you learn how.

1. For this exercise, you need to sit down with a pen and paper and imagine an assignment you might be given at work. Make it as large and complicated as you want. Perhaps you've been put in charge of organizing and hosting a two-day visit by the CEO of the parent company in Tokyo and his entourage.
2. Then, break the task down into manageable sections and as you write down each one, include the name or names of the people you would ask to take charge of that portion of the job. Picture yourself talking to your coworkers, explaining the tasks and their responsibilities, and describing your expectations.
3. Then, when the opportunity arises, implement this exercise. Your boss will see you in a different light, and you could be in line for even bigger and more impressive projects.

"All of us who are concerned for peace and triumph of reason and justice must be keenly aware how small an influence reason and honest good will exert upon events in the political field."

—Albert Einstein

Join a Political Action Group

Are you dissatisfied with politicians? Do you hope for change? Do you hold a brighter vision for America and the world? Mahatma Gandhi once advised people to be the change that they wanted to see in the world. That means getting off the couch, turning off the television, and going out into the world and doing something to bring about that change. Join with others who feel as passionate as you about creating a more meaningful life and a better future through political action. Living and working toward a more meaningful and purpose-driven life is an important path to achieving happiness.

MEET OTHERS LIKE YOU

Link up with other like-minded people. Make an effort to meet other politically active people by attending political rallies, working with charitable fundraisers, and joining environmental groups for hikes, bird watching, or biking trips. When you join communities of like-minded people, you have more power to effect change, get laws enacted, and do good works.

"I don't love studying. I hate studying. I like learning. Learning is beautiful."

—Natalie Portman

Support Your Friends' Education

Going back to school has become increasingly popular in recent years. Sometimes we're forced to put aside an ambition when reality comes knocking at our door, but it isn't too late to get back on track. Even if you're not going back to college and have no plans to do so, you probably know someone who is. It takes great resolve to jump back into a scholastic endeavor. The costs can be high, and the demands on a person's time can be enormous. Make sure you support your friends who are pursuing educational goals.

HELP YOUR FRIENDS STUDY

1. Think of all the friends you have who have taken this leap. Could any of them use a little help studying? Offer to be a study partner.
2. You don't need to be an expert on the subject they're studying. A study partner simply has to be there to help keep the other person focused on the task at hand.
3. You might give them prompts for memorization or check a paper for spelling, punctuation, and clarity. It all depends on what they need.
4. If nothing else, they could probably use someone to help them maintain their sanity!

*"My favorite sense is touch. I love the feel of a man's cold
skin, with goose pimples. I find it very erotic."*

—Tina Hobley

Seduce Yourself with Touch

We live in a very visual society. Unfortunately, this obsession with only what we can see leaves us in danger of missing out on some extremely erotic experiences. One of the most exciting senses of all is touch, and one of the best parts of sex is enjoying the sensation of touch. You can enhance the sensual side of touch before you even get to the bedroom. Focus on how things feel rather than how they look. How does the water feel as it shoots out of the shower head and down over your skin? Think about how silky your blouse feels as you slip it on. Caress your arms and feel the smoothness.

SEDUCE YOUR PARTNER WITH TOUCH

Your attention to the sensation of touch in your daily life could easily translate to a more pleasurable sexual experience.

1. To heighten your lover's awareness, make sure everything that touches his or her skin has an extra sensation added to it. You can do this with items like silky bedding or silky lingerie. You may also want to try a feather, something furry, or a rose when you touch them.
2. You can further heighten the sense of touch by removing the sense of sight with a blindfold. Of course, you'll want to make sure your partner is completely comfortable with this type of love play before doing this.

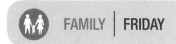
"Being selected Most Improved was a special individual award because when I speak to young people I always try to tell them the importance about it's not where you start but where you end up."

—Kevin Johnson

Hold Your Own Awards Ceremony

We're inundated with the best and brightest from television, music, and the movies, and every year there seems to be another group of people patting each other on the back. So, why not create your own version of an awards ceremony—one with a bit of a twist?

Once a year, hold a special awards night during which everyone receives recognition for something notable he or she has done during the previous year. Play games and serve snacks. Give your ceremony an air of importance.

CREATE YOUR OWN AWARD

You're not looking for the obvious or the earth-shattering for this award. You're looking for someone who has done a little something that went unnoticed or was overlooked by the rest of the family—by everyone except you. Perhaps your eight-year-old finally brushed her teeth for more than 30 seconds, or your teenager hung up the towels after his shower. Maybe your spouse or partner remembered to take out the trash. Create the award and give it to your loved one at a moment when he or she will appreciate it.

"An ideal museum show would be a mating of Brideshead Revisited *... with* House & Garden *... provoking intense and pleasurable nostalgia for a past that none of its audience has had."*

—Robert Hughes

Visit a Museum

Visiting a museum with your friends is fun and enjoyable, but if it's been a while or it's your first trip, it might be pleasant to go on your own. It's a delightful experience to spend time in a museum with absolutely no expectations.

Visit the website for the American Association of Museums, at *www .aam-us.org,* to find out everything you ever wanted to know about museums. With more than 17,500 museums in the United States, there's bound to be one near you that caters to one of your many interests. You might find something new to pique your curiosity, and if museums really appeal to you, there are plenty of volunteer and career opportunities available.

MEDITATE IN A MUSEUM

1. It doesn't matter what type of museum you pick. Choose one that matches your interests. Walk into a quiet museum on a quiet afternoon, and you'll suddenly find yourself surrounded by nothing but an abundance of culture and history.
2. The special ambiance of a museum can be extremely effective for soothing your frazzled nerves. The hushed, expectant atmosphere allows your mind to move across a landscape of sights and sounds designed to inspire you on countless levels.
3. When you're on your own, you don't have to rush or consider someone else's schedule. You can absorb what you see at your own pace.
4. It doesn't have to cost you anything—there are museums nationwide that offer free admission during specified hours or days of the week. Visit the website of a museum in your city to see what they have waiting for you.

"Tolerance implies no lack of commitment to one's own beliefs. Rather it condemns the oppression or persecution of others."

—John F. Kennedy

Open Your Mind to Other Faiths

No one is perfect, but that doesn't mean we can't strive to be. One of the ways to do that is to maintain a high level of tolerance and understanding for other religions. You may not believe in or even understand another religion, but millions of other people do. When you practice acceptance of this and other truths, it lowers your stress level, lowering your blood pressure, increasing your tolerance of others, increasing your levels of joy and happiness, and accentuating your wellness in general. Don't forget to introduce your children to other religious beliefs and traditions as well. For example, you could bless them with the traditional Jewish birkat kohanim prayer and make it part of their bedtime ritual.

VISIT OTHER CHURCHES

You can do more to increase your tolerance or understanding if you take time to visit some of the different places of worship in your area. No one is telling you to change your own beliefs. Visiting some of these places does not mean you're going to walk in the way you are and walk out a card-carrying member of that religion. Rather, it's a way of putting aside some of the things you may not completely understand about the world that exists outside of your own. Ignorance can be eliminated, and there are always things you can do to facilitate that. Dropping in on a church, synagogue, or other place of worship does that by increasing your education of what moves and inspires other people.

*"I'm a great believer in luck, and I find the
harder I work the more I have of it."*

—Thomas Jefferson

Think of Three!

You know you're good at your job. You hear it from your coworkers, you're praised by your boss, and your partner is impressed with your job successes. But it's been a long time since you've received a raise or a promotion. Perhaps it's because you haven't asked, but before you rush off to see your boss, you have some work to do.

You could present your boss with a giant list of your successful projects and admirable qualities, but you'd be more likely to hold his or her attention if you present three clear, succinct reasons why you're a great candidate for a promotion or raise. But first you'll need to review the work you've done and determine how you've benefited the company during the time you've been with them. You should write out a list of everything you've done in order to search out those three things that really set you apart. If you need help, ask a few trusted friends and coworkers. When you have three reasons, write them down and write down what projects you've completed that best illustrate those points.

MEET WITH YOUR BOSS

After you have requested a private meeting with your boss, let her know you understand she's a busy person. Instead of making small talk, get directly to the point. Let her know that you enjoy working for the company. Then:

1. Focus on the quality and quantity of your work.
2. Tell your boss the three reasons why you should be promoted to a new job.
3. Know what the new job will entail and be able to share details of what qualifies you to perform the tasks expected in the new job.
4. Explain you'll happily take new training and are eager to accept new responsibilities.

"What makes a good coach? Complete dedication."

—George Halas

Support Youth Sports

You probably know of several youth-league sports teams in your community. One of the most important ways these leagues sustain themselves is through the dedication of people who lend their time in any way possible. You don't necessarily have to be a parent to be a part of the team. Many of those who join in are people who simply want to be involved. They want to support youth sports and its countless benefits, and they want to support their community. If you find yourself nodding in agreement, there's a good chance that something can be found for you to do.

SUPPORT YOUR TEAM

There are many ways to be useful. There are likely several sports available to choose from, including football, soccer, basketball, hockey, and baseball.

1. If coaching is your dream, then by all means go for it. Just remember that a lot of these leagues often need more than just good coaches. They may also need help with selling tickets, running the concession stand, cleaning up the bleachers after a big game, or even maintaining the field through the busy season.
2. No job is more important than the other. All of them are vital to the continued health and success of these leagues. The kids might not thank you for cleaning up the stands, but they don't have to. They're already thanking you every time they go out there and have a terrific time.
3. You can get started by attending a few of the games for the different leagues. Get to know some of the people involved with each team so you can choose the one that fits your needs and interests.

"May those who love us, love us; and those who do not love us, may God turn their hearts; and if He cannot turn their hearts, may He turn their ankles that we may know them by their limping."

—Irish prayer

Laugh at Each Other's Jokes

Laughter has positive health benefits and also is a rational way to accept the totally irrational aspects of life, including disagreements between friends when they arise. Expecting two people to agree all the time is the most irrational expectation you can have. People are prone to asking unanswerable questions and taking life far too seriously. Friends tend to be more accepting when they can view an issue with humor because, let's face it, humor can make everything seem a little bit better. One way to navigate beyond disagreements and lighten things up is to make a little joke and then laugh together at the silliness of it. Self-deprecating humor is also effective in shifting the energy of negativity, darkness, or tension. Don't take yourselves too seriously. Poke a little fun now and again.

THROW A COMEDY PARTY

Laughter is good for your health and longevity, and comedy adds fun and frivolity to any gathering. So, the next time you're thinking of throwing a party, kick up your happiness quotient a notch or two and make sure that your guest list includes some people with a natural sense of humor. Give your comedic friends free rein to do a little standup work or try out some new material. Make sure they know ahead of time that you will have a receptive audience who enjoys a good laugh. Then join in the fun; laugh until your muscles hurt.

"A spark between two people can lead to a short circuit."

—Amanda Marteleur

Break the Cycle

Do you continually fall for people who are wrong for you? You're not alone. A recent study using information garnered from 2,000 adults on a dating website concluded that the average woman will kiss twenty-two men, enjoy four long-term relationships and have her heart broken five times before she meets Mr. Right.

It's time to break the cycle. For example, if you crave excitement, instead of winding up in a relationship drama all the time, try finding someone who loves to travel to exotic locations or who participates in high-adrenaline sports. By finding other, healthier ways to fulfill what you need, you're more likely to have a long-lasting and fulfilling relationship with less drama.

LOOK AT YOUR PAST

It's time to break the unhealthy cycle before you end up in another dead-end relationship.

1. For this exercise, you're going to need a quiet space and some time to take an unflinchingly honest look at your past love life. If you'd like moral support or some candid input, enlist the help of a trusted friend.
2. For each past romance, list why you were attracted to that person in the first place, and then write down why the relationship didn't work out. Did you find yourself interested in people who were unavailable because you liked the thrill of the chase, only to find they were unable to provide for you emotionally or otherwise? Did you seek out "bad boys" or "bad girls" because you found them exciting?
3. Brainstorm ways to get what you want in a healthy relationship.

"Having children makes you no more a parent than having a piano at home makes you a pianist."

—Michael Levine

Learn about Parenting

Talk about on-the-job training! Parenting is the career that comes with no preparation, no instruction manual, and no do-overs. Do you want to be more confident and more in control? Invest a little time in becoming a better parent if you want to raise strong, self-sufficient, well-adjusted, happy children. You can do this by reading parenting books, talking with other parents, and consulting with trusted advisers, such as your children's pediatrician.

TAKE A CLASS

If you want to be the best parent you can be, sign up for a parenting class. As these classes become increasingly available and widely acceptable, more parents than ever are seeking them out for help with the most difficult job they will ever have. Learning and implementing new parenting methods can help you now and give you critical skills and resources to deal with problems later.

1. Such classes often can be found through parent-teacher organizations, local adult education courses, the family court system, and even online.
2. Learn what to expect from your child as he or she goes through various stages to adulthood.
3. Discover techniques for discipline that do not involve yelling, spanking, screaming, or arguing.
4. Understand why children need boundaries and guidelines as they grow.
5. Networking is another one of the many benefits to taking parenting classes. One of the greatest sources of support and encouragement in any undertaking is someone who is going through the same thing.

"There is no mystique to Tai Chi Chuan. What is difficult is the perseverance. It took me ten years to discover my chi, but thirty years to learn how to use it. Once you see the benefit, you won't want to stop."

—Ma Yueh Liang

Practice the Art of Tai Chi

You may be familiar with the art of tai chi, because it has become a very popular form of exercise in the West. Its ability to bring relaxation to the mind and vitality to the body is well-known.

Tai chi emphasizes relaxation through gentle movement. Through specific exercises that emulate natural forces—animals, plants, and elements like the wind—*chi* is also transformed. This is an important part of the practice, because it enhances both the mind and the life force.

FIND A TAI CHI CLASS NEAR YOU

You might find tai chi classes at the local YMCA and fitness centers. Many tai chi instructors also offer private classes. You may also want to try a tai chi video—many are meant for beginners.

"For I was hungry and you gave me something to eat,
I was thirsty and you gave me something to drink,
I was a stranger and you invited me in."

—Matthew 25:35

See the Homeless

You see them on the street, but you try not to make eye contact. You want to avoid the possibility of sparking a conversation. Part of this desire to steer clear of a homeless person stems from your frustration and feelings of helplessness. What can you possibly do to help? One of the best ways to assist a homeless person is to show them respect. Make eye contact, talk to them with genuine interest, and give them a sense of dignity that they rarely experience. While homeless people living on the street suffer hardships that are difficult to imagine and are often treated like society's pariahs, pretending not to see them doesn't void the truth that they are part of society.

HELP THE HOMELESS

Although some may be mentally ill and a minority might even be dangerous, many are ordinary people with few resources and options.

1. Look them in the eye, flash a big smile, and say hello. Your smile can make a difference and brighten a moment or two for someone others most likely avoid. The look of kindness, compassion, or consideration is more beautiful than an expressionless person who treats others as if they weren't visible.

2. Carry cards that list the names, addresses, and phone numbers of local shelters and other nearby organizations that help the homeless. Hand these cards out to the homeless.

"Two heads are better than one."

—English adage

Consult with Colleagues and Friends

"Two heads" means the minds of two people thinking together to solve some problem or to figure out some great strategy for accomplishing a task. To build your skills and create more income, brainstorm ideas with your colleagues and friends. For example, if you have a specific skill that you use in your day job, maybe you could expand your skill, increase your knowledge, and make more money by consulting, teaching, writing books and articles, and even becoming a professional speaker on topics related to your areas of expertise. The point is to find ways to exploit what you know in ways that generate income streams. Your friends and colleagues can help you figure out these ways and point you in directions you might not have thought of on your own.

WORK TOGETHER

You can also work with friends and colleagues to create something new out of the skills each of you possess.

1. For example, let's say your husband works with computer-aided design (CAD) programs and mechanical CAD software. You are proficient in using Microsoft Office and several financial software programs. Together, your combined knowledge and skills are formidable.

2. Consider how to combine what you know to work together. With companies going global, you might think of combining your knowledge and talent to form a web-based company or offer to consult.

3. First figure out what you have to offer and whether what you have to offer fills a need in the current marketplace.

4. Then think about how you might function as a team to create income streams from what you know.

"An animal's eyes have the power to speak a great language."

—Martin Buber

Support Foster Programs for Animals

People are not the only ones in need in your community. Most cities and towns have some kind of animal foster program in place. These organizations perform many valuable services for animals, one of which is placing dogs and cats in foster care. This happens for a number of reasons. Usually, it's due to limited shelter space or the animal being extremely young or injured. You can support your local organization by donating money and supplies.

FOSTER A PET

You can also help support a foster program by actually fostering a pet.

1. Taking in one of these animals is a tremendous responsibility, but it provides remarkable rewards. You must be at least eighteen years of age to qualify.
2. It's also important to remember that your commitment may require a great deal of time and effort. This will depend on the physical and mental health of the animal you decide to foster, but you don't have to take on the sickest or youngest animal in order to do some good.
3. Several websites, including *www.paws.org, www.pets911 .com,* and *www.aspca.org*, have information on how to become an animal foster parent and lists of frequently asked questions. Your local animal shelter may also have a foster parent program, so give them a call and find out what they have to offer.

"Never doubt that a small group of thoughtful, committed citizens can change the world."

—Margaret Mead

Do a Charitable Deed Together

Take a cue from the many Hollywood celebrities as well as successful artisans, musicians, politicians, and others who support a favorite charity, and get involved. If you feel inspired to do a kind act or make a charitable donation that could change the life of someone else, talk about it with your friend. Decide together what appeals to the both of you and how much time, money, and commitment that together you could pledge.

FIND YOUR PERFECT MATCH

Booker T. Washington once said, "I think that I have learned that the best way to lift one's self up is to help someone else."

1. With your friend, visit *www.volunteermatch.org*. Using their search engine, enter your location and keywords describing the volunteer opportunity you are looking for. You can also enter the skills you have or the ones you would like to develop.

2. For example, you could work in a soup kitchen, be hospice volunteers, or host a fundraising party for your favorite cause.

3. You don't have to follow in the footsteps of Angelina Jolie, with her United Nations work, or Susan Sarandon's support of Heifer International. Whether you choose to help a local family or organization or work on the global scale, you and your friend will be earning good karma.

"There are things that we never want to let go of, people we never want to leave behind. But keep in mind that letting go isn't the end of the world; it's the beginning of a new life."

—Unknown

Accentuate the Positive

We've all been hurt by love. It's how you choose to react and move forward that matters. When you permit feelings of fear, jealousy, angst, the need to control, or resentment to take charge, it's easy to become bitter and defensive. By doing so, you erect barriers that prevent you from finding true love. In fact, we often attract what we put out, which means that if you're approaching love in this negative way, you're more than likely to find someone who is bitter, defensive, resentful, jealous, and so on. If you find yourself thinking and feeling negatively about love relationships, make an effort to reframe your thinking into more positive channels. Consider that your past experience has taught you what you don't want. Give yourself permission to move towards what you want—a more positive approach than trying to avoid more pain.

HEAL THE HURT

Take steps to heal past relationship hurts in healthy ways.

1. Do all of those things for yourself that your last partner didn't. Treat yourself with respect, and believe that you are deserving of respect from others.
2. Write about the experience in a journal to allow yourself to process all of your feelings. Look within yourself to see where you can improve and be a better partner.
3. Be a force of love, support, joy, and peace. Believe in the power of love and that you, too, will find someone who treats you as you deserve. You'll be impressed at how thinking positively and taking positive actions to support those thoughts will bring you what you want.

*"Another thing I like to do is sit back and take in nature. To look
at the birds, listen to their singing, go hiking, camping and jogging
and running, walking along the beach, playing games and sometimes
being alone with the great outdoors. It's very special to me."*

—Larry Wilcox

Go Camping

Camping can be incredibly fun and can teach you and your family about mutual respect, responsibility, resiliency, and survival strengths and weaknesses. Having the right gear and camping know-how can make the experience a lot more enjoyable. Talk with your loved ones about where you'd like to camp and for how long. Spending time together in nature can draw you closer to see the wonder of creation and enable you both to renew and recharge body and spirit.

CAMP WITH COMPANY

Get together with another family who would enjoy joining you on a camping trip.

1. Talk through any concerns. Make safety the top priority.
2. Make a reservation and become familiar with park regulations before you head out.
3. Check the weather and take along the appropriate clothing, and supplies. Plan on taking out of the park whatever you bring in.
4. Create a keepsake box or book of photos you take on the trip.

"Sorrow can be alleviated by good sleep, a bath and a glass of wine"

—St. Thomas Aquinas

Take a Long, Hot Bath

When was the last time you took a long, hot bath? If you can't remember, then it might be time to reconsider the idea of taking one as a way of distancing yourself from a long day and relaxing enough to think about getting to bed in decent time. Many people prefer a morning shower, and that's fine, but a leisurely bath isn't just about cleanliness. It can be one of the fastest ways to cut ourselves off from the rest of the world and find a little calm after a long day.

MAKING YOUR BATH SPECIAL

It shouldn't take you very long to fill up the tub or indulge in any other rituals you might want to include.

1. Some people enjoy a good book and a glass of wine.
2. Others prefer bubbles, dim lights, and a few candles.
3. You can even add some favorite music to the mix.

There's no right or wrong to relax in the tub. Anyone who has already added a bath to their routine already knows how great it feels. Try one tonight and discover the benefits for yourself.

"Integrity is what we do, what we say, and what we say we do."

—Don Galer

Keep Your Integrity Strong

How do you keep your integrity intact when the elements of life are threatening it all the time? You have to realize that you will be tested occasionally, and you must stick to your standards of what you know is the proper thing to do. The best way to fight a threat to your integrity is to understand what is right before the threat comes. Know right and do it when you're not faced with a challenge, and it will be easier to act with integrity when you *are* faced with a challenge.

CHOOSE INTEGRITY

Consider the following tips when faced with challenging situations.

- Keep the faith. Faith in what you know is just and right is a monumental tool in fighting threats against your integrity.
- Trust yourself. You know your heart, and you must trust in your own ability to do what is right.
- Keep your hunger in check. Don't let your desire for more or bigger or better or faster or prettier steal your integrity. Your hunger can be overpowering and can cause you to abandon your integrity in pursuit of fulfilling the hunger.
- Choose fairness. Being fair means that you are consistent with the rules of ethics, principles, and morality. It means that you will choose what is morally and ethically fair over what is easy.
- Practice loyalty. Being loyal to others is certainly important, but being loyal to yourself matters just as much. One of the most painful lessons learned is when you are disloyal to your own value system, moral code, and ethical standards. It is damaging to your self-esteem to betray yourself.

"The way of the world is meeting people through other people."

—Robert Kerrigan

Network Now

Some people falsely believe that you don't need to begin to network until you are looking for a job. That would be akin to starting to take better care of your body after you have been diagnosed with heart disease. At that point, the damage has already been done. It's a much better idea to try to stay healthy in the first place with regular exercise and a balanced diet. Think of networking the same way; it's something you can do to keep your career healthy.

> **BUILD A NETWORK**
>
> Building a network can seem like an overwhelming task, especially if you think you are starting without any contacts at all. Well, guess what? You already have contacts—unless, of course, you've been living in a cave all your life. It's likely you have relatives, friends, and acquaintances. Sure, not all of them can personally help you with your career—they probably don't even work in the same field you do—but they haven't been living in caves, either. They have friends and acquaintances who may be able to help.
>
> 1. There are many ways in which being part of a professional network can benefit your career. Of course, the first thing that comes to mind is the job search. Some career counselors believe that the best route to a better job is through somebody you already know or to whom you can be introduced. People such as former coworkers, friends of friends, neighbors, and even former classmates can be very helpful in your job search.
> 2. There are other reasons to network, too. Members of your network can offer you advice on work-related matters, provide information, hook you up with potential clients, and even help you find potential employees when you need to hire someone. The larger your network, the more opportunities you'll find to get help achieving your goals.

"Without a sense of caring, there can be no community."

—Robert J. D'Angelo

Volunteer at a Senior Center

You may know of someone, perhaps even a family member, living in a retirement community, an assisted-living facility, or a nursing home. Many such facilities have a center where residents may gather for special programs or for planned social events and activities. You can spread some good cheer by volunteering some of your free time to a senior center.

Today's senior citizens are not quite like previous generations of seniors. They like stimulation, care about good health, eat right, appreciate lifelong learning, and enjoy socializing, even if their options are limited to conversations with others living in their community. Most likely, whatever you do will be appreciated and the topic of happy conversation long after you've done your bit.

HOW YOU CAN HELP THE ELDERLY

Contact your local retirement community, assisted-living facility, or nursing home to find out what is needed there and how your interests and schedule can fit in. Visiting the residents, assisting with crafts, writing letters and cards, reading the papers and discussing the news, providing musical entertainment—the list goes on and on.

1. If you have a pet, ask if the home participates in a visiting pet program and find out how to have your pet approved to be taken along.
2. Recruit a group of friends and help to decorate a room or plant a flower garden. Learn more about health-related careers by assisting with medical records and nutritional services.
3. Offer your talents and abilities to bring inspiration and enthusiasm. You'll be delighted by what you receive in return.

"The most I can do for my friend is simply be his friend."

—Henry David Thoreau

Do Something New Together

Bringing someone along on a new venture can open your eyes. Another person might suggest something that you wouldn't have thought of on your own. Most of us enjoy experiencing new things, but we balk at the prospect of going it alone. A friend cuts right through that and eliminates any excuses. You might be doing that friend a favor by inviting her to join you, since she may also be reluctant to go alone. You won't have to worry about not having anyone to talk to because you'll have someone right there whom you already know. It should make those awkward first moments fly right by. After that, you'll be too busy having fun to worry about it.

TAKE A CLASS

Taking a course at a community college or rec center is a great way not only to spend your spare time but also to pick up a new, useful hobby or skill. You might be reluctant to give it a try on your own, but it might become a lot more appealing if you could convince a friend or two to join in. Half the fun may be deciding on the right course to take. Pick up a course catalog from your local community college and bring it along to the next coffee date or lunch with your friend. Show it to your buddy and propose your idea.

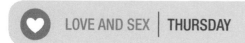

"You yourself, as much as anybody in the entire universe, deserve your love and affection."

—Buddha

Love Yourself

Begin by noticing how often you worry about what your lover might be thinking of your physical features, whether it's breasts, hips, or tummy (if you're a woman), or penis, muscles, or hair (if you're a man). Notice how you talk trash to yourself. And start talking back. Tell yourself what you appreciate about your body. When you appreciate the gifts you have been given, the journey toward learning to love and honor yourself—just the way you are—can begin.

TAKE BACK YOUR POWER

When you recognize that it is only you who hold yourself back, you can take back your power and discover your freedom. If you decide that as an adult, you do not agree with some of the things you were taught as a child, you can make the decision to reclaim your vitality and your capacity for bodily pleasure. Here is a simple exercise that will be useful in all areas of your life.

- Create an image in your mind of a situation or time in your life when you have felt really good about yourself. You feel empowered, smart, and capable.
- Close your eyes and breathe deeply into your belly for a few minutes while you hold on to that feeling. Really feel it and breathe it in.
- Now, imagine that you are feeling that way about your body: It is strong; it is healthy; it is beautiful. Drink in that feeling and bathe yourself in it for a few minutes.

This little exercise, if you practice it, will vastly improve your sex life. Practice loving yourself!

"Any problem, big or small, within a family, always seems to start with bad communication. Someone isn't listening."

—Emma Thompson

Avoid Communication Breakdown

It is important for everyone involved in the care of a child to know what is happening in that child's life. Due to busy work schedules, lack of time, and transportation challenges, sometimes the opportunities for caregivers to meet in person are limited. Make sure that communication is a priority.

USE A COMMUNICATION NOTEBOOK

A communication notebook can be a vital tool when parents share custody of a child and especially if that child has special needs or health issues.

1. The communication notebook can contain a list of medications, special foods or food restrictions, and allergy reminders. The notebook could also contain important phone numbers (pediatrician, dentist), medical plan and coverage info, and eating schedules and bedtimes.
2. The notebook can put your mind at ease when sending your children off to their grandparents, allowing them to sleep over at a friend's house, or taking them to the ex-partner's for the weekend. Everyone will be on the same page; for example, knowing the rules in your household about snacks before bedtime and what constitutes a healthy snack, and whom to call in an emergency, besides you.
3. Get your partner and children involved in making a communication notebook for each child. Let each child personalize his or her notebook with a picture, a fingerprint, and anything else that would make it unique.

"Tea began as a medicine and grew into a beverage."

—Kakuzo Okakura

Make a Bedtime Brew

Herbal teas have become increasingly popular with a tea for every mood. It's become a valuable tool for people trying to unwind and relax at any time of day, and for many, it has become a wonderful treat to enjoy and use for winding down before going to bed. The wide variety of herbal teas makes it possible for everyone to find something to suit their tastes. Some enjoy chamomile. Others prefer one of the lightly-flavored varieties that feature all kinds of fruits and herbs. Pour yourself a cup of a simple, enjoyable way to decompress and let your mind relax. Have a great sleep!

BREW UP A HOBBY

The enjoyment of tea can even turn into a hobby. For the time being, you'll do just fine buying a box of tea that appeals to you at your local grocery store. You can also shop online at sites such as *www.argotea.com, www.teavana.com,* or *www.celestial seasonings.com.*

- However, you can decide to get more involved in tea-making. There's a lot of information available to make sure that you're enjoying your tea to its greatest potential.
- To enjoy your tea drinking more fully, invest in a decorative pot and cups or mugs. You'll find some beautiful choices at *www .enjoyingtea.com.*
- Thich Nhat Hanh, the Buddhist monk, says that in order to enjoy your tea, you must put all stressful thoughts far away from you and focus on your tea experience. This is called "mindfulness" in Buddhist tradition.

"The measure of life is not its duration, but its donation."

—Peter Marshall

Contribute to Charity

If you're planning to donate to a charity, you certainly have a multitude of worthy causes to choose from. It's important to give, but it's also important to be satisfied with your giving. You have to connect to something that speaks to your humanity. You have to strive to go beyond your comfort zone and become a better-informed citizen of the world. That means making sure that any charities you give to deserve the time and money that you're able to give. One website, *www.charitynavigator.org*, evaluates the financial health and efficiency of more than one thousand charities. You can read reviews by other people who have donated and even submit your own review.

FIND A NEW CHARITY

If you already give to charities, one wonderful exercise in spiritual growth and edification is to venture beyond the known and familiar and to consider choosing another charitable organization as the recipient of your time and money.

1. Spend some time online and investigate some of the charities seeking assistance.
2. Think of a cause that you've always been interested in but know little or nothing about. That's a good starting point.
3. Digging a little deeper might introduce you to a charity you never even knew existed. It's a big and complex world out there, one that includes people and causes who need help, but don't get the same exposure as the more established charities.

"Youth is a wonderful thing. What a crime to waste it on children."

—George Bernard Shaw

Establish Financial Goals for Decades Ahead

With the recent economic crisis hurting plenty of people's retirement plans, longevity might be an expensive prospect for you and your spouse. But even if you are already a couple of decades into your marriage, you can still do some financial planning for the future. Start by sitting down and talking about the goals you have for the future.

WEEK FOURTEEN

MAKE A PLAN

Once you've decided on your goals, you can make a plan and start taking action steps to meet it.

1. For example, if you aren't already saving, you can start.
2. You might even take a second job or figure out if it makes sense to turn a hobby into a moneymaking enterprise. If you both decide to do that, you'll have many revenue streams to help you meet future financial goals.

As you approach your retirement as a couple, you'll be glad you gave some thought to the future when there was still time to affect it in a significant and positive way.

*"A characteristic of the normal child is he
doesn't act that way very often."*

—Unknown

Mentor at an After-School Program

When school is out for the day, most kids already have plans in place for their afternoons and evenings. Homework, sports, and other extra-curricular activities usually take care of what little free time they have. Still, there are many children who have nothing to do and only an empty house to welcome them. For these kids, there are many after-school programs in place. These programs can usually be found at your local rec center, and the activities can range from field trips to just watching a movie and hanging out. The organizations running these programs require volunteers to supervise the children. All you need is the ability to relate to kids and a little creativity.

GET STARTED

Children of all ages and from all walks of life need you in their life, so consider becoming a volunteer today.

- The website *www.americorps.gov* is looking for people to act as mentors, counselors, and tutors in after-school programs all over the country. Enter your location and the search terms "mentor youth" into their search engine, and you will be provided with specific volunteer opportunities in your area.
- Maybe you have some new ideas to change things up a bit and offer the kids a change from watching movies and playing cards.
- The most important thing to remember is that you're creating structure for kids who perhaps don't have enough. Numerous studies have shown that structure is critical in the development of healthy, mature, and successful adults.

"Loose lips sink ships."

—World War II slogan

Don't Give In to Gossip

Friends need to keep the trust they have placed in each other. You are your friend's most trusted ally; she can feel safe in venting or discussing her problems with you and knows it won't go any further. We live and work in worlds populated by friends, acquaintances, family members, and coworkers, and those people often are separated only by degrees. It really is a small world. Although a friend or relative might want to know all the latest gossip, don't share your friend's problems. That's no one else's business.

PRACTICE THOUGHTFULNESS

In addition to keeping your friend's secrets, give your friend the gift of mindfulness. Be attentive to every aspect of your relationship with her.

1. Notice how you listen, how you speak, whether or not you thoughtfully choose your words or just utter whatever your mind is thinking.
2. Do you ever remain silent or think about silence as a good thing and the best response in certain situations?
3. When you practice mindfulness, your focus is on only one thing at a time.

"Any man who can drive safely while kissing a pretty girl is simply not giving the kiss the attention it deserves."

—Albert Einstein

Improve Your Kisses

Keep your mouth fresh and healthy for a lifetime of kisses by maintaining good dental hygiene and taking care of your toothbrush. It's not glamorous, but it's important! You can effectively kill bacteria if you soak the toothbrush in Listerine or other antibacterial solution for about twenty minutes. Alternatively, you can buy your mate a packet of new toothbrushes to use on his pearly whites and toss his old brush.

GIVE A KISS

Kissing is an art and can be improved with practice. Our lips are extremely sensitive and receptive to stimulation. Many people hold their lips stiffly, not letting them relax and be open to the receiving and giving required for good kissing. Practice using your lips in a soft, open way. Part them slightly and keep them moist. This will heighten their sensitivity.

1. When you are about to kiss, lick your lips to wet them, open your mouth a little, tip your head very slightly, and go softly forward. At first, leave your tongue out of it. Use your lips to gently explore the interior of your partner's lips. Move very slowly, but with confidence. Go deeper, and open your mouth a bit more as you feel yourself going into the kiss. Create a slight amount of suction as you expand and open your mouth a little bigger.
2. Take your lover's whole mouth into yours. Do this lovingly, as if you were exploring it for the first time. Eat them up—but gently. Now, if you wish to, you can do some French kissing—probing with your tongue into your lover's mouth and letting your lover do the same. Let your tongue slowly investigate rather than force its way into your partner's mouth. Tease and let yourself be teased. The more subtle you are, the better. Kissing can go on for a long time if it's treated as a playful and erotic activity.

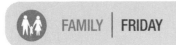

FAMILY | FRIDAY

"Straightforwardness, without the rules of propriety, becomes rudeness."

—Confucius

Set an Agenda for Your Family Meeting

Families benefit from calling meetings to air grievances or work through everyone's schedules, transportation, discipline, health, or financial issues. But if you try to accomplish too much at one time, you might accomplish nothing. Or, if no one knows what to expect, they may feel blindsided when a family member brings up a grievance against them. Set an agenda so that everyone knows what needs to be covered.

SET GROUND RULES BEFORE YOUR MEETING

Make sure you have some ground rules in place before your family meeting. Why? Because the conversation can move from civilized to heated and confrontational at warp speed. This is especially true in blended families and in dealing with exes.

- Avoid complaining about the past, and instead focus on the present issues.
- Make the meeting about finding solutions to problems.
- Keep the conversation positive.
- Try to communicate the issues and problems without blame or accusations.
- Ask everyone to offer their best solutions.
- Acknowledge the fact that everyone has hot-button issues, but ask everyone to set them aside for the sake of accomplishing the goals set forth in the agenda.
- Let go of expectations. When you have expectations, whether or not they are realistic, you are setting yourself up for disappointment if they aren't met. Accept the other people involved for who they are. You can't change them, nor should you try. Take responsibility for what you do, say, and feel and, if you can, try not to sweat the small stuff.

"I hold this to be the highest task of a bond between two people: that each should stand guard over the solitude of the other."

—Rainer Maria Rilke

Help Each Other De-Stress

Find a place of peace and solitude where you and your partner can relax and de-stress. Simultaneously give each other foot massages. Sit opposite one another with legs outstretched so as not to block the flow of the energy as it is released during the massage. Foot massage has long been used as a way to invoke deep relaxation. In fact, reflexology, an Eastern modality that focuses on the zones or meridians on the body through which vital energies circulate, involves deep tissue massage of the hands and feet, where some of the meridians are located.

TRY SOME DIFFERENT TECHNIQUES

You could also combine several relaxation techniques.

- Before or after the foot massages, drink cups of fragrant herb tea.
- Listen to soft relaxation music.
- Dim the lighting. Warm the room, if it's chilly, or cool it, if it's uncomfortably hot.
- Do deep breathing. Focus on eliminating chronic muscle tension that can decrease mental acuity and agility.

Use quiet, gentle speech with each other. Talk to each other as lovers do—that is, when lovers talk they don't have a list of talking points, don't stick to an agenda, and don't have an ulterior motive. Each enjoys every moment of the other's company and is reluctant to have such moments together end.

*"Striving for excellence motivates you; striving
for perfection is demoralizing."*

—Harriet Braiker

Accept that Nobody's Perfect

If you have perfectionist tendencies, you are less likely to take the blame for something gone wrong at your hand. It is out of your nature to be wrong or to have caused a problem, and thus, you may tend to pass the blame on to others to avoid the appearance of being imperfect. As you can imagine, this can make those around you unhappy—and thus contribute to conflict in your relationships with others. It's also no fun to be a perfectionist! It creates a lot of anxiety and conflict within yourself.

People with perfectionist tendencies have common traits such as the relentless pursuit of unrealistic goals, dissatisfaction with completed work, the belief that the less-than-perfect accomplishment equals the less-than-perfect person, an unrealistic fear of failure, and the false impression that perfection is tied to self-worth. Let go of the need to be perfect—or for others to be perfect—and you will be much happier!

DEFEAT PERFECTIONISM

If you feel that you are a perfectionist and want to work on being more realistic and kind to yourself, consider the following tips:

- Review your goals and make them more realistic.
- Understand that perfect is just a word, not a possibility.
- Enjoy your daily accomplishments and successes.
- Learn to celebrate mishaps of mood, action, and deed.
- Acknowledge your weaknesses as well as your strengths.

Choose one of the above tips and decide to implement it in your life for a week. Keep a daily journal detailing your successes and failures as you work to overcome your need for perfection.

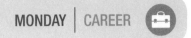

> *"The significance of man is not in what he
> attains but in what he longs to attain."*
>
> —Kahlil Gibran

Develop a Plan of Action

When you set goals for yourself and when you think about and work toward them day by day, you will feel happier about yourself. However, a goal must have an action plan, and that includes career goals. If your goal is finding a job with more security, how do you plan to do it? Will you research other careers of interest? Will you go back to college? What is your plan?

This is the place in your goal-setting process where you will need to use very specific statements. These statements will have to be realistic and doable to you. You may need to start simple and work toward complex, or start small and work toward big. With this type of goal setting and action planning, your goal is more likely to come to fruition. It is detailed, simple, doable, and reasonable. To say, "I'm going to go to college next semester" is a recipe for doing nothing next semester. However, a detailed list of ten specific statements outlining your plan is realistic, attainable, and will give you a genuine sense of accomplishment.

WEEK FIFTEEN

GET THE JOB DONE

Your action plan should look something like this:

- I will make an appointment with a counselor at a local college.
- I will research careers of interest.
- I will decide on my major.
- I will apply to college.
- I will apply for financial aid and scholarships.
- I will meet with a college adviser to plan my first semester.
- I will register for two classes for the first semester.
- I will buy my textbooks early so that I can begin to study early.
- I will attend every class meeting.
- I will seek tutorial assistance if I feel that I am getting behind.

"A good book has no ending."

—R. D. Cumming

Give the Gift of Reading

We often take our ability to read for granted while we complain of never having the occasion to enjoy a good book. We sometimes forget that there are people who don't even have the option to grumble about their lack of time to read because they are illiterate. This may be because of a learning disability, a language barrier, or simply because no one has bothered to take the time to teach someone. It doesn't take a lot of time to make the difference between illiteracy and the joy of reading. Take some time to find out what you can do to promote literacy. Literacy Connections, at *www.literacyconnections.com,* is a site where you can discover how to promote literacy.

LEND A BOOK—AND YOUR TIME

It's not important where you lend this kind of help. Anyone who needs this assistance will be grateful for the chance to love books the way you do.

1. Programs exist in most places. Check with libraries and community centers for programs that could use your help.
2. You don't have to make a huge time commitment. The training and time involved is a drop in the bucket compared to the gift you're imparting. A couple of hours on your part can open up a lifetime to someone else.

It isn't limited to the enjoyment of a good book, either. When someone has learned to read, the paths in other areas of work and life that will reveal themselves will be limitless.

> *"Nothing but heaven itself is better than a*
> *friend who is really a friend."*

—Plautus

Put Time and Energy into New Friendships as a Couple

In the first months of a new relationship, you might find that the people you used to pal around with sort of fall away—that is, they don't call you much anymore and don't seem very interested in putting time and energy into the friendship that they once did. It may seem strange, but actually, it's a fairly common occurrence. As our lives change, so do our relationships.

Extend the hand of friendship to other young couples whom you meet at church or possibly even when you go out to dinner. For example, if you sometimes eat in a restaurant with limited seating and there is a long line of couples waiting for a table, start a conversation with one or two couples. Invite them to share a table with you.

KEEP YOUR FRIENDS

All friendships require an investment of time and energy. Sometimes you just have to help your old friends understand how to interact with you as a part of a couple. Communication is always key.

1. Set aside time for you and your old friends to do things one-on-one, the way you used to.
2. If you are the only one who ever calls your friend to set up a date for getting together, you might want to verbalize that you view friendship as a two-way street and gently ask what's going on.
3. Your old friends simply may not get along with your partner as well as you'd like. That's okay. Don't push them, but let them know that you value their friendship.

"My ears turn me on like nothing else, they must be my most erogenous zone. Just having my ears kneaded is like a full body massage."

—Rebecca Romijn

Love Your Lover's Ears

The ear is one of your main erogenous zones; it has many nerve endings, and it is situated near the neck, another highly erotic area. The ear should be approached slowly, with a little teasing. Try a soft breath to start. Get close to the ear that is about to enjoy being the object of arousal. With slightly open lips, spread your warm breath around the ear and behind it. Move in with very soft and light kisses to the top area and the immediate hairline just above the ear. You might take a small piece of hair in your lips and give it a little pull, just to entice.

TAKE MORE ACTION

1. Move down the ear slowly to the fleshier areas and the lobe. Kiss and gently blow. Speak to your partner with barely audible words, teasing a little if you want to, or reminding your partner to relax and breathe. As your partner begins to react by moving and making sounds, begin to press your lips a little harder and with more ardor.

2. Take the lobe and lightly press and suck on it with your lips. Try a few light bites on the lower, fleshy part of the ear. Be gentle and playful. This is a bite to entice and show your passion; it is not meant to hurt. Above all, take your time, and find out what your ears have to offer to your sensual experiences the next time you make love.

"Children need boundaries and ground rules. When children don't have structure, they make up their own rules and negative behavior is what they use to get your attention."

—Jo Frost

Build Boundaries

Pediatricians and child psychologists have long noted that children do best when their lives have structure. The world can be a very scary place unless boundaries are in place to render a sense of security to children and teens. As teens go through the process of individuating, they push up against and even test the rigidity of parental and societal boundaries.

As parents, you are responsible for establishing boundaries for your children, including setting curfews, time frames, and limits that are acceptable for doing homework, eating meals, going to bed, getting up in the morning, dressing for school, staying over at a friend's house, and having friends visit in your home. In addition, assigning your children duties or chores teaches them perseverance, time management, and sense of purpose—all necessary for success in life.

HOLD REGULAR MEETINGS

Have weekly family meeting to go over curfews and other boundaries, as well as to review each child's duties and responsibilities. Make sure everyone knows what the limits are. Praise the good. Avoid focusing on negatives and use gentle redirection, as necessary.

"God put me on this earth to accomplish a certain number of things. Right now I am so far behind that I will never die."

—Bill Watterson

Tackle a Simple Project

Spring-cleaning or any kind of cleaning is not how most of us like to enjoy our time off. For many people, the idea of relaxing is to do as little as possible. That's okay, but you can also do something around the house and still find the tranquility you've been seeking. Certain projects around your house would probably lend themselves quite well to accomplishing something without sacrificing your sense of leisure.

MAKE A LIST

To facilitate getting small projects done in your spare time, make a list of the little projects that need to be done around your home. Select uncomplicated jobs you've been wanting to tackle, but just haven't been able to find the time. Here are some suggestions:

- That desk in your office could probably use some tidying.
- Maybe you have an attic, garage, or basement that you've been meaning to organize and clean.
- Go through that out-of-control linen closet or your grandmother's hope chest, or sort through a small drawer full of letters and papers.
- If a little bit of redecorating appeals to you, choose a color and paint one of the rooms in your house. Choose some matching wallpaper borders and create a new look that will lift your spirits as well as providing a wonderful sense of accomplishment.

"Influence may be the highest level of human skills."

—Unknown

Find Teachers—and Prophets

Not every person who is fascinated by the teachings of Buddha is a Buddhist. Not everyone who finds comfort in the words of Christ is a Christian. Usually, the admirers of a religious leader or prophet are disciples of that particular faith, but that's not always the case. You can study teachings and look for strength, comfort, or inspiration in religious and spiritual teachings outside your personal belief system. You are exposed to a lot of information as you travel the path of your life, and if you find something remarkable in the teachings of another faith, then more power to you.

DIG DEEPER

There is always more to be learned.

1. Revisit the words and ideals of a spiritual teacher or leader who has brought you enlightenment. Try to go beyond what you already know and glean even more from their philosophies. Be grateful for the positive influence these words have exerted over you and continue to wield over you. These teachers or prophets can leave an impression that will follow you for the rest of your life.
2. Have lunch with a friend with different religious beliefs. Engage him in a discussion of the teachers and prophets associated with his faith. Make sure he understands that you are asking to be enlightened and not to create a confrontational situation.

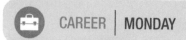

CAREER | MONDAY

"Pollution is nothing but the resources we are not harvesting. We allow them to disperse because we've been ignorant of their value."

—R. Buckminster Fuller

Recycle at Work

If you've had some success with recycling at home, why not set up a recycling program at your company? Not only will you have the opportunity to broaden the huge positive impact of recycling, you'll be seen by your superiors in a favorable light—as an altruistic individual with widespread concerns for the future and for the businesses and individuals doing this important work.

ORGANIZE A RECYCLING PROGRAM AT WORK

1. The first thing you'll need to do is to meet with management to get their support for your program. Be prepared for your meeting with facts and figures to show how implementing a recycling program would be both realistic and advantageous. As soon as management gives you the green light, you're ready to start recycling.

2. Determine what materials need to be recycled. Start simple and focus your recycling program on the largest volume of waste materials being thrown away. For example, if you work in an office, you might want to start with paper and cardboard. The next step is to ask your garbage hauler if they will collect and recycle these items. If not, you will need to find a recycling company. You can use different companies for different materials. Once this matter is settled, you need to set up the containers. Mark them clearly and place them in an area where they will receive the most use.

3. Educate your fellow employees through e-mails, motivational posters, and ongoing progress reports. Don't forget to include the custodial staff and new employees. Generate enthusiasm by offering incentives and rewards to those who participate.

WEEK SIXTEEN

"The charity that is a trifle to us can be precious to others."

—Homer

Meals on Wheels

Since 1976, the Meals on Wheels Association of America has worked to provide seniors with the nourishment they are unable to get for themselves. They offer their services at senior centers across the nation and through delivery to individual homes. They supply more than one million meals per day and have the largest army of volunteers in the nation. With millions of seniors in the country facing hunger, they need all the help they can get. Volunteers do a variety of jobs including meal delivery and preparation, office tasks, fundraising, and much more.

GET INVOLVED

There are approximately 5,000 Meals on Wheels programs operating, which means there is probably one near you. They provide meals, but they also offer a critical support system in the form of real people who care.

- All you need to participate in this worthy endeavor is time and energy. It's your efforts along with the efforts of countless others that create the powerful force that improves the lives of almost a million people.
- Volunteering for Meals on Wheels is as simple as visiting the MOWAA website at *www.mowaa.org.* They'll help you find a job to fit your schedule and skills. They can easily provide you with the opportunity to literally save the life of someone from your community.

"Good friends are like stars. You don't always see them, but you know they are always there."

—Unknown

Find a Long-Lost Friend

At one time or another, we have all wondered about that old friend from elementary school, high school, or college. We remember what he was like when we knew him and speculate on what he might be up to now. Until a few years ago, your best bet was to wait for the class reunion to arrive and hope to run into him. Thanks to the advent of such social networking sites such as Facebook, you don't have to wait that long. Finding and reconnecting with people you haven't heard from in years is easier than ever. Take some time today to reach out to an old friend you haven't heard from in a while.

CONSULT—OR CREATE—A SOCIAL NETWORK GROUP

1. If you're using Facebook or MySpace, you can also try your luck looking for a group built around a particular graduating class or school. Hundreds of these groups exist, so the chances of finding a particular school is good. Not only could you possibly find the person you're looking for, you might run into someone else from your past.

2. Start a Facebook or other social network group based on a theme from your childhood. Perhaps you could start a group of alumni from your elementary school or one for former players in your Little League team or friends from your old Girl Scout troop.

"Love is a cunning weaver of fantasies and fables."

—Sappho

Explore Sexual Thoughts and Feelings

Powerful fantasies can be the prelude to incredible sex. Indeed, the mind may be the most erogenous zone of all. Some people report being capable of having orgasm solely through fantasizing, without any accompanying physical stimulation. If you haven't been using your mind to help get you turned on, you should consider giving it more focus. This is particularly true if you have any difficulty sustaining arousal or achieving orgasm. Sexual thoughts and feelings come in many forms. Here are a few:

- Being in love or lust and thinking about the object of your desire
- Mental images of something or someone that turns you on
- Fantasies of something erotic happening to you

FULFILLING YOUR FANTASY

Crawl between the sheets before bed while your lover is in the shower and begin your fantasy. Use any or all of the three items from this list to shift away from the cares of the world into a magical, sensual, erotic fantasy world. When your spouse slips into bed beside you, keep the fantasy going while playing it out to completion with him or her.

- Fantasies of witnessing something erotic
- Anticipating sexual touch by yourself or another
- Anticipating a sexual encounter with someone you lust after

 **FAMILY** | **FRIDAY**

> *"We must not promise what we ought not, lest we
> be called on to perform what we cannot."*
>
> —Abraham Lincoln

Keep Your Promise

Partners and parents who do what they say they will do and who follow through when they say they will are seen by their significant others and children as dependable and trustworthy. Keep your promises, and everyone in your family will know that they can always count on you.

Write your promise on a piece of paper and tape it to your computer. It's a constant reminder. Do what it is you promised to do and do it quickly. That way it won't hang over you like a duty. Knowing you haven't yet kept your promise is a burden that becomes harder to bear each day.

BE MINDFUL OF YOUR PROMISES

Before you give your word, take a minute to consider if keeping the promise in question is reasonable. Being sensible and not going too far beyond what you are capable of will help you keep your promise successfully. Try to think of all the details involved in keeping a specific promise. Endeavor not to break your promises, but if you must, then at least be honest and forthcoming about why you made the promise in the first place and the reason or reasons why you couldn't keep your word. Relationships can be seriously damaged by a pattern of broken promises. You can ensure that your bonds stay healthy and buoyant by keeping your word.

"The way you treat yourself sets the standard for others."

—Sonya Friedman

Treat Yourself to Tickets

Maybe your favorite band has just come to town or that Broadway hit is finally playing somewhere nearby. When we read about these events online or in the newspaper, we usually think that we'd like to go, but then we decide that we probably can't afford it and leave the matter at that. Why give up on the idea without even really considering it?

Describing a concert or show in detail and sharing anecdotes with your friends online or at work the next day sounds a lot more appealing than telling them you wish you had gone. Go online and see if you can score some tickets to whatever you want to see before it's too late.

GIVE YOURSELF A SPLURGE BUDGET

Maybe you can't afford it. It's better to be frugal than spend money you don't have.

1. However, if you give it some thought and come to the realization that you could splurge a little on some great concert tickets or a chance to see a show you've wanted to see, then what's stopping you? If you see yourself as someone who doesn't treat themselves often, this might be the time to change that. Do you really want to think back and wish you'd spent a few bucks on a memorable night out?

2. Make small treats like this a line item on your budget and set money aside for them. That way, you don't have to feel guilty about treating yourself. Put some fun money in your budget—and then don't forget to spend it on something fun!

"For everything there is a season, and a time
for every purpose under heaven."

—Ecclesiastes 3:1

Understand the Cyclical Nature of Life

Life is rhythmic, cyclical, and always evolving. It's difficult not to notice repetition and renewal going on all around you. Just as darkness comes at the end of each day, so also comes the dawn to spread light across the land. Just as plants must die at the end of their life cycle, the seeds they have produced will emerge as new plants in the spring. Understanding the cyclical nature of life will reassure you that difficult times won't last forever, and you will feel joy and happiness again. The rough times must be endured and taken as they come, but they are not constant, nor do they last forever. There will always be good times and bad, feasts and famines, hot summers and cold winters. Whenever you feel stuck, spiritually dry, or just plain gloomy, take time to remind yourself that change is on its way.

PLANT A GARDEN

Plants are a great way to let you know that life is cyclical in nature. Create a small garden somewhere in your home or backyard. It doesn't have to be large or complicated. An herb garden or bonsai tree can serve as that reminder you need.

Visit an online bonsai nursery such as *www.bonsaiboy.com* and buy a miniature tree. Just like their larger counterparts, bonsai trees lose their leaves in the fall and bloom in the spring. Pay close attention to the nursery recommendations and care instructions for your selection.

"While one person hesitates because he feels inferior, the other is busy making mistakes and becoming superior."

—Henry C. Link

Live and Learn

Are you learning from your mistakes? You may view mistakes as embarrassing incidents that you'd like to forget, and certainly not as something you want to review and examine for potential life lessons! But if you're going to have a successful, rewarding career, you're going to have to learn that mistakes are an essential part of learning, and they're often the path to new and exciting opportunities. Spend some time looking at a recent mistake and understanding why and how it happened. You're not trying to place blame; you're trying to grow! But don't beat yourself up over the mistake. Learn what you can and move on.

DON'T TAKE EXCUSES AT FACE VALUE

Perhaps one of your major clients recently left the company for another vendor, citing the bad economy as a reason. This doesn't give you a lot to go on, but you still need to take an in-depth look at your history with this client to search out any other possible reasons for his departure.

1. You might realize that you didn't give him the same attention you gave your other clients.
2. You might discover an error that you had failed to notice.
3. Even if you don't find any further reasons for the client's exodus, you can still learn something. Is there action you can take to prevent further client loss? Perhaps you should take a look at your other client relationships and see if you need to do anything else to ensure their security.

"Any good therefore that I can do or any kindness that I can show to any human being, let me do it now."

—Mahatma Gandhi

Do a Good Deed Today—and Every Day

You have an opportunity every day to lift up another person—a child, a homeless veteran, a friend, a struggling single mother, and countless others in your community. Look for one act of kindness to perform each and every day. You don't have to save the whole world by yourself. If you try to do good deeds every day, your acts will make the world a better place.

MODEL SELFLESSNESS TO OTHERS

Some acts can generate good karma, such as helping a sick child get medical treatment when her parents have no financial resources to pay for it, or cleaning out your pantry to feed the homeless.

- You can also use these opportunities to teach selflessness to your children.
- Be an exemplar of selflessness. Parents are their children's first teachers and thus are in a better position than anyone to demonstrate acts of altruism.
- Teach your child to share with other children and to donate their unwanted toys to organizations that serve needy families.

"You get whatever accomplishment you are willing to declare."

—Georgia O'Keeffe

Encourage Your Friend to Develop Her Talents

Your friend has the voice of an angel, but sings only in the shower. She can whip up a meal fit for a royal entourage from what she finds in a nearly empty pantry and dreams of attending a culinary school, if only her day job paid more. Or she creates beautiful, one-of-a-kind purses from silk fabric and embellishments and gives them to her nieces and friends as gifts . . . but can only make those lovely creations when she isn't studying, working, or caring for her children.

The demands of marriage and family, not to mention a busy career, leave little time and energy left over at the end of the day for many women to fully express or improve their talents. Yet, psychologists say that doing activities that involve our natural talents often boost self-esteem levels and give meaning to our lives. Tell your friend how talented she is. Ask her how you can help her develop, express, or pursue her talent to wherever it might lead her.

SUPPORT YOUR FRIEND'S DREAM

- Brainstorm with your friend to help her find a way to pay for a coach, classes, or a conference.
- Assist her in developing an action plan with specific steps to achieve her goal.
- Show that you really mean what you say and that you will do your part to support her. Encourage her to reach the full potential of her life, including claiming and developing all her talents.

"We are not machines that blindly fall into some stereotyped behavior in response to an odor, but we may be machines that are nudged towards a type of behavior by pheromones in concert with our higher intellect."

—David Wolfgang-Kimball

Use Your Sexy Scents

Pheromones are chemicals found in body secretions that attract the opposite sex. They don't have a discernible smell or odor, but humans have special detectors in their noses for pheromones. We respond physiologically to another person's pheromones, even if we cannot consciously smell them.

Body temperature, skin conductance, heart rate, and blood pressure are just some of the functions that can be affected by our reactions to our partner's pheromones. Pheromones have also been isolated as the cause for synchronized menstruation cycles among women who live in close proximity over a period of time.

Most research on pheromones in humans indicates that the main odor-producing organ is the skin. These odors are largely produced by the skin's apocrine and sebaceous glands, which develop during puberty and are usually associated with sweat glands and tufts of hair. Some men and women are greatly attracted to the smell of their partner's underarms and hair. Try burying your nose in your partner's hair the next time you want to become aroused.

FIND PHEROMONES

Sebaceous glands are located everywhere on the body surface, but tend to concentrate in six areas.

- The underarms
- The nipples (both sexes)
- The pubic, genital, and anal regions
- The lips
- The eyelids
- The outer ear

"If there is any one secret of success, it lies in the ability to get the other person's point of view and see things from that person's angle as well as from your own."

—Henry Ford

Experience a New Point of View

Each person in a relationship usually views situations and circumstances from his or her point of view and personal concerns. That's not wrong; it's just the way it is. Male and female brains often see things differently, so it's a good idea to at least try to see your partner's point of view. Ask your significant other to share his ideas about how best to solve a particular problem. Hear him out as he explains his take on it. If you rush to judgment, criticism, and rejection, he will likely shut down and tune you out. Show him whenever possible that you can not only see but also appreciate his point of view.

PRACTICE A NEW POINT OF VIEW

Consider the following example.

1. You ask your mate if his consulting business could spare him long enough to fix the leaky faucet in the kitchen because the water bill is straining the family budget. He agrees to try to fix it first thing Saturday morning.

2. When Saturday comes, he instead takes off for the golf course for a round with a potential new client. You believe that he has totally forgotten his promise to fix the faucet. All day, you listen to the drips, steaming with anger. When he comes home, you let him have a piece of your mind.

3. But what if, instead of criticizing and judging him, you try to understand his point of view? You might arrive at the conclusion that he saw the potential new client as a means to increase his income, an event that would greatly benefit the family finances, and the means with which he could hire a plumber to do something that he isn't sure he knows how to fix.

---

*"Find a place inside where there's joy, and
the joy will burn out the pain."*

—Joseph Campbell

Rub Your Lover's Temples

Headaches are a common symptom of many maladies, such as tension, stress, eyestrain, sinus inflammation, food allergies, the common cold, flu, depression, anxiety, meningitis, diabetes, and a host of other illnesses too numerous to list.

It's little wonder that our fingers go right to our temples when we have a headache. We all need the human touch to feel safe, secure, happy, and loved. Offer to gently massage your spouse's temples if he is suffering discomfort. Crawl up behind him on the sofa or in bed. Cradle his head in your lap, and gently massage his temples in a slow circular motion, using the third finger of each hand. Try using white flower oil—ingredients are wintergreen, menthol, eucalyptus, peppermint, lavender, and camphor—as an analgesic balm to soothe away his discomfort.

TRY THIS FOR HEADACHE RELIEF

Offer to massage the midpoint between your partner's eyebrows. Use your index finger to apply a little pressure and massage in a circular motion. Then push gently into the forehead for twenty to thirty seconds and release. This same technique can be used on the sinuses.

"News is something that happens that matters to you,
which is not most of what we watch on television."

—Val Kilmer

Choose Your News

With all the negative messages coming at you every day from myriad directions, you may wonder how you can possibly feel optimistic about anything. Seeing or hearing news stories about the downward slide of the global economy, the escalation of armed conflicts that Americans are fighting, and the lies told by financiers and world leaders make optimism an increasingly elusive goal. A global peace seems ever-elusive.

One strategy to combat this problem is to be more selective about the news items you read. Websites like *www.alternativenews.net* and *www.world-newspapers.com* have lists of alternate news sources as well as magazines and newspapers from all over the world.

TAKE A BREAK FROM THE NEWS

Another way to avoid all of the negativity and to maintain a more positive, balanced emotional state is to take a break from the news for two days.

1. Turn off the television and radio.
2. Don't click on Internet news stories.
3. Stop the bombardment of negativity from virtually every media outlet.

Take a well-deserved break from the news, and after two days, evaluate just how much of an impact the news has been having on your sense of well-being. The answer may surprise you. After that, you may need to more closely examine your relationship with these media outlets. By taking that break, you will have the insight and tools necessary to be able to do this.

"Everyone wants to be appreciated, so if you appreciate someone, don't keep it a secret."

—Mary Kay Ash

Appreciate Someone

You know how it feels to be unappreciated. Now, stop for a moment and remember the last time someone at work appreciated what you did and told you so. Think about how good that felt. Most people associate appreciation at work with a boss expressing gratitude towards his employees. But since everyone needs to be appreciated: your colleagues, coworkers, and yes, even your boss need to be included, too.

There are immediate and long term benefits for everyone involved. You build a good reputation with your coworkers and manager. You provide the opportunity for getting to know the other people in your workplace and for strengthening relationships already in place.

WEEK EIGHTEEN

PICK THREE

Here's how to start appreciating the people you work with.

1. Every week for the next four weeks, choose three people at work and find a way to express your appreciation for something they have done. You can send them an e-mail, a letter, or a thank-you note. Better yet, thank them face to face; perhaps you can even have lunch together. The important thing is to make your gratitude sincere. Be specific about the experience in which this person helped you.

2. If you enjoy your appreciation "exercise," there's no reason why you shouldn't continue. Of course, you can expand your efforts to include more than three people.

"The nice thing about the gallery shows is that without having to pay any money you can just go and see it."

—Yoko Ono

Appreciate Art

You've probably been to your local art gallery a few times. For many of us, it can be a nice way to occupy an hour or two. It also gives us the chance to be completely surprised by some astonishing piece of art that we weren't expecting to see. It's a terrific way to enrich our soul and fuel our own creative spark. Take an afternoon to visit your local art gallery— or, even better, get in touch with your child's teacher and volunteer to help plan a field trip to the gallery for your child's class at school.

HELP ART OUT

The vast majority of people who work behind the scenes to keep these galleries running are volunteers who love art and love to be around it.

1. If that description fits you, or if you would like the chance to increase your appreciation of art, then it couldn't hurt to call up a local gallery and volunteer your time.
2. Offer to perform tasks such as conducting tours, organizing events and benefits, or doing maintenance.
3. The work you do will enable others to enjoy that gallery in the same way you have. You might be the person who takes the next Vincent van Gogh or Georgia O'Keeffe on his or her first tour of the gallery.

"Confidence can get you where you want to go, and getting there is a daily process."

—Donald Trump

Help Your Friend Brainstorm

We all have situations where we can't see a way to move past a road-block. If your friend is experiencing this in any area of his life, offer to brainstorm ways to move past the roadblock. This is an excellent exercise, since brainstorming through a problem together can produce innovative ideas that your friend might not readily see in his "stuck" place.

HELP YOUR FRIEND THROUGH JOB DIFFICULTIES

Your friend is at a juncture in his career and has turned to you to help him brainstorm about where to go next.

1. Offer your support, suggestions, and opinions.
2. Talk about the pros and cons of a lateral move—for example, if he's a law officer, he could join another department, albeit in a different community. It may mean a move away from friends and family but on a positive note, it could be a new start with potential for advancement.
3. Propose a more significant job change. For example, if he's a city police officer, he might seek positions with the FBI or the Department of Homeland Security.
4. Do some footwork for your friend. Do an Internet search, downloading those position descriptions and applications you think would be most appropriate for what he seeks in his career.

"For the millions of us who live glued to computer keyboards at work and TV monitors at home, food may be more than entertainment. It may be the only sensual experience left."

—Barbara Ehrenreich

Erotic Edibles

An aphrodisiac is a substance (generally, a food or drink) that you use to enhance pleasure or susceptibility to pleasure. The list of possible aphrodisiacs is probably endless, since everyone's tastes are different. Plus, a substance can have aphrodisiac effects if it reminds someone of an enjoyable experience. Many people become aroused when exposed to certain foods, odors, or environments that their brain associates with sex. Some substances that are commonly believed to have aphrodisiac qualities are oysters, chocolate, and wine. Certain spices and plants are also said to be aphrodisiacs.

HAVE FUN WITH FOOD

Try an evening of lovemaking that involves blindfolding your partner and offering her different sorts of fruits, chocolates, and desserts that are suggestive of softness or juiciness. This is more about sensing than it is about eating. Keep the bites very small and offer the food gently for smelling and brushing across the lips first, before letting your partner take the bite into her mouth.

1. Whipped cream and chocolate syrup are fun (though messy!) in the bedroom, but allowing these types of substances to dry and remain on the skin, especially in or near body openings, can cause all sorts of problems. A good solution: enjoy a shower together after a food-enhanced sexual romp.
2. While the stereotypical aphrodisiacs may indeed have an erotic effect on you, it can be fun to try to find new and unusual alternatives. Try lots of different foods, and you just may discover some exciting new arousal boosters.

"I am thankful for a lawn that needs mowing, windows that need cleaning and gutters that need fixing because it means I have a home. I am thankful for the piles of laundry and ironing because it means my loved ones are nearby."

—Nancie J. Carmody

Divide Up the Chores

According to a recent survey by the Pew Research Center, sharing the household chores is a very important factor in a successful relationship. Some couples decide that the person who makes the dinner does not have to do the dishes and cleanup because the other one will take care of it. If they make dinner together, both have to share in the cleanup and associated chores such as taking out the garbage and putting away the linen and dishes.

Many couples also designate a certain day to do the general house-cleaning and other chores. Children, from toddlers to teens, can and should help with household chores as well. You and your mate can choose to compensate them with allowances or other rewards. The point is to get everyone to pitch in to help keep the family home and pets clean and cared for.

CREATE A CHORE CHART

To avoid squabbles about whose turn it is to empty the dishwasher, make a family chore chart.

- You can create a chore chart for each member of the family, showing what they are responsible for and then using stickers or gold stars to show when each chore has been accomplished appropriately, or you can create a chore chart for the entire family that shows who should be doing what when.
- Alternatively, search the Internet and find chore charts and lists already compiled and ready to download. You can personalize them with photos, affirmations, or quotations.

"Every now and then a man's mind is stretched by a new idea or sensation and never shrinks back to its former dimensions."

—Oliver Wendell Holmes, Jr.

Explore the Outdoors

Blaze some new trails. Do you live near a lake? Help your better half load up the canoe or kayak. If the lake is fully frozen because it's winter, rent some ice skates. If it's summer and blazing hot, grab a hard hat, helmet light, and spelunking ropes and explore the coolness of a cave. Climb a wall at your local outdoor gear shop, or pack your camera and drive to the desert, the beach, the woods, or a mountain to take in the scenic wonders of nature. If you're longing for company on your outdoor adventure, and your mate loves to fish, you can spend the afternoon searching for new fishing holes. Plan a camping trip for the two of you to one of America's national parks. Enjoy exploring with the one you love.

GO BERRY-PICKING

Invite your significant other to join you for an afternoon of berry-picking.

1. Take along a galvanized bucket for the bounty you hope to find.
2. If you don't know a place where wild berry vines grow and aren't up for exploring your local area to find one, visit a farm that has a pick-your-own-berries program.
3. The website *www.pickyourown.org* has a comprehensive list of fruit and vegetable farms all over the world where you can pick your own produce. You'll also find recipes, weather reports for the different locations, and instructions for canning and freezing.

"Without the spiritual world the material
world is a disheartening enigma."

—Joseph Joubert

Understand Spiritual Symbols

There are literally thousands of symbols, from ancient to modern. Some may have obscure meanings, while others are universally understood. While certain symbols may be associated with myths and cultural traditions, others hold special meanings only for certain groups or even certain people. Some symbols have represented a specific meaning for centuries. However, these same symbols may have other meanings associated with them. It depends on the culture in which they were created.

Take some time to understand the meaning behind various symbols you encounter in your daily life or meditate on the symbol as a way to divine its nature.

CHOOSE A SYMBOL

If you don't have a spiritual symbol that you personally identify with, it's never too late to choose one. Pick a symbol that resonates with you (a dragon, the yin-yang symbol) and research its various meanings—or decide on its meaning for yourself. If you're looking for a symbol to represent a metaphysical truth or a transcendent state of mind, consider the Hindu symbol of Aum as a point of reflection. It is believed to be the sound of the cosmic vibration of the very universe itself.

---

*"We're supposed to be perfect our first day on the
job and then show constant improvement."*

—Ed Vargo

Put Out the Welcome Mat

First days are memorable. The first day on the job is difficult for a variety
of reasons with perhaps the biggest challenge being surrounded by a
group of strangers. How do you react when a new person arrives at your
workplace? If you're like a lot of busy people, you smile, shake hands,
and then leave it up to someone else to make the new person feel at
home.

Consider inviting the new person to lunch. Invite two or three of your
coworkers or colleagues to give the new hire a chance to get acquainted
with other people in the workplace. You could also buy a festive cake for
the staff to share on their coffee break.

KEEP THE WELCOME MAT OUT

Although most companies arrange for someone to give the new
hire a customary orientation, there is so much more you can do
to make him or her feel welcome.

1. The first day can be overwhelming, so you need to be percep-
   tive and sensitive.
2. If the hire is surrounded by people or swamped with work,
   step back and wait.
3. The initial commotion will die down, and the new person will
   probably need some help. He or she might be reluctant or
   self-conscious, so your sincere offer of support will almost
   certainly be welcome.
4. Make sure the new employee has company for lunch and
   coffee—and not just on the first day.

WEEK NINETEEN

"We think sometimes that poverty is only being hungry, naked and homeless. The poverty of being unwanted, unloved and uncared for is the greatest poverty. We must start in our own homes to remedy this kind of poverty."

—Mother Teresa

Giving It All You've Got

Giving does not have to involve volunteering your time, but that may be one way that you can give back to the community. Volunteering is a more structured, formal means by which to offer your services, talents, and energy. Study after study on altruism, giving, and volunteerism suggests that the people who are more involved in these activities report an increased quality of life for themselves. In giving, the gifts are returned tenfold.

GIVING BACK TO YOUR COMMUNITY

Following are some seldom-thought-of, informal ways that you can help others and your surrounding community:

- Cook a meal for a family that you see struggling.
- Recycle and try to get others to do it as well.
- Volunteer to read to children at the library.
- Serve meals at a soup kitchen.
- Be a model of good manners and polite behavior.
- Sit with an Alzheimer's patient so the family can have a night off.
- Send out one "thank you" or "I'm thinking of you" note every day.

"I awoke this morning with devout thanksgiving
for my friends, the old and the new."

—Ralph Waldo Emerson

Include Your Significant Other in Your Friendships

You undoubtedly had friends before you established a committed relationship with your partner, and you're bound to make new friends as you go through a life together as a couple. Talk with your mate about including him or her in those relationships. Although most couples find it important to retain independent interests and friends and thus give each other "time off" from being part of a duo, the question is degree. Some couples live substantially separate lives, while others prefer more togetherness.

If you didn't talk with your partner before you became a couple about how much socializing you'd like to do individually and as a couple, make it a topic of conversation now. Partners who have trust issues or insecurity issues may feel discomfort with the other person socializing with members of the opposite sex. For example, your mate wants to have her usual weekly lunch date with a girlfriend, whom you've met, but suddenly the plan includes two guys, whom you haven't. You trust your lover, but you don't know the men, and you have concerns. The best course of action is to talk over your concerns with her and keep asking questions until you are satisfied that neither safety nor impropriety is an issue.

CULTIVATE MUTUAL FRIENDSHIPS

A great way to make sure your partner is part of your friend relationships is to cultivate friendships as a couple.

1. Cultivate friends around interests that you share with your life partner, whether gardening, art, music, sports, cars, remodeling, or food and drink.
2. Plan activities around those interests and involve your mate.
3. Sharing your passion and knowledge with others and learning new things from them can add layers of meaning and purpose to your life and build a strong social network, an important factor in longevity and life satisfaction.

"Outward beauty is not enough; to be attractive a woman must use words, wit, playfulness, sweet-talk, and laughter to transcend the gifts of Nature."

—Petronius

Spell Out Your Lust

For both men and women, words can be powerful erotic stimuli. In general, men will prefer lusty, teasing, more explicitly sexual language. Women tend to respond to more indirect language—hints, words of love and desire, and compliments. Regardless of what you like, the idea is to start the erotic play before you get to the bedroom. The longer we are juiced up, the stronger our reactions will be when we get there. Don't hesitate to use words liberally when making love and make sounds to let your partner know how you are feeling.

SPEAK WORDS OF LOVE

Don't just talk about how much you lust after each other, though. You can increase intimacy and rev up your sex life by talking about how much you love each other.

1. Sit facing each other and take turns.
2. Give each other the gift of one minute of compliments. Just say loving, complimentary words and phrases as they come to your mind. Don't think too much—just let them flow.
3. If either of you is feeling hurt or vulnerable, use words of compassion, care, and sympathy as they come to your mind.
4. Use words of gratitude and thanks for one minute each. This practice helps us remember to speak about how precious our lives are. Use this one generously!
5. Make up your own version with themes that fit your life.

"Children have never been very good at listening to their elders, but they have never failed to imitate them."

—James Baldwin

Set a Good Example

As parents, you and your partner are exemplars for your children. From your behaviors, they learn to show restraint, be respectful, and engage in moral reasoning, from early childhood through their teenage years into young adulthood. Not only are you teaching through example, but you're also teaching them how to think and reason through moral dilemmas they may face in their relationships with others at home, in school, and in all other activities. Through the way you and your mate deal with family members, friends, business associates, strangers, and everyone with whom you interact, you demonstrate for your children what patience, kindness, understanding, empathy, self-discipline, self-restraint, and self-reliance look like.

KEEP A JOURNAL

One way to make sure you remember that you're a role model is to write about your child's spiritual development.

1. Start a journal that documents your child's developing spiritual and moral character. Write about moments when your child had said something or done something you consider profound or just shows his unique way of being or view of the world.
2. Review your child's progress over time to see if you and your spouse need to reinforce any particular values or beliefs through your own behaviors and counsel.
3. You can also keep a family journal or a personal journal on the same topic.

"The art and science of asking questions is the source of all knowledge."

—Thomas Berger

Study for Fun

By the time we're finished with high school or college, we're more or less finished with learning anything that isn't absolutely essential. We become busy with career, family, and hobbies and tend to think of knowledge as something we just happen to pick up as we move along. Sometimes we come across something that makes us think how great it would be to learn more about it, but we rarely make the effort to do so. The next time you sit down to check your e-mail, think of something that has piqued your interest or something you've always wanted to know, and type it into the Google search engine. Check out some of the dozens of links that come up, and you're bound to learn something new.

GO ON A SEARCH FOR KNOWLEDGE

Keep track of those things that cross your mind that you'd like to know more about. Then set aside some time to do some real research.

- The Internet can be more than just a way of watching videos on YouTube or playing games on Facebook. It remains an enormously powerful tool for obtaining information. You can put it to use the next time you're eager to learn more about a particular subject.
- Google's search engine is a terrific starting point, and from there, the possibilities are seemingly endless.
- Your quest for knowledge can involve a lot of work, but getting absorbed in that work might be a great way to lose yourself in something completely different than your list of daily duties.

"For those who wish to climb the mountain of spiritual awareness, the path is selfless work."

—The Bhagavad Gita

Change the World

You can help others by putting your interests and passions to good use. Read books on how to turn your passion into profits, products, services, humanitarian aid, or change in the world in some way. Check out the book *1001 Ways to Do Good* (Adams Media). It is full of ideas about allowing your passion to do good works, including some that cost you nothing but that can make a big difference to others.

CONSIDER HUMANITARIAN RELIEF WORK

Many societies have a history of religious and cultural traditions that include charitable giving or personal sacrifice for the good of someone else without seeking recognition for it.

- Couples who engage in charitable work or service make themselves and the world a better place. If you and your spouse feel the urge to help others less fortunate than you, don't hesitate to get involved.
- Find some charity or charitable work that has meaning for you both and join.

Two people, a couple, whose hearts beat as one, sharing a common vision, can make a huge difference in the lives of others. Indeed, they are sharing a part of their lives with others, perhaps people they don't even know.

"Soon silence will have passed into legend. Man has turned his back on silence. Day after day he invents machines and devices that increase noise and distract humanity from the essence of life, contemplation, meditation."

—Jean Arp

Encourage Quiet

Does the noise level in your workplace send you home each day in a rotten mood or suffering from a blinding headache? Does it feel as though the intensity and variety of noise has gotten worse? Researchers in Europe have found that office noise disrupts concentration, decreases productivity, and erodes good health by increasing stress.

Here's one thing you can do today. Don't forget that you, too, produce sounds that interfere with your coworkers. Keep your voice down and your music low, and maybe your efforts will catch on to create a more peaceful and productive atmosphere for everyone.

ASK FOR NOISE REDUCTION SOLUTIONS

Of course, there are other solutions to the noise problem, but some of these involve major changes in the work environment. But depending on how bad the problem is, it may be worth discussing solutions with your boss and other decision makers.

1. Present information on how sound can be absorbed by ceiling tiles, fabrics, and carpets. Other modifications to the work space include walls, panels, partitions, and other barriers that can block the sound.
2. If your company can't make these types of big changes, recommend smaller ones. Sounds can also be masked with other sounds, such as a radio playing softly, or a noise machine that can make a variety of sounds, such as waves crashing on a beach.

WEEK TWENTY

> *"A civilization flourishes when people plant
> trees under which they will never sit."*

—Greek proverb

Celebrate Trees

If you go to the Arbor Day Foundation website at *www.arborday.org* you will discover that the great work done on Arbor Day doesn't end with planting trees. The site offers a wealth of information and a multitude of ideas to encourage people to plant, cultivate, and appreciate trees every day of the year. Plan your own Arbor Day celebration.

PLANT A TREE

In the United States, Arbor Day is held on the final Friday of April. Every year on this day, we are encouraged to get together under the wonderful act of planting and nurturing trees. An estimated one million trees were planted on the first Arbor Day in 1872.

- You can probably think of quite a few places where some greenery would be nice. It can be as close by as your own backyard, somewhere in your neighborhood, or the local park a few blocks over.
- Recruit friends and neighbors! This project can be even more exciting when you get others involved. Organize your neighborhood and talk to your city officials, schools, and local businesses.
- Invite children. It's a great way to get kids to participate in something that guarantees fresh air, group spirit, and a lasting impression on their surroundings.

"Culture is the sum of all the forms of art, of love, and of thought, which, in the course of centuries, have enabled man to be less enslaved."

—Andre Malraux

Host an International Night

Persuading your friends to help you host an international night probably wouldn't be that hard. We love to learn about other cultures, and we often try to think of fun and unique ways to go about doing that. An international night can accomplish both. It's a good idea that lends itself well to a creative mind.

LEARN MORE ABOUT OTHER CULTURES—TOGETHER!

Choose a culture you and your friends would like to explore—maybe a place you've always wanted to visit—and then go online for resources that will help make the experience authentic. Then try the following ideas:

1. Visit the local library and look for international cookbooks, books about customs, language, and clothing.
2. Download some international music to listen to.
3. Encourage everyone to learn as much as they can over the course of a week.
4. Then get together on the weekend to demonstrate their knowledge and enjoy some fringe benefits like international cuisine or films.

You might learn some history, popular culture, language skills, and other things that stimulate conversation and create an atmosphere of discussion, education, and collaboration among you and your friends.

*"I'm certain that most couples expect to find intimacy
in marriage but it somehow eludes them."*

—James Dobson

Create a Safe and Sacred Space

Intimacy doesn't always come easily, even with someone you love. But you can create intimacy between you and your partner through effort and practice. One way to help enhance intimacy in your relationship is to create a safe, sacred space.

It's tough to truly relax and open yourself up to another person if you are tense or uncomfortable in your environment. This is especially important with your romantic relationships. You and your partner should have your own special love nest where you can enjoy each other's company without distractions or annoyances. That's why you need to create your sensual, sacred space. This is where you go to enjoy sensual lovemaking or to talk about matters of importance. To sanctify this space, you might light a candle, burn some incense, or smudge by burning herbs. Whenever you enter this space, even if there is disharmony in the air, you enter it with an attitude of openness—with willingness to speak about and hear whatever is ready to be revealed.

SPEND QUALITY TIME IN YOUR SPACE

Your sacred space isn't doing any good if you hardly use it. Even if your schedules are very busy, make it a point to spend some time alone together doing something fun in your sacred space.

1. Ideally, this would mean leisurely lovemaking sessions.
2. It could also include quickies, massages, or adult games.
3. You can also use the space to watch romantic/erotic movies, or whatever else you two enjoy doing together.

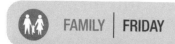
"I think what destroys Hollywood marriages is our work schedule, not so much infidelity."

—Eva Longoria

Control Demanding Schedules

Demanding schedules involving work, children, and community obligations can deflate even the most buoyant of relationships. Regaining control means giving up something to create blocks of time to be with your partner. Marriage and family therapists strongly recommend this as something a couple needs to do to build and strengthen their relationship, but many couples resist. When both people have jobs requiring long hours or extended periods away from home, it makes it difficult to find even a small chunk of time to be together. It may feel as though you are attempting the impossible—but for the sake of your relationship, you have to try.

COMMISERATE TOGETHER

Although there is no substitute for quality time together, commiserating over the situation is one way couples can convey their sense of longing for the other and their displeasure at not having a time for togetherness.

1. Talking to your mate forms a bridge that allows you to reconnect with each other. Communicate often, sharing your feelings of love.
2. Establish small marital rituals, such as sharing morning coffee, an evening walk, or kisses before bed.
3. Do volunteer activities together when possible.
4. Eliminate time wasters such as watching television.
5. Make a master schedule of a month of activities for the whole family and pencil in appointments with your mate for a half-hour coffee, a shower together, a lunch, a lovemaking session, or a time to talk about how you can get a better handle on your schedules in the future.

"Don't worry that [children] never listen to you;
worry that they are always watching you."

—Robert Fulghum

Get the Kids out of the House

Having a full house can be a blessing, but during the times when we could really use a moment to ourselves, it can also be something of a curse. Wanting a few hours or even a full weekend away from your children doesn't make you a bad parent. Chances are they, too, would love to get out of the house for a little while. You're not the only one who could use a vacation, however brief it might be.

PLAN YOUR GETAWAY

You may find it tricky to get started on the path to renewal and rejuvenation if you don't create an environment that supports it. Make it a priority.

1. You probably have a friend or family member who would love to babysit. Take advantage of someone you know who has made the offer.
2. You can use the time in whatever way you want. If you long to sit on the couch and watch television, that will be as beneficial as anything else you might think of doing.
3. Creating some alone time is the first step, and anything else you do beyond that is certain to be a rest and relaxation bonus.

"I saw the angel in the marble and carved until I set him free."

—Michelangelo

Discover More about Angels

You don't have to belong to a particular faith to believe in angels. They are a universal element of the unseen world and have been so since the beginning of recorded human history. When you feel the weight of the world upon your shoulders, seek out some angels and read more about them. Millions of people look to them as celestial companions that many of the religious traditions of the world have placed as intercessors between humans and a supreme being. Visit the Internet Movie Database (*www.imdb.com*) for television series, movies, and documentaries about angels.

LOOK FOR ANGELS EVERYWHERE

Images of angels can be found everywhere. Their presence in art and literature can provide you with a source of strength and encouragement. Consider these points:

1. When you feel as if your world is full of challenges and difficulties, a belief in the notion of a higher power and angelic helpers might help to lift your spirits.
2. Your discovery of angels and their spiritual qualities might resonate with the beliefs you once held and left behind. They can help you return to an inner oasis of peace and love.
3. For an entertaining look at guardian angels, watch the television series *Saving Grace* with Holly Hunter.

"My career has developed where I get to do an interesting range—television commercials, campaigns for big companies such as Victoria's Secret, designing shoes, jewelry, even my own candy . . . so I get to do a lot of different projects."

—Heidi Klum

Create One River with Many Streams

If you see yourself locked into one job and collecting one paycheck for the rest of your working life, then it's time to think again. Try to visualize not just one source of income, but many, from a variety of sources. This is another exercise that will take some self-examination, so be prepared to take a good, honest look at yourself.

1. The first thing you need to do is take a look at your hobbies and the other things you like to do. Write each one down in the center of a blank piece of paper and draw a circle around it. For example, if you like to prepare gourmet meals, write down "cooking" inside your circle. Draw a set of lines radiating from your circle, with each line ending in another circle. You might write "catering on the weekends" in one circle, "writing a cookbook" in another, and "teaching cooking classes" in yet another circle.

2. Using these diagrams, you need to make an honest assessment of the ideas you've come up with. What is your skill level for each item? How much knowledge have you accrued? These are only two of the many questions which you'll need to ask yourself, but with a little creative thinking, you can come up with a way to implement your income.

WEEK TWENTY-ONE

TURN YOUR JUNK INTO CASH

Do you have a house full of things that you no longer need or use? Turn these things into cash by selling them on eBay (*www.ebay.com*), at a consignment store, or in the classifieds—either in the newspaper or online. Then, have a yard sale to sell the rest.

"If the money we donate helps one child or can ease the pain of one parent, those funds are well spent."

—Carl Karcher

Contribute Even Small Amounts

Happiness researchers say that when you perform a selfless act of generosity for someone else, it increases your happiness. If you think you can't donate to a charity because you can't make a major contribution, think again. Most, if not all, charities are eager to accept and eternally grateful for any amount you are thoughtful enough to give.

By some estimates, the average American household has as much as $90 lying under the sofa cushions, in dresser drawers, and even in laundry room, where a lot of it comes out in the wash. There are myriad ways to donate your loose change—drop the coins into charity boxes in grocery store checkout lines, give it to your church or temple, or simply convert it to larger bills and donate it to a favorite charitable organization.

SEARCH FOR TREASURE

For a quick dose of happiness, gather up that loose change lying around the house and give it to a good cause. For younger children, you can turn this activity into a game.

1. Turn the search into a contest with a small prize for the person who collects the most money.
2. Look in those places where money seems to gather: the sofa and chair cushions, under the rugs and the beds, in the car, in coat pockets and unused luggage.
3. Designate a tin or jar for loose change. When it's full, hold a family meeting to discuss which community charity should receive it.

"Where there is an open mind there will always be a frontier."

—Charles F. Kettering

Try Something New

Most of us like to imagine we're capable of trying new things, new foods, new places, meeting new people and the like. Unfortunately, most of us don't have the inclination or ambition to follow through on our ambitions. This is where a good friend can come in handy. Our friends often want us to try something new, and we sometimes turn them down. This could be due to a lack of free time, a lack of energy or interest or even a fear of leaving our comfort zones. The first two excuses are understandable, but the third one shouldn't hold you back. The next time a friend suggests something new, take them up on it. It could be as simple as trying some different food at a new restaurant, but it could also be something like skydiving or rock-climbing.

ASK YOUR FRIENDS TO ENCOURAGE YOU

The adventure of trying something new is one of the great things about being alive. Having friends who encourage us and expand our horizons is another. Put the two together sometime, and see what comes out of it.

- Ask your friends to give you an extra nudge when you're settling for the familiar.
- Call a friend who's been pushing you to try something new. Tell her you're up for an adventure, meet her for coffee, and come up with an idea together.
- If you spot something you'd like to try but feel unsure, call a friend and ask her to do it with you.

"Passion is the quickest to develop, and the quickest to fade. Intimacy develops more slowly, and commitment more gradually still."

—Robert Sternberg

Don't Be a Statistic

Problems will develop in your relationship if you don't talk, don't touch, and don't make love. A recent estimate put the number of U.S. marriages suffering lack of physical intimacy at a whopping 20 million. Don't let your marriage be a statistic—prioritize each other to ensure you both feel loved, respected, and cared for.

DEEPEN INTIMACY

Many experts suggest intimacy must be learned and practiced if a relationship is going to develop and strengthen. As you embark on your voyage toward greater intimacy and mutual awareness, you can practice this nurturing exercise that will help you to restore and harmonize your energies after a fight or disagreement. This is an excellent way to clear negative energy that can arise from everyday fights and disagreements.

1. Lie on your side with your partner, with one of you in front of the other, like spoons in a drawer. If you are in back, place your top arm over your partner and hold your hand to her heart. If you are in front, have your partner place her hand on your heart. Relax and breathe together. Do this for at least five minutes.

2. After a few minutes, you can also try some slow, gentle undulating together. One of you starts and begins to rock from the hips. Cradle your partner in your arms and hold firmly. This is a good tool for getting in sync or harmonizing.

"Family traditions counter . . . alienation and confusion. They help us define who we are; they provide something steady, reliable and safe in a confusing world."

—Susan Lieberman

Embrace Your Traditions

Most families have rituals unique to their family that they celebrate year after year. Activities such as decorating eggs at Easter, opening stockings on Christmas morning, or eating roast turkey at Thanksgiving create memories that fill your mind with love and peace. According to Dr. G. Scott Wooding, bestselling author and leading Canadian authority on parenting teenagers, traditions help to determine family boundaries and help children feel more secure by giving them a sense of belonging to a clearly defined unit. So embrace your family traditions, no matter how traditional or silly! They'll help your family stay connected.

CREATE A NEW TRADITION

If your family is lacking in traditions, go ahead and create some! They don't have to be extravagant or elaborate.

1. Brainstorm with your children and spouse about making a new family tradition. Perhaps something wonderful and spontaneous occurred as you were preparing to leave for summer vacation, the night before Thanksgiving, the afternoon of the first snowfall, or on the way to the pumpkin patch. Or maybe you had a pillow fight that ended with everyone making popcorn and s'mores and watching old movies in their pajamas. If it still evokes powerful memories for all of you, make it a tradition.

2. Other ideas might include an annual family cleaning day (when everyone pitches in to tackle the mess in the garage, basement, or attic), an annual family fun day (let a child choose what the family does for the day, even if it's bug hunting), or an annual plant-a-garden day.

"Pets are humanizing. They remind us we have an obligation and responsibility to preserve and nurture and care for all life."

—James Cromwell

Get a Low-Maintenance Pet

Doctors have aquariums in their waiting rooms to calm and entertain their waiting patients. Studies have shown that watching fish in an aquarium can actually lower your blood pressure. There is some cost involved, but if you're willing to spend a little money and to invest some time in research and maintenance, an aquarium can be a wonderful way to enjoy your free time. Many people claim that they can feel themselves relax simply by staring at the small world going on inside four glass walls.

FIND YOUR NEW FISH BUDDIES

Visit a nearby pet store to check out the tropical fish. Knowledgeable staff can help you select the aquarium and fish perfect for you—and your budget. Shop online at *www.petsmart.com* or *www.drsfostersmith.com*.

- You have to first decide how much you're willing to spend, whether you want a freshwater or saltwater tank, and, of course, what kind of fish you think you'd like to own.
- There's a lot to do, but after getting the right tank and the right fish, you'll have a lot to enjoy. You'll have a pastime that includes living creatures and their environment, the chance to learn more about a very popular hobby, and something that's going to look nice wherever you put it.
- Most hobbies don't reward you with that many benefits. And remember, you won't have to take your pet fish for a walk three times a day!

"Knowing trees, I understand the meaning of patience.
Knowing grass, I can appreciate persistence."

—Hal Borland

Spend Time in Nature

Some people say that nature isn't really for them, but check with them again after they find themselves in the middle of a national park. See what they say about nature when they're surrounded by oak trees with centuries of age in their roots, or see the sun rising over a horizon of beauty untouched by humanity. Even the most hardened city lover can probably find nothing to complain about when they happen upon a deer grazing undisturbed just after sunrise. Nature has a powerful ability to resonate with our desire to strip away everything that clogs our spirit and bring our life back to a simple, level playing field.

CREATE A NATURE PHOTO ALBUM

What better way to celebrate and appreciate a connection with nature than to create a photo album to remember your experiences by?

1. Visit a local nature trail or one of those national parks and take as many pictures as you like.
2. Take your photos home and post them to a social network like Facebook or a blog provider like Tumblr.
3. Share your experience with the rest of the world. Show everyone the unparalleled beauty of the nature that exists around you every day. It may inspire them to make their own discoveries out in their own backyard or on a local nature trail.
4. Create a physical album for you to keep on a shelf in your home to help you remember the experience.

"Destiny is not a matter of chance; it is a matter of choice. It is not a thing to be waited for; it is a thing to be achieved."

—William Jennings Bryan

Reaping the Rewards

When you go to bed at night, are you filled with delight that when you wake up you will get to go to work? Do you look forward to the next day of work? Or do you dread getting up and going to work the next day? These feelings can be a perfect indicator of whether you are doing or being, whether you are in the right vocation or not. Your vocation enhances your life both personally and professionally. If you are in the right vocation, you know it in your heart.

IDENTIFY THE BENEFITS

If you have a vocation where you are "being" and not just "doing," you should be enjoying the following rewards. Ask yourself the following questions:

- Do you feel that your work matters to you and others?
- Do you know that you make a difference?
- Do you know that you are contributing to the good of humanity?
- Are you eager to go to work?
- Does your work bring you energy and excitement?
- Do you make the most of your time at work?
- Do you enjoy your colleagues and respect them?

If you answered yes to most or all of the questions above, then congratulations are in order. You're in the right place at this time in your life. However, if you found yourself making excuses, rationalizing, or flat-out disagreeing with these criteria, then it's time to rethink your career options.

"If you support the community, they will support you."

—Jerry Greenfield

Get Rid of Graffiti

There aren't too many populated areas that haven't been affected by graffiti. It's one of those things to which we've grown accustomed: buildings, bridges, and signs desecrated by a meaningless mess of spray-paint. We drive by it all the time. You might shake your head, mutter something under your breath, and drive on. But instead of driving by, ask the owner or property manager of an old building if you can remove or paint over the graffiti. He might not only be grateful, he might also offer to help you purchase the supplies you need.

PITCH IN

1. If you don't know the first thing about removing graffiti, do a little research first. Visit *www.ehow.com and* type "remove graffiti" into the search engine for step-by-step instructions.

2. You and your friends or family can change the landscape in no time at all.

3. The simple act of cleaning up just one or two buildings in a single day can have immediate positive effects on a street. The surroundings will look nicer. People driving by will have something to look at besides incomprehensible scribbling. Property values will go up, too.

"A real book is not one that we read, but one that reads us."

—W. H. Auden

Start a Book Club

Many of us have tried to go beyond simply enjoying a book by finding others who share the interest of literature. Book clubs can be wonderful and have worked out just fine for a lot of people. Some of us unfortunately have a hard time getting our foot in the door. It can be difficult to just walk into somebody else's group and pick up as though you've been there the whole time.

Starting your own book club might be a better, more interesting idea for you. You should have no trouble finding enough friends to get excited about the idea. Just bringing people together to enjoy a cup of coffee and some lively discussion about the book you're reading is enough for a great club. Visit Amazon.com; they have an entire section devoted to book clubs. You'll never run short of potential reads for your club!

BRING A BOOK TO LIFE

A book club doesn't just have to be a conversation about the book. It can be a chance to bring that book to life.

1. You can come up with dinner party ideas based on recipes or dishes found in whatever you're reading.
2. You could discuss the history or culture behind the characters, plot, or story locations.
3. You could even have a party and dress up as your favorite characters.

The mileage you get out of a great book doesn't have to end with the last page!

"Enjoy the little things, for one day you may look
back and realize they were the big things."

—Robert Brault

Do the Little Things

Setting the stage starts with romance—the little things two people can do any time of the day or night to communicate, "I love you. I want you. I'm glad I'm with you. I'm looking forward to being intimate with you." The word "romance" means different things to different people. In a sense, it's whatever turns you on.

People feel more romantic when they feel valued. We all want to be appreciated and acknowledged. That's really all that romance is. There's nothing mystical or difficult to get. Just hold your partner in your thoughts, and the little gestures will follow.

TRY A FEW SIMPLE THINGS

If romantic little gestures don't come to you automatically, make yourself a list of some of the simple things you could do to let your lover know you find him attractive or to make life a little nicer for him.

- Smile when your partner comes into the room.
- Listen to his stories.
- Make the bed in the morning.
- Open the door for your partner.
- Cook a meal or do the laundry without being asked.
- Take the dog for a walk, mow the lawn, or clean the garage.

It is amazing how much benefit comes from these actions.

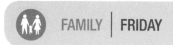

"A child needs a grandparent, anybody's grandparent, to grow a little more securely into an unfamiliar world."

—Charles and Ann Morse

Connect with Family Treasures

If your children have grandparents or other significant older people involved in their lives, they are truly lucky. Senior citizens are repositories of memories and details of a bygone era and as such are often treasure troves of information for younger generations. Their stories may be about other family members, historic events within the family, traditions, or their own childhood. As their memories are passed on, the children in the family gain a positive image of aging and a sense of identity.

Grandparents provide encouragement and support to the family in times of crisis. They serve as nurturers and mentors, and as role models, they provide children with examples of hard work and loyalty. Freed from the responsibility of daily parenting, grandparents are often the ones who are always there to play, to listen, or to help shoulder a burden.

BUILD A BOND BETWEEN GENERATIONS

Encourage lively discourse between the older and younger generations of your family. Teach your children why their grandparents are so special.

1. Get a piece of poster board and draw a family tree to show your children how they are connected to their grandparents. Depending on the ages of your children, the tree can be as simple or complicated as you like.
2. Budding filmmakers and historians can use a video camera to interview their grandparents for true stories about growing up in a different time (and possibly place) in the world.

"Flowers really do intoxicate me."

—Vita Sackville-West

Make Room for House Plants

Flowers and indoor plants add touches of nature to home interiors and help create a soothing and relaxing environment. Plants also improve the air quality in your home by removing the carbon dioxide and releasing oxygen and also increasing humidity levels. Some plants have medicinal value; for example, a piece of aloe vera can soothe a minor burn, leaves of mint can be used to create a mouth rinse, and the scent of lavender in soaps, sachets, and essential oils have been used to reduce stress.

USE HOUSE PLANTS

- Cut flowers or healthy plants are a welcoming presence in the foyer.
- Pretty pots of blooming African violets on a windowsill brighten a dining room or kitchen.
- A bamboo or money plant in your home office can serve as a reminder of good fortune and prosperity.
- Houseplants, like humans, need food, water, and light to live. They need to have dead leaves removed, an occasional misting and dusting, and now and then new soil, a larger pot, or both.
- Caring for your living décor can be calming and restful activity in itself.
- The website *www.guide-to-houseplants.com* has everything you need to know in order to select some greenery for your home. From the common to the exotic, you'll find care tips, suggestions for easy-care plants—including a list of ten house-plants you can't kill—and troubleshooting advice for pests and diseases.

"The essence of the beautiful is unity in variety."

—William Somerset Maugham

Understand Your Friends' Beliefs

Our friendships define so much of our lives. They reveal our personalities, ambitions, interests, and feelings. We tend to make friends with those people who match our likes and dislikes and who respect our values and opinions. Spirituality can be the great exception. If you know enough people, you're bound to be acquainted with both ends of the spectrum. You probably know someone of deep faith, but you're also likely familiar with someone who is an atheist. Spirituality has such a vast array of viewpoints and opinions that it's extremely difficult to find someone who matches your thoughts and feelings on the subject. We may consider people of varying faiths to be our friends, but how much do we *really* know about their thoughts on the subject of belief? Make sure you take the time to truly understand your friends' beliefs.

EXPLORE BOTH ENDS OF THE SPECTRUM

Increase your understanding of not only your friends but also of varying religious and nonreligious opinions by sitting down with two people who hold the most wildly different opinions you know.

1. Speak to them one at a time about their beliefs, and to what extent they think those beliefs influence their decisions and lives.
2. Compare notes afterward and then apply these notes to your own spiritual values. How are your friends' beliefs different from yours? How are they the same?
3. Examine these questions, gain valuable perspective, or even increase your tolerance through the answers. You may discover something you want to incorporate into your own belief system.

*"The soul which has no fixed purpose in life is
lost; to be everywhere is to be nowhere."*

—Michel de Montaigne

Live Purposefully

People who work to find meaning and purpose, and who live their lives making decisions and choices based on their purpose, are the people with the healthiest self-esteem. Finding your purpose is best explained by Parker Palmer as finding the thing that you cannot *not* do. That statement may sound somewhat abstract, but it means that you have found the talent, the passion, the miracle inside you that must come out. For some, it's music or medicine or repairing things or being around people. For others, it is surfing or writing or teaching or working with animals. It is sometimes described as "your calling."

Living purposefully means that you have found your calling, your passion, and all of your efforts, desires, goals, and actions are directed by this purpose.

WEEK TWENTY-THREE

FIND YOUR PURPOSE

Ask yourself the following questions:

- "Why am I here?"
- "What is my calling?"
- "What does my life want from me?"

There are no easy or clear cut answers to these questions, but hopefully they will encourage you to bring some purpose into your life—and your career.

"A community needs a soul if it is to become a true home for human beings."

—Pope John Paul II

Make a Beautiful Mural

Have you thought about ways of making the locale a little more eye-catching? Have you ever considered a mural? You may have seen one on the side of a school or another building before. Murals can be beautiful works of art and compelling narratives expressed through paint. Some murals feature one distinct vision expressed over a massive canvas. Other murals can feature contributions from any number of perspectives. Suddenly, the years of abuse and neglect fall away, and you're left with something that looks beautiful and promotes creativity in your area.

BEAUTIFY A BUILDING

It can be quite an inspiring sight to drive past a wall that explores a variety of outlooks, dreams, ideas, and artistic styles. It can be a testament to your town's culture and history, something well worth sharing with the rest of the world. Consider making a mural on one of those walls:

1. Since any murals must first meet with state and federal regulations, your first step is to contact someone in your local government.
2. Look for an established group. Some larger communities even have programs in which young people who have been arrested for vandalism are hired to create murals.

"A loyal friend laughs at your jokes when they're not so good, and sympathizes with your problems when they're not so bad."

—Arnold H. Glasgow

Rid Yourself of Toxic Friendships

Friends help shape your self-esteem and friends aid in good health and long life. In California, over 7,000 people were studied over a nine-year period. The people who had the best health, lived longer, avoided disease more often, and dealt with life's difficulties better were the people with strong social support.

Conversely, people who were isolated did not enjoy these benefits. When you are in caring relationships, you are not lonely, and the less lonely you are, the longer you live and the better you feel about yourself. On the other hand, when you see others in caring, loving friendships and you do not have them, your self-esteem and health suffer. This can affect you over the course of your life.

Countless people are in "friendships" to combat loneliness only to find that the relationships are abusive, controlling, and unhealthy. These friendships are called *toxic* or *contaminated*. Friends like this infect the way you act, think, and feel. They bring poison into your life and it takes a great deal of work to cleanse yourself of the debris. It also takes time for your self-esteem to heal because of these relationships.

DETOXIFY YOUR RELATIONSHIPS
1. Write down the names of your most significant friends.
2. Under each name write down some of your most honest and heart feelings about that person. How does this person make me feel? Act? Think?
3. You may discover that someone does not enrich your life and, in fact, may be a toxic or damaging influence.

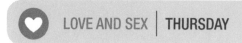

"When I am with you, the only place I want to be is closer."

—Unknown

Try a Tryst!

Don't wait for Valentine's Day. Try a chocolate-themed tryst. Book a hotel or bed-and-breakfast someplace where you'd like to spend the weekend with your lover, or take a staycation, if you're on a budget. If you're pressed for time, sneak off with your spouse for a lunchtime tryst!

MAKE IT SPECIAL

1. Choose your spouse's favorite chocolate truffles and wrap each in a photocopied image demonstrating an ancient Kama Sutra position. It's pretty much assured that in the time it takes that chocolate to melt on your lover's tongue, and for him to study the image, thoughts of the two of you engaged in that position will have flooded his brain. That, in turn, will trigger all the right responses in his body, ensuring you both will enjoy the tryst.

2. Book a flight to some exotic destination for a *really* special tryst. Ask your spouse how golf, buttery scones, and steamy sex in a Scottish castle sound. There's a good chance he won't reply, "Uh, sorry, no. I am planning to clean out the garage this weekend."

"What is important for kids to learn is that no matter how much money they have, earn, win, or inherit, they need to know how to spend it, how to save it, and how to give it to others in need. This is what handling money is about, and this is why we give kids an allowance."

—Barbara Coloroso

Give Them an Allowance

Numerous child rearing experts suggest that the only way for children to learn money-managing skills is to give them an allowance. No one is born knowing how to handle money, and many parents ignore the matter until the children are adults. By then, lifelong bad habits may have already developed. Receiving an allowance will help children distinguish between needs and wants—an important skill they will need their whole lives.

SET GUIDELINES FOR THE ALLOWANCE

1. Let your children know you are going to start giving them an allowance. If they will be required to do chores to earn it, explain what they need to do. Discuss the purposes of an allowance—spending, sharing, and saving.

2. Give them the option of earning extra money for special projects.

3. Teach your children how to wisely spend, save, and, depending on their age, invest. When it is their own money they must spend for the things they want, chances are they will learn to make better-informed purchasing decisions. And you will feel happier when your children are no longer treating you like you're the bank.

"A cheerful frame of mind, reinforced by relaxation . . . is the medicine that puts all ghosts of fear on the run."

—George Matthew Adam

Take a Solo Spa Day

Resist the temptation to call up your friends and set up a group trip to the nearest day spa. It doesn't matter if it's your first time, or if you have a favorite spot that you like to visit whenever you're feeling overwhelmed. Take the opportunity to enjoy the amenities of a day spa on your own.

Do away with the wants and needs of others, the headaches of coordinating schedules and what each person might want to do. Strip away the unnecessary until you get to the essential and singular task of relaxing at your own pace and according to your own interests.

TREAT YOURSELF

Do you have an important business meeting coming up, or is there another stressful date in your future? Give yourself something to look forward to, and make an appointment at a spa for a visit after your demanding day.

1. When you feel like life has become a treadmill and you need to step off, treat yourself to a day at the spa. Get a manicure, a pedicure, or a skin-rejuvenation facial.
2. Or if you'd like to try something a tad more radical, get a colon cleansing, take a mud bath, or slip into a sensory-deprivation tank.
3. For a healthy state of mind and body, try some treatments at an upscale med-spa center that integrates innovative, cutting-edge therapies and holistic healing modalities with ancient practices of other cultures.

"We need to find God, and he cannot be found in noise and restlessness. God is the friend of silence. See how nature—trees, flowers, grass— grows in silence; see the stars, the moon and the sun, how they move in silence. . . . We need silence to be able to touch souls."

—Mother Teresa

Spend Some Quiet Time

Has anyone ever told you that you talk too much? Have you ever found yourself saying the same thing to someone after reaching the end of your rope? Both scenarios are probably right. Most of us talk too much. You may feel like everything on your mind is worth expressing, but if you think about it, you'd realize that there are times when silence is ideal. The only problem is that most of us are uncomfortable with long periods of silence. We don't have the ability to truly enjoy silence or welcome it as a respite from our chaotic lives. If your world provides too little time and space for reflection, prayer and contemplation, you can take your own vow of silence any time you want. Decide on a time frame (one to two hours would be best to start) and maintain complete silence.

TAKE A VOW OF SILENCE

1. The word for observing silence in Sanskrit is *mauna*, and it involves quieting the chatter of the mouth and also of the mind. The path of silence is an ancient method of spiritual renewal.
2. Some monasteries and novitiates permit visitors to join their communities for personal retreats. During the span of the retreat (often one to several days), silence is observed. This isn't silence with conditions, or silence that can be broken as soon as you get bored.
3. If you are intrigued and would like to give it a try, search out a silent retreat in a religious or spiritual center.

*"Before I can tell my life what I want to do with it,
I must listen to my life telling me who I am."*

—Parker Palmer

Leave the Moment

Thinking backward can help you find your vocation, your joy in work. Think back to the first thing you ever wanted to be. Was it a firefighter, a law enforcement officer, a doctor, an astronaut? Why did you want to be that? If you aren't doing it now, what stopped you? Think back to a job where you were truly happy and felt that you were making a difference. Is it still true? Does your current work bring you peace? If not, why? What did you have in the past that you do not have now? Looking back can be an important step in working forward.

Leaving the moment also asks that you move to tomorrow and beyond. While the past is a great teacher, the future is where promise lives. Where do you want to be next month, in a year, in five years? What do you want your legacy to be? These questions are not only a part of the past, but are also a part of the future.

GAZE INTO YOUR CRYSTAL BALL

An interesting but often scary thing to do is to consider the end of your life.

1. Pretend for a moment that you have just passed away at the old age of ninety. What do you want people to say about you? What do you want your life to have meant? This may seem morbid and strange, but thinking about this can help you clarify what really is most important to you.

2. If you seriously listen to your heart, examine what your strengths and weaknesses are, study your past, and make vocational decisions based on these things and based on your overriding life goals, the future can start at any moment of your choosing.

"You really can't beat that. Having some good friends and going out to eat some good barbecue."

—Andrew Ray

Organize a Community Barbecue

When the weather finally begins to warm up, one of the things we look forward to the most is the opportunity to fire up the grill. Our Sunday afternoons can be spent relaxing outside, relishing a reprieve from winter, and enjoying the company of our friends and family.

It's a summer tradition, but it doesn't have to involve only the people you already know. Block parties were a staple of neighborhoods for years, but they seem to have become a thing of the past. There's really no reason for this. Many neighborhood parks have places for grilling, and if they don't, you might consider hosting a get-together in your own backyard. It's a wonderful way to welcome new neighbors, but it could also be a nice introduction to those neighbors you've been meaning to get to know. Very few things break the ice faster than good food, cold drinks, and interesting conversation.

PLAN A POTLUCK

Everyone can bring something, and don't forget about vegans or vegetarians! The variety of grill-friendly food now available guarantees that everyone can be included. Make sure you pay attention to the special dietary needs of diabetics and those individuals with food allergies, too.

1. Sit down with your family and select the date for your cookout.
2. Then create an invitation for the best party on the block! Coordinate who's bringing what so you have a variety of dishes.

"Babies are such a nice way to start people."

—Don Herrold

Host a Baby Shower

Sharing in the joy of a friend's pregnancy is one of life's great moments. We love to be there as she gets ready to welcome a new life into the world. It doesn't matter if it's her first baby or her fourth; we want to make it a truly special experience. Baby showers remain a popular way to celebrate one of life's greatest miracles. It also presents a perfect opportunity for friends to gather and participate in a particular kind of silly, harmless kind of fun. It's a chance for the expectant mother to stand in the spotlight and receive some well-deserved attention before the baby arrives.

PLAN A BABY SHOWER

Be a true friend and offer to host your friend's shower. Planning one is surprisingly easy, but Google can be an easy resource of tips and inspiration. Websites like *www.punchbowl.com* and *www.babyshower101.com* offer everything from supplies to planning advice and even tips for games and activities.

- If someone else is hosting the shower, offer to share the planning responsibilities.
- As a special gift for the mother-to-be, make up a book of coupons good for things like free babysitting, a trip to the nail salon, or lunch at her favorite restaurant.

"Sex appeal is fifty percent what you've got and fifty percent what people think you've got."

—Sophia Loren

Look Good for Your Lover

Beauty may start on the inside, but it's a pretty safe bet that no one is going to compliment you on your gorgeous gall bladder. While taking care of your body is important (exercise, eating right, reducing stress, getting enough sleep, and being positive) so, too, is keeping up your appearance. Put another way—don't stop looking nice for your partner just because the relationship has stood the test of time. Try a new look from time to time. Keep that sexy, confident attraction going between you.

INVEST IN YOUR LOOKS

1. Women: Buy a new lipstick. Invest in a facial once in a while. Get your nails done. Color your gray. Buy a bra that pushes your boobs north and wear it with a low-cut blouse.
2. Men: Purchase cologne with a sexy scent that she loves. Get a GQ haircut, grow a mustache (or shave it off), get the hair between your brows waxed, and invest in a new cut of jeans or slacks.
3. Consider the expenditures as the vitally important cost of looking good for each other. If finances permit, invest a little more in your sex appeal. Book an appointment for yourself and your spouse at your favorite nail salon for his-and-her manicures. Also try his-and-her massages and his-and-her facials.

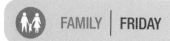
"Writing is a way of talking without being interrupted."

—Jules Renard

Send a Message

The next time someone in your family turns a deaf ear to your point of view, try a new strategy. Write her a succinctly worded note. A note is a terrific way to communicate your feelings and send a clear and direct message unencumbered by spontaneous emotion. It can reopen the lines of communication that were perhaps closed by an angry, disruptive conflict. Writing a note gives you the time to choose your words carefully and to put love and consideration into your side of the story—something that's not always easy in the heat of a discussion.

AVOID MAKING MISTAKES

1. When you write your note, resist the urge to call names, to point out someone's stubborn streak, or make threats. Instead, create a lens for her to see your position on the subject.
2. Argue your point without finding fault with her as a person.
3. Show respect for her view, but reveal why you've arrived at the opposite conclusion. She's not your enemy. Tackle the problem, not her, and you may find that she isn't all that attached to her point of view after all.
4. If the opportunity arises, apply the same strategy to talking with her and you may even find her listening.

"A well-spent day brings happy sleep."

—Leonardo da Vinci

Make Sleep a Priority

Rather than living your life exhausted and stressed out, make it a point to let go of the tension accumulated throughout the day so that you can get deep, restorative sleep. Your body and mind will thank you the very next morning. You'll find yourself more eager to seize the day and its challenges. Those long days won't seem quite as long. You might even be able to avoid the dreaded afternoon crash that so many people experience. Just try to go easy on your coworkers when you see them at work in the morning. They probably didn't sleep as well as you did!

RELAX BEFORE YOU SLEEP

After a long day at work, are you tense? Do you toss and turn while you try to go to sleep at night? Release stress before you go to sleep, and you may find that you are able to fall asleep more quickly, have a better quality of sleep, and wake up more rested and refreshed. There are myriad ways to calm your mind and let go of the tension held in your body.

- Take a warm bath.
- Sip a glass of warm milk.
- Do some deep breathing.
- Pray in order to release any concerns that might be troubling you.
- Tuck lavender under your pillow. Lavender is known for its soothing and calming properties and may help you sleep.

"Prayer is not asking. It is a longing of the soul. It is daily admission of one's weakness. It is better in prayer to have a heart without words than words without a heart."

—Mahatma Gandhi

Find Comfort in Prayer

Prayer can center you when things are going right in your life, give solace and lift you when you feel down, and remind you that you aren't alone. Praying can help you move forward when you feel stuck or provide hope when you need healing. Harold Koenig, associate professor of psychiatry and medicine at Duke University School of Medicine, has observed that religious people tend to have healthier lives.

RECITE A PRAYER

Recite a prayer that gives you comfort. Or, if you prefer, you can make up your own prayer.

- A simple "thank you" is a powerful prayer of gratitude. "I need your help" or "Please guide me" are also excellent points of departure into prayer.
- Pray and then be still like an empty vessel waiting to be filled. Gratefully receive whatever inspiration, answers, relief, peace, joy, and bliss may come.
- Visit the website *www.worldprayers.org.* You'll find dozens of prayers for all occasions that represent numerous faiths and traditions. Some of the prayers are thousands of years old, while others are contemporary. They represent our attempts to connect with a divine creator or spirit.

"A country should be defended not by arms, but by ethical behavior."

—Vinoba Bhave

Make Ethical Decisions

We all know stealing is wrong, but is it okay to take a few ink pens and a pack of Post-It notes home from work every week? Everyone does it. Yes, lying is wrong, but a little lie could save your job. What's the harm in that?

Perhaps the most important word associated with ethics is betrayal. Is there a worse word or act? Ethics demand that you consider this word. When you are making a decision, evaluating whether to act or not, or when you consider the consequences of a decision or act, is there any betrayal? That one word can be your guiding force in ethical behavior.

WEEK TWENTY-FIVE

CONSIDER THESE GUIDELINES

If you have concerns about whether a decision you are about to make is ethical or not, or if how you have treated someone is ethical or not, consider the following guidelines:

- Will this decision hurt your reputation or the reputation of others?
- Can you tell others about this decision or action with pride?
- Would you do it to your mother?
- Is it legal?
- Have you considered every angle and option?
- Is it right? (Yes, you do know!)
- Is it balanced and fair to others?
- Does your conscience approve?
- Have you betrayed anyone to make this decision?

These simple but important questions can help you learn to make ethical decisions. They can also help you build positive self-esteem, in that you know that you have done right by others.

"Social media is not a media. The key is to listen, engage, and build relationships."

—David Alston

Join Facebook

If you don't have a Facebook page yet, consider joining. It's quickly become the best way to share information, post photos, meet new people, and re-establish connections we haven't met in years. But Facebook has developed into more than that. It can be used to raise awareness for a cause, promote entertainment, and generate interest for an upcoming event.

START A COMMUNITY FACEBOOK PAGE

Like any social network, Facebook is constantly improving. One of their most impressive improvements has been with their groups section. Now, it's easier than ever to start a community group. This is a way to bring your neighborhood together under a single, immensely useful banner. Keeping people in your community up to date will be much easier, and you'll have a much better time planning any possible events or get-togethers.

1. Decide whether the group should be private or public.
2. Invite members.
3. Keep everyone up-to-date on important events significant to them. You can even open a "members only" chat for your group.

"As teammates, we are always there for one another
. . . everyone has everyone's back."

—Whitney Barrett

Join a Team

Get active and you will feel better. If you prefer team sports to those you do solo, join a softball or bowling team or organize one that includes people from your circle of friends or business colleagues. Softball teams and bowling leagues play other teams, so even as you are having fun with friends on your team you are also potentially making new friends with players from other teams. Psychologists say those who live isolated lives or without strong social networks are not as happy as those who have strong bonds, social connections, and ongoing support from friends and family.

JOIN A BOWLING LEAGUE

1. There are leagues to suit all sorts of people and their different tastes. The types of leagues include youth, adult, adult and youth, all men, all women, senior citizens, and groups with men and women together. Playing times can be during the day, mornings, afternoons, or evenings, which can be early, such as right after work, or late at night. Leagues can take place during the week or on weekends.

2. On an adult team, there are usually four or five bowlers. On a youth league team, there are three or four. Bowling leagues can be made up of people with different backgrounds and interests. Religious organizations, companies, fraternal groups, and many others form leagues. The format of a league is usually three games, which take approximately two and half hours for a traditional bowling league.

3. League bowlers often compete for individual and team awards, such as plaques and trophies. Also, many leagues will collect extra money at the end of the season or host a dinner or dance for the league members and their guests. Some organizational leagues will donate money to a charity that they represent.

"Sing and dance together and be joyous, but let each one of you be alone/Even as the strings of a lute are alone though they quiver with the same music."

—Kahlil Gibran

Understanding Unrealistic Ideals

Write down three ideals about marriage that you harbored before you were married. Ask your spouse to do the same. Then discuss whether your ideals were too far-fetched. When spouses bring unrealistic idealization to their marriage, the marriage can be vulnerable. Strengthen your bond by accepting your partner's real self, flaws and all.

LEAVE A LITTLE MYSTERY

However, while you need to be realistic, you can also enhance your appeal to each other by keeping some things private. The minutiae of feminine products and breast pumps could probably be kept out of daily conversation. Relegate such information to the realm of female mystery.

- The truth is that husbands and wives really don't need to know *every* teensy weensy bit of detail about each other. Who wants to see a woman shaving her underarms or a man clipping nasal hair? You just want that finished, well-groomed look, right?
- Also, to get too up-close and personal is to start feeling somewhat suffocated. Although early in your marriage you might desire to cleave to each other as only newlyweds can, later on that same intense closeness pushes you away from each other again to reclaim your individuality and a little self-focus. Marriage provides a fertile ground for both oneness and separateness and that, like other aspects of marriage, is one of its mysteries.

"Other things may change us, but we start and end with family."

—Anthony Brandt

Reunite with Your Family

While coping with your chaotic life, you might not see your cherished relatives as much as you'd like. A picnic reunion is one way for you and your family to catch up on what is happening in your respective lives while enjoying a time honored tradition. A gathering such as this encourages a celebration of your shared identity, calls up memories of past eras and perhaps historical events, and strengthens family bonds.

SHARE THE RECIPES

Ask each family member to make a special dish from a treasured family recipe and bring it to the picnic.

1. Encourage them to write down the recipe and share their memories of the recipe.
2. Who first made the recipe? What makes it so special? Was the recipe involved in a special family tradition?
3. Ask them to make enough copies of the recipe so that other people at the reunion can receive a copy. Encourage them to pass it along to their children and grandchildren.
4. Those beloved relatives who made those dishes, perhaps even centuries before your time, have long since passed on, but you can all remember them whenever you make it.

"The time to relax is when you don't have time for it."

—Sydney J. Harris

Try a Sauna or Steam Bath

If you believe that time spent in a sauna or steam bath is healthy because sweating releases unwanted material from the body and improves circulation, you are correct. Make sure that you are in good health by checking with your physician before stepping into a sauna or steam room. The warning on the door is there for a reason, and it should be taken seriously. Taking a sauna or steam bath can eliminate toxins and excess sodium, loosen tense and sore muscles, and enable you to relax into your happy place.

MAKE THE MOST OF YOUR SAUNA

1. Savor the feeling you get when you open the door to leave the room. The rush of cool air hitting your skin after spending time in a steam bath or sauna is one of the best natural highs there is. It is an energizing and exhilarating way to end a relaxing activity. With a clear head and a relaxed body, life might not seem so difficult after all.
2. It's important to drink lots of water to replace what you lose from perspiration.
3. Buy yourself a flattering new terry robe for your visit to the sauna. You'll feel even more pampered and special when you wrap yourself in something soft and luxurious.

*"Failure will never overtake me if my determination
to succeed is strong enough."*

—Og Mandino

Identify Your Spiritual Strengths and Weaknesses

Physical well-being is something we're all familiar with. Not everyone takes care of themselves as they should, but most people are aware of the concept of good physical and mental health. The path to physical well-being can be as clear as we want it to be. We can exercise, take vitamins, watch what we eat, and get a decent night's sleep every night. There's more, but the basic idea is pretty simple.

What doesn't get mentioned often is our spiritual well-being. Too many of us just don't have the blueprint for it. Perhaps that's because there isn't one single blueprint; every human being is unique. There are, however, some general principles you can consider. Spiritual well-being can result from living a life filled with integrity, believing in nonviolence, caring for your family, performing your work and worldly duties, and practicing your religious or spiritual traditions. It is also important to show respect and reverence toward that which is considered sacred.

EXERCISE YOUR SPIRITUAL SIDE

Work for change from the inside out and try to turn your spiritual weaknesses into spiritual strengths. Create your own "exercise" plan for spiritual well-being and stick to it.

1. Separate your life into five areas and write them down. For example, you could write family, friends, career, religion, and leisure time.
2. The next step is to write down your greatest spiritual weakness for each area.
3. Now that you've identified the things that need work, you can brainstorm ideas for turning those weaknesses into strengths.

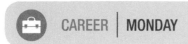

"We are what we think . . .
All that we are
arises with our thoughts.
With our thoughts
we make our world."

—Buddha

Understand the Law of Attraction

The law of attraction is based on the theory that we create our world through our thoughts. It's based on the belief that what you focus on is what you get or create for yourself. Proponents of this law believe that if you go through life smiling, full of gratitude and recognition that life is abundant, you will act with honesty and generosity of spirit.

Your subconscious doesn't know real experience from imagined. According to the teachings of the law of attraction, you just have to believe the experience can be yours and supercharge it with emotion in order to manifest it in your life. Let those happy feelings permeate your dream and your time at work.

CREATE IT AND BELIEVE IT

You can use the law of attraction to draw to yourself the fame you desire. For example, the work you do is satisfying, but you want recognition for those big accomplishments and milestones.

1. Before you retire for the night, take five minutes to clear your mind.
2. Focus. Use your imagination to create a scenario in which you are receiving accolades, praise, and ovations by industry leaders, your business colleagues, and others.
3. Now, add your emotion to your imagined scene. Concentrate on your emotional feelings and mood as you listen to the words spoken by others about your achievements and accomplishments.

"Crafts make us feel rooted, give us a sense of belonging and connect us with our history. Our ancestors used to create these crafts out of necessity, and now we do them for fun, to make money and to express ourselves."

—Phyllis George

Put Together a Craft Show

All of us have been to a craft show at one time or another. We've marveled at some of the amazing creations people have for sale, taken the opportunity to purchase unique items, and appreciated the chance to contribute to a local artisan. What makes these shows unique is their ability to exist almost anywhere. They can be held anywhere from a spacious outdoor venue, to a monstrous convention center, to a small church basement. Like yard sales, the size of the event has little to do with your chances of finding something wonderful.

Finding a venue should be easy enough. Keep those church basements in mind, and don't be afraid to hold it in someone's front yard. It can be a fundraiser for a worthy cause, or it can simply be an excuse to get together and make some money for the artists to continue their work. Whatever the reason, you'll be giving creative people a chance to network and show off their wares.

FIND VENDORS FOR YOUR CRAFT FAIR

You probably know a few people whose hobby or work produces distinctive creations. Why not invite them to participate in your own craft show? Visit the principal of your local high school and invite creative students to participate in your craft fair. Not only are you encouraging budding artists, but also the school may provide the perfect venue for your endeavor.

"Wine lets secrets out."

—Chinese proverb

Don't Let Drinking with Friends Become a Problem

The occasional drink with friends who invite you out for an evening of catching up and talking about the old days can be a lot of fun. But if meeting your friends always means excluding your mate and if the meeting always involves drinking at a bar or club, you have to be concerned about the impact on your relationship. Drinking alcohol can lower inhibitions, and while you may see no harm in having drinks with friends in a setting like a bar or nightclub, unhealthy situations can develop. Your relationship may be strong and loving, and you and your mate may trust each other. But what if you have let down your guard and aren't thinking quite as clearly as you normally would because of the alcohol you've consumed? It's flattering when someone finds you attractive and flirts with you. Do you flirt back because you think it's harmless, maybe because it gratifies your ego? Do you leave? Do you tell your significant other? If not, what happens when your mate finds out the truth? The prudent choice is to exercise caution and restraint; think through your choices before going out with friends for drinks on a regular basis, and ask if your partner is invited, too.

FIND AN ALTERNATIVE TO GOING OUT

Spend some time with your friends at home instead of at the bars or nightclubs. Partners get to know each other's friends and acquaintances, and frequent outings with the focus on alcohol won't be necessary.

1. Throw the party at your house.
2. Invite your friends over for a tea party, a potluck, or a poker game.
3. Watch a sporting event together.
4. Find an activity everyone can participate in, like a trivia game night.

"There's no half-singing in the shower, you're either a rock star or an opera diva."

—Josh Groban

Join the Glee Club

Who cares if the singing is off-pitch or out of key? You and the other half of your darling duo are in the shower, for goodness' sake, naked, soaped up, and ready to belt out a Puccini aria. Or maybe a little ditty by Fergie and the Black Eyed Peas is more your style. Go ahead, shake your booty and belt out that number. It will likely endear you to your partner. You can wash her hair and she can scrub your back to the rhythm of the music.

SET THE STAGE

1. Heighten the shower singing experience by ensuring that you've got everything you need in the stall before you step in. Set out a basket with scented shower gel, shampoo, conditioner, a back scrubber, and a loofah or two.
2. There is a saying in Spanish, *dímelo cantando,* that means "Say it singing." So, go ahead. Say it, and sing it: "I love you."
3. Put some waterproof adult toys in your shower basket. Make the bathing experience a lot more fun and give it new meaning when you invite your lover to join you. Warning: Shower singing and hot sex can be habit-forming.

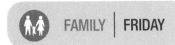
*"If you can give your son or daughter only
one gift, let it be enthusiasm."*

—Bruce Barton

Set Aside One Hour for Crafts

After the dishes are done and the homework has been put away, turn off the television and turn on your creativity. Get the craft box out and create something fun, whimsical, or beautiful with the kids. This exercise will require some planning ahead on your part. Before you choose your craft, consider the ages of the children involved and base your choice on difficulty, safety, and any time constraints or short attention spans.

GET MESSY

Resign yourself to the fact that doing crafts with kids is usually messy. Remember the point of this activity is for everyone to have fun, so ignore the pictures of how the craft is supposed to turn out and have a good time.

1. Allow your children to use their imagination and be creative. Quality time with your children is never time wasted. They need time with you to feel loved and wanted. Instead of allowing them to sit in front of the television and get bombarded with undesirable messages, establish an hour of family fellowship and watch them thrive.
2. Get crafty ideas online at sites. Or you can visit a crafts store like Michael's for hands on inspiration and to pick up the supplies you will need.

"As I was snuggling back into my bed after getting up to use the bathroom, I breathed a little, 'This must be like heaven.' I love my bed. I love the 'ahh' that comes with getting warm and smelling fresh sheets."

—Jan Denise

Snuggle a Little

A survey of 6,000 British adults by the hotel chain Travelodge found that 35 percent admitted to sleeping with stuffed animals. So why might someone still have affection for a shabby old blanket or a tattered stuffed dog? Part of the reason is probably nostalgia, but most people also retain a deep emotional attachment to the objects as well. It's called "essentialism," or the idea that objects are more than just their physical properties.

As a child, you probably had a teddy bear or a security blanket that helped you get through the night. As an adult facing crisis, you may wish you had something tangible like that to give you comfort. Give it a try.

PICK YOUR TEDDY

If you don't have a favorite blanket or stuffed animal, you need to pick one! As a child, you loved your blanket because it was yours and yours alone. Wrap yourself in your blanket or hug your bear and let your inner child feel protected and comforted. This exercise can match a wide array of moods and soothe you gently into a deeply relaxing place by appealing to your need to find comfort through touch.

1. Visit your linen closet and see if there's a comfy throw, a worn afghan, or a silky coverlet that might suit you.
2. Go to the clearance table at your local department store and pick something out that could become your new security blanket.
3. If you want to treat yourself, go ahead and indulge in a truly special teddy bear, like a mohair Steiff.
4. Go to Build-a-Bear with your kids, and build your own bear!

"The spiritual path, then, is simply the journey of living our lives. Everyone is on a spiritual path; most people just don't know it."

—Marianne Williamson

Walk a Spiritual Path

We're familiar with the concept of a "lonely road." The term implies going through a difficult period without any support, guidance, or advice to guide us as we go. Indeed, there can be some truth to that. It shouldn't be the norm of your life, however. If it is, you may want to re-examine the entire concept of walking a road that, according to your perspective, is perpetually lonely. Sometimes you have no choice but to travel through life in that way, but sometimes the choice is entirely up to you.

TAKE A PILGRIMAGE

Some paths have been trod by pilgrims seeking spiritual renewal for centuries. Jerusalem's Via Dolorosa or the pilgrim's path leading to Mecca are two examples. Another path leads to the Bodhi tree in Bodhgaya, India, the place where Buddha became enlightened.

1. Perhaps there's a spiritual trail or road in your part of the world. If so, follow it.
2. If not, consider walking along one of the ancient routes that spiritual pilgrims have traveled over the centuries.
3. If you can't travel to one of the traditional and well-known spiritual paths, you can take a walk in nature. Seek something that will reacquaint you with that feeling of wonder and renewal that exists all around you.
4. If you are in the right frame of mind, you can find that in a walk down a quiet, tree-lined street.

"Sometimes it's important to work for that pot of gold. But other times it's essential to take time off and to make sure that your most important decision in the day simply consists of choosing which color to slide down on the rainbow."

—Douglas Pagels

Take a Mental Health Day

Maybe your career has been particularly demanding recently, or your life outside the job is taking its toll. Either way, you're feeling depleted and discouraged. Working under the deadline of a stressful job and a heavy workload can be harmful to your physical, emotional, and mental well-being. Your productivity drops when you are mentally and physically exhausted.

Give yourself the gift of time. What would you do if you didn't have to be anywhere or do anything? Break your routine and take a day or two to regroup. Get away from work, stress, deadlines, and other job-related challenges and difficulties.

GET THE MOST OUT OF MENTAL HEALTH DAY

1. Do nothing that is related to your job. This will be particularly difficult with the 24/7 lifestyle that includes text messaging, e-mail, and BlackBerrys, but a mental health day means avoiding anything that resembles work.
2. If you can take a day when your mate and children are at work and school, then you can really make it a personal day.
3. Spend your day doing something that you truly enjoy. Make sure it is something that will clear your mind and invigorate you. Bring one of your daydreams to life.
4. Finally, guilt is forbidden. You are only allowed to feel refreshed and relieved. You've worked hard to earn your mental health day. Now enjoy it!

WEEK TWENTY-SEVEN

"Until you have become really, in actual fact, as brother to everyone, brotherhood will not come to pass."

—Fyodor Dostoyevsky

Honor Your Mentor

Do you recall someone who made a difference in your life? Someone who instilled you with the values and beliefs that you cherish today or who helped you through a difficult and challenging time? Say thank you by writing them a heartfelt letter. If this isn't possible, post a tribute to them on your Facebook page.

PAY IT FORWARD

Another way to honor your mentor is to play that role in someone else's life. Consider mentoring a child who could use your guidance.

1. Try the Big Brothers and Big Sisters program. For more than a hundred years, this organization has worked to make a substantial difference in the lives of children in need of guidance during their most formative years. Eighty-three percent of children who have participated in the program agree that their life was changed for the better.

2. Visit the Big Brothers and Big Sisters website, *www.bbbs.org*. It's a terrific resource for learning more about the program and making the decision as to whether or not you'd like to give it a try. With approximately twenty-one thousand boys and ten thousand girls waiting for a big brother or sister, the need is definitely there.

3. Finding something to do with your new little "brother" or "sister" is the easy part. A trip to a museum, a baseball game, the bowling alley, or a theme park are all good examples. Your investment of time will pay you back in ways you might have never imagined, and for the child, the benefits will probably last for the rest of his life.

"There are three hundred and sixty-four days when you might get un-birthday presents . . . and only one for birthday presents, you know."

—Lewis Carroll

Celebrate an Unbirthday

Even if haven't read *Alice's Adventures in Wonderland* (or seen a movie version), you may have heard of an un-birthday. It refers to the days of the year when it's not actually your birthday. The concept was invented by Lewis Carroll for his classic novel, and it's an idea that's gained popularity through the years. Celebrate your un-birthday today!

DO IT ANY WAY YOU WANT
People celebrate un-birthdays for all different kinds of reasons.

- Perhaps you just feel like throwing a party to celebrate the gift of knowing a cherished friend.
- It's a humorous and touching way to let someone know you care. As Carroll so wisely observed in his writing, an unbirthday can be just about anything you want it to be.
- Do you have a friend who needs cheering up? Or one who recently received a promotion at work? Celebrate in a new and quirky way by throwing an un-birthday party in her honor.

"The pressure of the hands causes the springs of life to flow."

—Tokujiro Namikoshi

Bask in the Afterglow

All humans need physical touch to feel safe and connected. In psychology, there is something known as the attachment theory, which postulates that distressed infants and young children need to be held and touched in order for them to learn how to soothe and calm their own nervous systems. Research in the fields of neuroscience and psychology is finding a significant link between emotional needs being met in the first years of life and the ability to form healthy adult relationships.

The pleasure our bodies can feel is a great gift. Combine that gift with a sense of connection to someone you care about and you can open yourself to even greater satisfaction. Don't shortchange each other by rolling over and falling asleep after sex. To lie together in a loving embrace after sex is to enjoy an important part of the process. Having your lover to play with creates many new options for enjoying your sexuality. It can also invite more complexity and complications. It helps to attend to your relationship and keep it in harmony, making sure you both get what you need. When you feel relaxed after lovemaking and are wrapped in the warm cocoon of loving arms, you feel contentment and security that you may not experience any other way during your day.

RELAX AND DRIFT AWAY

Play soft music on the radio or iPod. Make sure you set a time for it to shut off, then relax after lovemaking and take your time drifting off to sleep. Pray, meditate, or incubate a dream as you sink deeper into the in-between state between wakefulness and sleep.

"Kids: they dance before they learn there is anything that isn't music."

—William Stafford

Get Your Kids Moving

According to the Center for Disease Control and Prevention, approximately 17 percent of children and adolescents aged two to nineteen are obese. Since 1980, obesity prevalence among children and adolescents has almost tripled. Encourage your child to be more active now in order to maintain good health later.

GO OUTSIDE AND PLAY

It wasn't too long ago that children came home from school, changed into their play clothes, and went outside until their mother called them for supper. However, today's world has cable television, video games, and interactive websites competing for and winning your child's attention.

1. There's no better way to encourage your children to get off the couch and go outside than to spend time outdoors with them. Children love to participate in activities with their parents.
2. When your children are old enough to run around, get out a soccer ball and take it to the yard or park. As you demonstrate a competitive spirit, team cooperation, respect for the rules of the game, and good sportsmanship whether you win or lose, your child learns through observation, listening, and participation.
3. If soccer isn't your thing, make up a game. The point is to play, set a good example, and have fun with the little (or not so little) ones in your life.

"Wine is bottled poetry."

—Robert Louis Stevenson

Unwind with Good Wine

Unwind with a glass of your favorite wine at the end of an exhausting day or difficult period. According to a number of studies, wine is good for you if you drink it in moderation and as part of a healthy diet. There are different wines for different meals. One of them is bound to go perfectly with that special dinner you're going to cook on Saturday night.

Wine has nonalcoholic phytochemicals (flavanoids and resveratrol) that prevent free radical molecules from damaging your body's cells. Studies show that wine could reduce the risk of getting certain cancers and heart disease and might slow the progression of Alzheimer's and Parkinson's disease.

DRINK RIGHT

For women, one five-ounce glass a day is good, but keep in mind that the health benefits are forfeited if you drink more.

1. Find the wine that fits your taste buds perfectly.
2. Pour yourself a glass and feel your body relax as soon as you take that first delicious sip.
3. Enjoy treating yourself to something that both tastes good and is good for you.
4. To learn more about wines, wine festivals, and even wine vacations, visit *www.localwineevents.com*.

"Vision is the art of seeing things invisible."

—Jonathan Swift

Reconnect with Your Spiritual Side

It's human nature to maintain connections that are important to us, such as with friends and family. If we lose that all-important connection, then we do what we can to get it back. When it comes to our spiritual side, we often don't make the same kind of effort. Losing our connection to our spirituality is much like the domino effect. We lose one thing, then another, and another until we get to a point where we feel drained and struggling to keep ourselves intact from the inside out. Make an effort to spend time reconnecting with your spiritual side. Rest, reflect, read spiritual readings, or talk with a spiritual adviser.

GO ON A VISION QUEST

- One way to reconnect with your spiritual side is to undertake a vision quest. Generally, these are accomplished during periods of aloneness (often with fasting), under the guidance of an experienced mentor.
- Use the opportunity to commune with a higher power or force to gain a sense of purpose and direction for your life.
- Done correctly, a vision quest can help you sense the wholeness in the fabric of the universe and yourself as a thread in that fabric.

> *"One of the great undiscovered joys of life comes from doing everything one attempts to the best of one's ability. There is a special sense of satisfaction, a pride in surveying such a work, a work which is rounded, full, exact, complete in all its parts, which the superficial person who leaves his or her work in a slovenly, slipshod, half-finished condition, can never know. It is this conscientious completeness which turns any work into art. The smallest task, well done, becomes a miracle of achievement."*
>
> —Og Mandino

Take Pride in Your Work

People who pay attention to detail and present polished, professional work not only feel a sense of satisfaction for a job well done, they also gain respect and appreciation from their superiors. You'll enjoy your job more if you feel confident and efficient. You can help accomplish this in several ways. Avoid embarrassing mistakes by getting into the habit of rereading all of your writing before showing it to others. With the ease of spell-checking, you might get into the habit of assuming your work is fine, but there can still be a lot of errors even when the words are spelled correctly. Reread everything that you write, whether it's an e-mail, a report, or any other work-related document, especially after using the spell-check function.

IMPROVE YOUR WRITING SKILLS

- Work constantly on improving your writing skills. Putting together your reports, letters, proposals, and other written information in an effective way is a valuable skill that will get you noticed.
- Developing solid writing skills is something that may benefit you in other areas of your life. You may just discover you have a flair for writing and pen the next bestseller!
- The website *www.dumblittleman.com* has hundreds of interesting tips for just about everything—including writing, grammar, and other career-related topics.

"How wonderful it is that nobody need wait a single moment before starting to improve the world."

—Anne Frank

Help Teens in Crisis

Teens run away from home for a variety of reasons, some more compelling than others, but they may not be aware of the dangers they face living on the streets. Crisis hotlines and teen shelters are necessary for assisting these young people who are not yet adults and who have no means of support. If this cause resonates with you, check out *www.standupforkids.org* or volunteer at a local teen shelter.

VOLUNTEER AT A CRISIS CENTER HOTLINE

Giving your time to a crisis center hotline enables you to reach people who are sometimes the most difficult to help. Many people who call those numbers are doing so because they see no alternative. The aid provided by the volunteers at the other end of the phone line has saved many lives. These voices can provide the encouragement and inspiration a person requires to seek the help he needs. This can be in the form of supplying contact information for other services, helpful advice, or just a sympathetic ear. Contact your nearest crisis center for volunteer opportunities:

- There is some training involved, but anyone who becomes involved with a crisis program must also possess strong listening skills and the ability to provide tactful and sensitive advice.
- Crisis work is not for everyone, but if you feel drawn to help, you should investigate it more fully.
- Making yourself available to those who see no other way of reaching out for help is one of most critical and compassionate ways to serve the people who live and work in your community.

"I've been on a diet for two weeks and all I've lost is fourteen days."

—Totie Fields

Join the Club!

If you need to lose a few pounds, buddy up with two or more friends who are also trying to lose weight and form a weight loss club. Share weight-loss ideas, low-fat recipes, and information on how to cut salt in the diet. Eat smaller portions of healthier foods. Drink water instead of sodas and other sugar-laden beverages. Replace high-calorie sweets and desserts with lower-calorie counterparts such as fresh fruit with a dollop of creamy soy yogurt. Help each other remember to do these things, and support each other during successes and challenges.

SUPPORT YOUR FRIEND'S EFFORTS TO LOSE WEIGHT

If one of your friends is struggling with her weight while you're not, you know that you need to be careful about how you help her.

1. Model good eating habits instead of asking her how her diet is going or criticizing her food choices.
2. Encourage your friend to exercise by asking her to walk with you around the block (to start).
3. Celebrate her accomplishments, however small. Offer encouragement. Everyone needs that.

"A kiss can be a comma, a question mark, or an exclamation point. That's the basic spelling that every woman ought to know."

—Mistinguett (Jeanne Bourgeois)

Never Stop Kissing

Often couples slip into routines that can become ruts, forgoing intimate touching such as kissing. Some become so lax in expressing affection that they won't even give the most perfunctory of kisses, a peck on the cheek. Your partner is your best friend, helper, sounding board, confidant, and lover. To keep your relationship exciting, use the sense of touch to express your love, and use it often. It brings a sense of comfort and closeness that both men and women crave. A touch can be electrifying, especially for someone who hasn't been suggestively touched in a while. Kissing can be so expressively erotic.

Some women may think that even spending an hour kissing their lovers would not be enough to get them really turned on. But kissing for any amount of time, if done tenderly, slowly, and sensuously, can really get you going and serve as the prelude to hot and heavy intercourse. This would include oral sex. Using your mouth to kiss and caress your lover's body all over is a very erotic experience. Kissing, licking, blowing warm air, and even light sucking on the neck, face, and other areas add to the sensuous arousal.

KEEP YOUR KISSES SPECIAL

Kick the kissing up a notch. Purchase a creamy, flavored lip balm for him, and some sensational, lip-plumping, palate-pleasing lip gloss for you. Brush your teeth, floss, and finish with a nice-tasting mouthwash. Set a timer for five minutes. Now lube your lips and let the kissing begin.

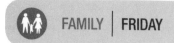
"There was a star danced, and under that was I born."

—William Shakespeare

Send a Birthday Card

In this age of instant e-mail, not many people have the pleasure of opening real cards sent by snail mail anymore. Send a loved one a birthday card instead of just relying on an e-mail or Facebook message.

MAKE A BIRTHDAY CARD

Get the rest of the family involved in making a card for the special birthday person.

1. A sheet or two of colored paper, paste, scissors, colored pens, and some magazines are all you need to make a great, personalized birthday card guaranteed to evoke smiles of appreciation.
2. Find birthday quotations and greetings on the Internet or make up your own. Use the magazines for images or words.
3. Making a birthday card is a great tradition to create memorable family birthdays. And you never know—maybe your children will pass it on to their own kids someday.
4. You can add something extra and invite everyone to write a special, personalized note to enclose in the card.

"A whole lot of (travel) volume and a whole lot
of weather means a whole lot of delays."

—Rally Caparas

Distract Yourself from Travel Delays

When your train doesn't arrive on time or your flight is delayed, see it as an opportunity. Calm down and accept that travel carries with it a certain set of problems that will be out of your control no matter what you do. We take on so much unnecessary stress and waste a lot of valuable time when we let things we can't control dictate our mood.

Think of the delay as a blessing that gives you some extra time to use in myriad ways. Or you can do nothing at all. Sit back and stretch your feet out, secure in the knowledge that you'll reach your destination.

MAKE USE OF YOUR DELAY

- Make some phone calls.
- Catch up on paperwork.
- Study a map.
- Network with others.
- Brainstorm some new adventures.
- Write some postcards or e-mails, or even outline a book.
- Get a cup of coffee and enjoy some people-watching.
- Pull out that book you've been meaning to finish.

"Silent gratitude isn't much use to anyone."

—G. B. Stern

Be Grateful Today

There is nothing so terrible that it should prevent you from reminding yourself of what's good and decent in your life. We lose sleep, spoil special moments, and develop new wrinkles and gray hair by focusing on the negative. Our contentment becomes cloudy, and we let our minds venture too far into the negative. Anything good is rendered invisible, and it can be a long time before we are able to find it again.

Concentrate on what you love about your life. Engage your intellect, your emotional side, and your spiritual nature, and allow yourself to become enthused and excited. Your passion will create a ripple effect in your life. Your appreciation for the blessings in your life helps you feel both fulfilled from within and more positive when looking to the next day, the day after that, and the rest of your life from that point on. Those feelings of gratitude and joy enable you to attract more of the same.

PUT IT ON TAPE

Get a tape (or digital) recorder and verbalize aloud five things for which you're grateful today. This trains your brain to focus on love and the pleasant experiences that you have had in the past and the present.

- Focus on what it is about your life that makes you feel young, spiritually strong, and happy.
- If you're grateful to someone, send a taped message of gratitude to them so that they can play it for a lift to their spirits.

"Boundaries build mutual consideration and respect."

—Jane Bluestein

Set Your Personal Boundaries

If you are one of those people who has trouble establishing and enforcing personal boundaries, consider the power of the word "no." It has a purpose and place in every life. If you haven't established personal boundaries, people can take advantage of your kindness and you may unwittingly allow them to either use you or waste your time. When that happens, you get angry at them and perhaps also at yourself, and that's counterproductive—even damaging to your career. Ensure that you have firm personal boundaries in place and reinforce them with a "no" as necessary.

PUT IT INTO PRACTICE

Decide on one personal boundary that you will implement immediately. Don't be discouraged if you find it difficult at first to establish your boundaries. You will become more skilled as time passes and you discover how much freedom and control can be gained by creating and executing a few personal boundaries.

1. For example, if someone is always interrupting you at work to chat about topics unrelated to the job, establish a boundary.
2. Insist that the door to your office is to be considered closed when you are working and that visitors need to knock first.
3. Remind anyone who violates your rule. If they enter and start chatting, tell them, "No, not now."
4. In the long run, having personal boundaries in place can help you lighten up by ensuring that your work is not interrupted, that you don't feel angry at others and yourself, and that you are empowered to set and hold firmly in place your own rules.

WEEK TWENTY-NINE

"It's what you learn after you know it all that counts."

—Attributed to Harry S. Truman

Share Your Knowledge

Teaching is a wonderful way to engage the people around you. Contact your state's department of education for information on how to become an adult education instructor at a community college. Adult education offers courses on a wide variety of subjects ranging from child care to budgeting for emergencies.

HOST A HOW-TO WORKSHOP

1. What better way to do that than to create a chance for others to discover something new? Your local community center may provide you with the time and space to host a workshop of your own design.

2. The details are entirely up to you. Perhaps you want to teach people how to make the perfect lasagna. Or maybe you want to show off your idea of basket-weaving. Then again, you might want to get people started on the rewarding pastime of creative writing.

3. You will have the opportunity to engage people as teacher, bring strangers together, and perhaps learn some interesting things yourself. We can gain as much from imparting what we know as we can from learning something new. It's a situation that can have far-reaching rewards throughout your community.

4. A great how-to workshop will send your students out into the world with knowledge to enrich their lives. They might even be inspired to run a how-to workshop of their own.

"When we are dreaming alone, it is only a dream.
When we dream with others, it is the beginning of reality."

—Dom Hélder Câmara

Form a Dream Support Group with Others

You may need the emotional support of others to achieve a dream. You are not living in a vacuum, but rather in a world of people who may harbor the same or similar dreams that you hold dear. People who share common interests often form groups with other like-minded individuals, in everything from astrology, metaphysics, and esoteric topics to New Age healing practices, music, art, literature, the environment, politics, ecology, green jobs, and other topics. Find one—or start one—today! You will find many new friends along the way.

REALIZE YOUR DREAM—WITH A LITTLE HELP FROM YOUR FRIENDS

If, for example, if you have a dream of owning a green vineyard—that is, a vineyard where pests are controlled without the use of dangerous chemical pesticides—you could ask for a little help from others.

1. Find information on like-minded vintners and wine aficionados on the Internet or by visiting vineyards in California, Europe, and elsewhere.
2. Read books on the topics that relate to the dream you want to manifest.
3. Gather contact information about websites that relate to some aspect of your dream.
4. Use blogs, RSS feeds, Usenet groups, and social networking sites to find others who share your passion. You can also find Usenet groups for virtually any subject in which you are interested and read or post information or participate in discussions with people the world over.

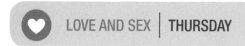

"We must always change, renew, rejuvenate
ourselves; otherwise we harden."

—Johann Wolfgang von Goethe

Renew

Keep your relationship vibrantly alive and interesting through an ongoing process of renewal. Renewal is one of those cultural buzzwords that you often hear at the beginning of a new year when people are busy making resolutions or during early spring when everyone sees the natural world undergoing a renewal process following winter.

Renewal strategies can be implemented throughout the year by changing the way you handle the relationship or by shifting your perspectives and attitudes. For example, practice flexibility, talk openly, give up control more often, find ways to balance your togetherness with your individuality, work on managing your differences, and put more thoughtfulness and energy into your relationship. Some of the things to give up or at least work on would be the tendency to hold on to resentments, nagging, and forgetting to be respectful.

DOCUMENT YOUR LOVING PROMISES

Make a promise book, a blank journal in which you and your partner can write messages to each other whenever you feel inspired.

- Use the book to write of renewed hope, trust, belief, and love.
- Also, you can record new promises in the book, such as "I promise to keep your confidences and earn your trust, putting you first before all others in my life."

*"The perfect family board game is one that can
be played each time with fewer pieces."*

—Robert Brault

Play a Board Game

What children want most is to spend time with their parents. Many studies support the premise that children thrive when they are in a family that spends quality time together. Their bonds to each other and their parents are strengthened as well as their sense of identity and belonging. And you may find that you enjoy the time together just as much as they do. It's just another way to build happy relationships. You probably have some favorite board games stashed away in a closet. Go online or visit a toy store to find something new. Schedule your next game night and invite the family to play!

TEACH SKILLS WITH BOARD GAMES

Playing board games is an easy and terrific way to spend leisurely, enjoyable time together. Board games also have abundant learning opportunities.

- They fill your children's need for competition and their desire to master new skills and concepts.
- The games can stimulate your children's imaginations.
- They don't have to be labeled "educational" to have intrinsic value. Children of all ages learn important social skills.
- Younger children learn critical lessons such as waiting and turn-taking, while older children receive practice in life lessons such as interaction and conflict resolution.
- Even the simple act of winning or losing can provide numerous teachable moments.

"Some places speak distinctly. Certain dank gardens cry aloud for a murder; certain old houses demand to be haunted; certain coasts are set apart for shipwrecks."

—Robert Louis Stevenson

Take an Intentional Wrong Turn

We often seek out the familiar when we need to unwind on vacation. We are frequently eager to take the straightest, shortest path from our place of stress and anxiety to a place of calm and relaxation. There's nothing wrong with that, but it could be a waste of a good opportunity. If you opt for surprise and adventure the next time you're traveling, you'll most likely collect some wonderful stories to share when you return home.

Sometimes, the most memorable places you'll find while on vacation are the discoveries you made off an alley, down an interesting side street, or along a path that lead to a river's edge, a shady courtyard, or a butterfly garden. Be adventurous when traveling.

TRANSFORM YOUR TRIP INTO AN ADVENTURE

Discover places beyond the familiar path that will make your trip unique and special.

- Explore the neighborhood where your accommodations are located.
- Drive to a nearby town or village and sample their food and wines.
- Discover a deserted hill town.
- Take off with your walking stick into the hill country.

"How people treat you is their karma; how you react is yours."

—Wayne Dyer

Understand How Karma Works

Karma is a far-reaching concept that has managed to filter into our society and into the everyday lives of even those who claim to have agnostic, indifferent, or atheist beliefs. It's an easy idea to accept and plant in even the deepest parts of our psyches. Even those who don't believe in reincarnation and in an afterlife of reward or punishment long to believe that the world around them is dictated by something other than chance or chaos.

The Sanskrit word *karma* comes from a root that means "to do or act." Karma is not punishment or revenge as many in Western civilization have come to believe, but simply an consequence of one's actions. Hindu philosophy maintains that every action and every thought has a consequence which will show up in a person's present life or in a succeeding one. It believes that karma functions automatically, making certain that the evil person suffers and the righteous prosper.

REAP THE REWARDS

Find out how you can tap into the remarkable power and positive energy that comes from giving, and discover the wonderful rewards that are possible when you give to others without the expectation of getting anything in return.

You may not embrace all the tenets of Hindu philosophy, but owning your actions and recognizing that they have consequences is a critical step in developing a healthy, fulfilling spiritual life.

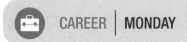

> *"From the backstabbing co-worker to the meddling sister-in-law, you are in charge of how you react to the people and events in your life. You can either give negativity power over your life or you can choose happiness instead. Take control and choose to focus on what is important in your life. Those who cannot live fully often become destroyers of life."*
>
> —Anaïs Nin

Make Peace with a Cranky Coworker

You can find them in every workplace. They whine and grumble about absolutely everything: too much work, not enough work, the clients, the furniture, the cafeteria food, the bathrooms, and the temperature in the office. They even complain when they get a raise or increased benefits, because it wasn't what they wanted. They're impossible to work with and their presence is sheer aggravation, but they're not going anywhere, so what can you do? Make peace with them. Lower your expectations. Do something nice without expecting anything in return. You can consider the cranky coworker a chance to work on your patience.

WEEK THIRTY

BRING SOME COOKIES

1. Bake some cookies or buy them from the bakery. If someone in your office often scowls, chronically complains, or flies into a tantrum with little or no provocation, offer that person a plate of warm chocolate chip or peanut butter cookies. Even if the cookies are refused, you can be assured that you at least tried to bring a little pleasure into that person's life.

2. The gesture may work or it may not. Some people get so used to being unhappy and feeling like the whole world is against them that they are outside their comfort zone when someone does something unexpected and nice for them. The truth is that they are more likely than not hungry for friendship and attention. And even if your cookies don't soothe the savage beast, it's quite certain they will warm the hearts of your other coworkers deserving of a sweet treat.

"Movement is a medicine for creating change in a person's physical, emotional, and mental states."

—Carol Welch

Hold a Walk-a-Thon

One way to help out a cause that's important to you is to hold a community walk-a-thon. Donors agree to donate a certain amount of money per mile walked; the more miles you walk, the more money you raise.

Don't limit your fundraising ideas to walking. Events such as read-a-thons, bike-a-thons, and skate-a-thons have also proved successful for raising awareness and funds for worthy causes.

MAKE IT SUCCESSFUL

Walk-a-thons are consistently successful in a number of ways:

- They bring attention to and raise money for a great cause.
- Your local area may have one or more walk-a-thons planned. You can even organize your own.
- Think of a cause that's near to your heart—one that may need some public awareness. Talk to some of your neighbors and friends to see if they're interested.

"You've got bad eating habits if you use a grocery cart in 7-Eleven."

—Dennis Miller

Go Grocery Shopping Together

Too often we let the little things in life drive us crazy. Grocery stores may well be at the top of the list for creating the trivial things that can make a day stressful when it shouldn't have been. Perhaps synchronizing your trip to the grocery store with a friend can banish those little things quickly and painlessly. Letting go of those minor irritants is a lot easier when we're busy talking to someone who lifts our spirits.

MAKE IT FUN

1. A friend can help you maintain a budget, if that happens to be something you're trying to do. It can be difficult to stick to a spending limit on your own. It helps to have a friend along who's in the same predicament.

2. Grocery shopping isn't necessarily fun, but it shouldn't be a hassle either. Doing it with a friend means you can catch up with each other while you're getting a chore done.

3. The next time you head off to the grocery store, invite your friend to go along. Make plans for a special lunch after you finish your chores.

"Growth begins when we begin to accept our own weakness."

—Jean Vanier

Tell the Truth

In the movie *Fatal Attraction,* the character played by Michael Douglas has an extramarital affair with the character played by Glenn Close. When she discovers that he is married, she begins to use information she has learned against him, information that will be damaging to his personal and professional life. It is not until he actually tells his wife about the affair that his lover loses the power of negotiation and her tool of destruction.

ADMIT YOUR SHORTCOMINGS

Many people will learn your weaknesses, your fears, and your shortcomings, and some of them will use this knowledge against you at every turn. The only way to combat this is to be comfortable in admitting your own shortcomings, thus taking the power away from other people to use this against you.

1. If you've lied, admit it to the person you've lied to.
2. Don't take it so seriously. Our human foibles can be funny.
3. Take steps to change. If your short temper gets you into trouble, work on ways of lengthening your fuse.

"The rules for parents are but three . . . love, limit, and let them be."

—Elaine M. Ward

Consider a Curfew

Curfews are a traditional and tested way of helping teens and young adults stay safe. A curfew allows them freedom to go out with friends but ensures that they are home under your protection during times when the likelihood of irresponsible behavior increases. It also helps your peace of mind.

ESTABLISH AND ENFORCE A CURFEW

If you decide to establish and enforce a curfew, there a few things you can do to get ready.

1. First, you might want to talk to the parents of your child's friends to see how they feel about curfews. There is strength in numbers, and no child will be singled out as having oppressive parents. Prepare your reasons for creating a curfew.
2. Have a family meeting to discuss your reasons for establishing a curfew. Explain to your child that his life may depend on honoring that curfew. Make sure you include lots of positive comments such as, "I am doing this because your safety is my number one priority." Agree upon a curfew time and listen carefully to your teen's viewpoint on this issue. Be firm but flexible. Don't disrupt the family peace and alienate your child for the sake of fifteen minutes.
3. Finally, decide what the consequences of breaking the curfew will be. Again, listen to your teen, but remember, the final decision remains with you. You will rest easier knowing you have done something to ensure your child's health and safety.
4. Many American cities and town have legislated curfew times for teens. For example, some communities have established a weekend curfew for teens without an adult chaperone. Other cities have partnered with parents to have law enforcement return teens to their homes if caught out and about after curfew and before 6 A.M.

*"There is something about the outside of a horse
that is good for the inside of a man."*

—Winston Churchill

Go Horseback Riding

If you want to own a horse of your own (and if you have the space, time, and money to do so), then by all means go online or visit a farm auction and make your dream come true. Most of us don't have those luxuries where a horse is concerned, but that doesn't disqualify us from being able to enjoy the thrill of horseback riding. It might take a couple of tries to gain some confidence and skill, but once you start riding you might find it difficult, even impossible, to stop. It takes you away from the modern world and into a timeless place of indescribable freedom.

Imagine bundling up in a sweater and scarf on a chilly spring or fall morning and riding horseback along a beach past crashing waves or through a leafy forest glade, replete with dew-laden spider webs and small animals scurrying out of your path. The world looks and feels fresh and unspoiled from the back of a horse. It's a comprehensive work-out that leaves you feeling accomplished and content, and the joy you feel observing the world from the back of a beautiful animal is beyond description.

FIND A RIDE

Finding a horse to ride in the middle of a busy urban area may sound like a difficult proposition. Visit *www.horserentals.com* to find a riding stable in your area. In the meantime, watch some riding videos on *www.youtube.com* for some helpful tips and confidence boosters.

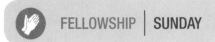
"Knowledge is only one half. Faith is the other."

—Novalis

Heal Through Belief

A survey from the Pew Forum on Religion showed that a majority of Americans, nearly 80 percent, believe in miracles. If you or a loved one is in need of healing, use your faith belief and ask for a miracle. Pray for miracles on behalf of others, even strangers.

SHOW THE POWER OF FAITH

Modern medicine should never be discounted. Miracles occur every day, but knowing this and taking it to heart should never replace legitimate medical treatment. In order for belief to be at its strongest, every logical avenue of treatment and rehabilitation must be pursued and measured in reasonable terms. It gives your faith the necessary weight to survive even the toughest tests.

1. Demonstrating your faith is especially important if you're in need of healing. At such a time, spiritual renewal is often also needed. It is often difficult to assess whether or not a chronically ill person has experienced a miraculous cure. Certainly doctors can bear witness to the inexplicable recovery and contribute to it, but explaining such a sudden phenomenon in someone who has been diagnosed with a chronic affliction or terminal disease is often impossible.

2. Still, many people do recover through the power of their faith and unshakable belief that they will become healthy again. When they have a steadfast faith coupled with a belief in the traditional avenues of treatment and care, they are setting up a powerful force for attracting and sustaining recovery.

"If you tell the truth you don't have to remember anything."

—Mark Twain

Notice Your Lies

It's one of our first life lessons. From the moment we come up with our first little white lie, we are taught that our word is sacred. However, as the years go by, telling the truth changes from an easily understood concept to a confusing notion rife with gray areas.

Many people tell little white lies, half-truths, or useful falsehoods to evade blame, deceive others, deny reality, or to feel better about themselves. A little white lie, in some instances, might be motivated by a desire to prevent someone from being hurt. For example, you know that a coworker is about to be fired. When she asks you if you've heard anything about her possible termination, you tell her no. It takes more effort to think about how to answer her truthfully and still not hurt her feelings than to just lie. The first step in breaking a habit of lying is to notice when you're doing it and why. Bring mindfulness to bear on the problem and you will find yourself more inclined to tell the truth.

WEEK THIRTY-ONE

TAKE THE TRUTH CHALLENGE
- Telling the truth, like thinking positive thoughts, is a skill that requires lots of practice, but if you live and work from a place of truth, others will trust your word and appreciate the honesty.
- In the long term, truth may be the most powerful tool you have in your career toolbox. Can you go through an entire day telling the truth and only the truth? Try it tomorrow and find out!

"When a singer truly feels and experiences what the music is all about, the words will automatically ring true."

—Monserrat Caballé

Go Holiday Caroling

The holidays aren't just about feeling good ourselves. It's also about to trying to extend that good feeling to others. It might be worth giving something a try if it can accomplish both of these things. Caroling through your neighborhood may seem a bit old-fashioned to you, but since it's one of the oldest traditions of the holiday, chances are it still holds some appeal. Most of us don't like to be out on a cold winter night, but that chill is easily forgotten when you're in good company.

LET THE SPIRIT MOVE YOU

- You might feel a bit awkward at first, but any embarrassment should be long gone by the time you're halfway through the first song.
- When you start singing you're bound to notice something quite wonderful on the faces of your audience. It might be a neighbor you know or someone you've never met before. Either way, they'll enjoy the music and be touched that you thought of them. You get the best of both worlds—giving and receiving.
- You can really get into the spirit of the occasion and dress in traditional Victorian costumes. Research Victorian era clothing and visit a website with images of dresses and suits from that time period.

"Health is a state of complete harmony of the body, mind and spirit. When one is free from physical disabilities and mental distractions, the gates of the soul open."

—B. K. S. Iyengar

Invite a Friend to Help You Get Healthier

If you've decided to live a healthier lifestyle, maybe it's time to get your friends involved. Go shopping together for the ingredients to make a healthy, homemade meal. Enlist one or more friends to help you discover interesting ways to prepare heart-healthy entrees. Split the cost of a cookbook for healthy meals or find some recipes online and, with your friends, cook something a little spicy, saucy, or just sensational, certain to delight your senses.

PLAN A PARTY

After experimenting with your new way of cooking and eating, make plans for a informal dinner party.

1. Invite the friends who helped you make such significant changes to your lifestyle.
2. If you love to cook and try new recipes, share one of your adventurous creations with a neighbor. There's nothing like cooking and eating together to create a bond between people.

LOVE AND SEX | THURSDAY

"When the spirits are low, when the day appears dark, when work becomes monotonous, when hope hardly seems worth having, just mount a bicycle and go out for a spin down the road, without thought on anything but the ride you are taking."

—Sir Arthur Conan Doyle

Cycle on a Pleasant Afternoon

If you ask your partner to join you for some exercise on a Sunday afternoon, the reply quite possibly will be no. But if you entice your partner out of the house on a Sunday afternoon with a promise of a bicycle excursion, you might get a different answer. Cycling invokes a completely different image than exercising, yet it's an exceedingly effective way to work out.

Don't have a bike? Go bike shopping with your significant other. Select a bike that you can easily navigate over the terrain in your local area, since studies show that most people don't ride more than five miles. Therefore, you need not buy an expensive professional mountain bike, but do invest in a helmet.

FEEL THE BENEFITS

1. You'll have some together time and enjoy some aerobic exercise, which can reduce the risk of high blood pressure, heart disease, obesity, and diabetes.
2. Out in the fresh air, breathing heavily but not out of breath, you will experience optimum results.
3. Some studies show that riding a bike briskly for twenty minutes results in fat burning for twenty more minutes after the ride has ended, because doing a faster exercise is more effective than exercising slowly.

"A vacation frequently means that the family goes away for a rest, accompanied by a mother who sees that the others get it."

—Marcelene Cox

Plan a Stress-Free Vacation

Are you looking forward to your next vacation? Even if your family doesn't include children, you still have the stress of dealing with your spouse and other family members. You may chuckle, but everyone knows that you can get sick of anyone if you spend too much time together. A poorly planned family vacation can be exactly that sort of nightmare.

IDENTIFY POTENTIAL PROBLEMS

Why do family vacations go sour? The stress around family vacation has many sources. Just a few include:

- Adults hit a vacation burnout or are tired already.
- Long rides in the car, train, or other source of transportation tire family members out.
- Eating out and trying new cuisine upsets the body's usual dietary habits and digestion.
- Lack of planning creates irritation when a hotel is booked, a restaurant is bad, or activities don't appeal to everyone.
- Spending the entire vacation together crammed in a hotel or other small space, when families don't usually spend so much time together at home.
- Family members have different expectations and conflict arises when everyone's expectations are not met.

"The soul becomes dyed with the color of its thoughts."

—Marcus Aurelius

Use Color in Meditation

Colors may be visualized in meditation for healing and maintaining certain states of mind. For this, select colors of matte board that can be cut into medium-size pieces, either 8" × 10" or 9" × 12". Place the board in a quiet place without visual distractions. It should be to the right or left of your sitting area, but not in front of it. You want to be able to move your attention elsewhere if necessary.

1. Devote at least fifteen minutes to a color session. Give the overall subject a distant gaze for the first five minutes, then close your eyes. Look at the subject with attention to detail for the next five minutes, and then close your eyes. Gaze at the overall subject again for the last five minutes.
2. After the color visualization exercise, begin the color breathing exercise. Take slow, moderately deep breaths. Allow yourself five minutes to do this. As you inhale, visualize the color on the easel lifting off and entering the body, circulating through it. As you exhale, the color fills the space around you and becomes part of the body aura. This may be done to "carry" the color's influence for a time.

CHOOSE YOUR COLORS

Color meditation should be limited to one color per session to allow the color to affect mental and emotional levels.

1. Red is associated with fire, blood, and vitality. It stimulates the immune functions.
2. Orange is associated with action, excitement, and warmth. It is said to influence the body's organs to function optimally, and is especially good for digestion.
3. The breath of life is seen in yellow by many cultures. It has a positive effect on the nervous system and stimulates thinking and communication.

"With the gift of listening comes the gift of healing."

—Catherine de Hueck

Forgive by Communicating

The first step is yours. If you wait for the other person to reach out to you, you may never find the peace you need and deserve. Time is of the essence when reaching out. True, you can reach out at any time, even decades later, but the longer you wait, the harder it will be to take that first step.

The first step in reaching out is to ensure that the lines of communication are open and that the other person knows this. Communication is the essence of any relationship; without it, the situation becomes nearly hopeless, and the thought of reconciliation and forgiveness is even direr. Listening is perhaps the most important thing that you can do when reaching out to another person. You will need to understand the other person's side of the story, and oftentimes the only way to do this is to stop talking and start listening.

BECOME A BETTER LISTENER

Following, you will find some helpful hints to aid you in becoming a more effective listener:

- Stop talking.
- Listen for what is *not* said.
- Listen between the lines.
- Listen to how something is said.
- Give the other person your undivided attention.
- Leave your emotions behind.
- Don't jump to conclusions.
- Ask the other person questions.

Think back to your last listening "experience" and read the list of tips above once again. Now, make a list of the areas in which you believe you can improve the next time you are listening to someone. Do this again and consult your original list of improvements to see if you're making progress. And keep listening!

 CAREER | MONDAY

"When people go to work, they shouldn't have to leave their hearts at home."

—Betty Bender

Let Your Boss Know

Developing a relationship with your boss can be an intimidating and confusing task. You want to be remarkable without being a showoff, you want to be friendly without being pushy, and most importantly, you'd like to initiate some positive interaction without being too demanding or intrusive. One way to open the lines of communication and build some rapport is to make a list of the work-related tasks you love to do. Do you love pulling together data for your company's due-diligence binders, working on payroll and reconciling the bank statements, writing press releases, researching, or working on the company website? Let your boss know!

GET MORE OF THE WORK YOU LOVE TO DO

- It's possible that just by letting your preferences be known that you will get more of that kind of work. If necessary, you may need to work longer hours in order to highlight your skills and abilities and really impress your boss.

- And if you really like doing those tasks, you'll be happier and more enthusiastic. Those feelings can spread around the office. Just imagine if everyone is doing what they most like to do. Contented and competent employees can give any boss an easier life!

"Be at war with your vices, at peace with your neighbors, and let every new year find you a better man."

—Benjamin Franklin

Organize a Neighborhood Holiday Progressive Dinner

Get into the holiday spirit this year and include neighbors on your street. In December, ask five neighbors to join with you in hosting a progressive dinner party that begins at one house for the first course and proceeds to other houses for subsequent courses. Suggest that your neighbors select one out of five possible courses to host at their homes: appetizers, soup, salad, entrée, or dessert. Then put fliers out at each house on your street inviting all your other neighbors to join in the festivities.

MAKE IT INCLUSIVE

1. Each family who will attend is asked to contribute one item to one of the courses. Be sure to inform everyone to RSVP so that you can keep a running tally of how many people will participate. Ask each family to make a special holiday recipe.

2. A number of religious and cultural holidays occur in the month of December, so even if the neighbors on your street are from differing ethnic and cultural backgrounds, you can still get them together for a progressive party and some wholesome family fun.

3. As an alternative, host a holiday dessert exchange where each family brings one tray of any kind of dessert. Planning and execution take less than a day, but the good feelings generated can last all year long.

"From the end spring new beginnings."

—Pliny the Elder

Celebrate New Beginnings

A new beginning is a wonderful gift. Unfortunately, that gift sometimes has to come out of a difficult period in our lives, such as divorce or losing a job. Some people prefer to use that time for personal reflection and would like to move on by themselves. For others, those can be the times when they need to know they have a support system of people who care about them. If nothing else, send your friend some flowers to show that you're thinking about her, that you care, and that you are there to support her.

THROW A NEW BEGINNINGS PARTY

Throwing a party for a friend to celebrate and emphasize the idea of a new beginning can be a great way of making sure they know that their support system is in place. It can be a tricky area to walk through, though.

- You have to know for sure that this is something your friend wants. You don't want to overwhelm him or place him in an uncomfortable position. How we process a dramatic change in our lives is a very personal thing.
- You should be mindful of this with a friend and be ready to offer your services if it becomes clear that they're needed.
- No matter how many people you invite, or whatever type of party it might be, a celebration of new beginnings can be a useful, even fun way of closing the door on one chapter and getting ready to open another.

"Don't ask yourself what the world needs; ask yourself what makes you come alive. And then go and do that. Because what the world needs is people who have come alive."

—Harold Whitman

Share Your Passions

What's your passion? Does your partner share it? When couples share a passion for something—a hobby, a cause, a noble belief—they strengthen their pair bond. It's the sharing of common interests that keep relationships going when that intense sexual attraction and passionate form of love cools a bit.

Humans are wired for pair bonding, which means that when your visions and passions are in tune with your mate's, the altruistic acts of generosity you do together can promote healthy bonding and closeness to each other. That, in turn, suggests positive implications for your satisfaction and longevity as a couple.

FIND YOUR PASSION

Find ways to get more deeply involved in what stirs your mind and heart. For example, if you believe that there are way too many abandoned dogs in the world, join your partner in volunteer work with your local animal shelter. Become a member of a rescue team. Help find families for abandoned or mistreated animals. Pay for getting some dogs and cats spayed or neutered. The following list includes some interests couples might share:

- Protecting human rights
- Working to get better labeling of genetically altered food
- Fighting racial, gender, and cultural intolerance
- Saving women and children from human trafficking
- Finding ways to feed the hungry
- Saving the planet and endangered species

> *"Television has proved that people will look at anything rather than each other."*
>
> —Ann Landers

Stop the Invasion

If you complain about technology invading your family's life, ask yourself—what's stopping you from pulling the plug? Every cell phone has an off button, as does every television and every computer monitor. The technological device can run forever as long as it's charged and electricity flows. Only you have the power to turn it off. Call a family meeting and announce that one evening a month (two or three hours) is going to be technology-free—no computers, no televisions, and no cell phones. No exceptions. Try it, and though everyone may experience stress from changing that habit, in the long run they may just find that they have a life to live that technology can enhance, rather than dictate.

DEALING WITH TEMPTATION

1. Remove the temptation altogether: A wise history teacher at a small university in the Midwestern United States insists that students place their cell phones and other hand-held electronic devices on her desk while they are taking tests. "Your network is not invited to take this test with you," she instructs the students. Even though the university has a policy prohibiting electronic devices in the classroom, she cannot get her students to turn their phones off during class. Rather than keep beating a dead horse, she simply confiscates the phones.

2. Take personal responsibility: How sad that a generation of Americans cannot even make it through an hourlong college class without checking Facebook, returning a text, or surfing the Net. Like a science fiction movie, they cannot function without their technological brain extensions. Only you can turn off your phone, wait on the e-mail, and ignore the temptation of losing an evening surfing the Web.

"We now have evidence to support the claim that exercise is related to positive mental health as indicated by relief in symptoms of depression and anxiety."

—Daniel M. Landers

Give Skating a Try

When's the last time you went skating? You can still rent skates and get a workout in a roller skating rink or ice skating facility. Ice skating is particularly fun in the winter at an outdoor rink. Roller rinks still offer the young and young-at-heart a place to get a workout, complete with music and a light show. It can offer enjoyment for every skill level, with the novice having as much fun as the professional. Another option is to buy some inline skates designed for skating on paved surfaces such as streets and sidewalks. Inline skates are sleeker and more stable and lightweight than their traditional counterparts.

So grab your mate or a friend or even your favorite canine for an afternoon skating adventure at the park. Take along a picnic lunch, a bottle of water, and your inline skates. Don't forget to bring some gloves to protect your hands, and pads for your elbows and knees.

DISCOVER SKATING'S BENEFITS

- You're bound to get a pretty good workout. Skating works the thighs, calves, and buttocks, and when you see the results on your body for doing that type of regular exercise, you'll exercise your facial muscles into a big smile.
- The benefits aren't limited to your physical health. Researchers at Duke University discovered that 60 percent of people who exercised regularly found relief from their depression without using medication.

*"Each place is the right place—the place where
I am now can be a sacred space."*

—Ravi Ravindra

Make a Sacred Corner in Your Home

Our home should be the beginning of all that we find sacred in the external world. It should be the first physical line of defense against everything that exists and moves beyond our front door. Without it we become prone to the danger of leaping into the great unknown with no foundation inside ourselves to keep us from being sucked into the blackness of that unknown. The place where you live is one of the easiest aspects of your life that allows you some measure of control.

Don't let that go to waste. Create an area in your home that can serve as a sanctuary for yoga, prayer, writing in your journal, sipping tea, reading, and reflecting. Regularly retreat to your sanctuary to reconnect with your own inner joy. When you need it the most, you should be able to find this without having to go out.

CREATE YOUR SACRED SPACE

- Make your sacred space private. Add a screen, a large plant, a curtain, or something that defines and separates that space from the rest of the house.
- Add a small table to hold your spiritual texts, sacred objects, candles, incense, holy oil, or prayer beads.
- A window or door with a view of a lake or garden is an added bonus. Otherwise hang a piece of silk, a batik, or spiritual art.

"I have always imagined that Paradise will be a kind of library."

—Jorge Luis Borges

Create a Company Library

If you can't find the most recent due-diligence binder, the latest industry trade magazine with a profile of your boss, or timely reference books that you need to complete a project, consider volunteering to establish a library for your business. Not only will it benefit others in your company, but it could be a career booster for you, especially if you not only brainstormed the idea but also got it approved and have sacrificed some personal time to spearhead the project.

CREATE A RECREATIONAL LIBRARY

You don't have to limit your library to work-related materials, either. Stock your recreational reading section with donations from your coworkers.

- Invite your coworkers to bring in their very-good-quality reading materials: novels, nonfiction, poetry, and magazines.
- You'll increase the numbers of readers per book, which gives the environment a break. You could encourage some interesting conversations during lunch and coffee breaks. You might even change a life with an inspiring story.
- Whether it's a business or recreational library—or both—your initiative and foresight most likely will set you apart as a visionary with a can-do attitude, the type of individual that many companies like to recruit and retain.

"The duty of helping one's self in the highest sense involves the helping of one's neighbors."

—Samuel Smiles

Give a Farewell Gift to a Neighbor

A thoughtful way to send off a longtime neighbor who is moving away is to give her a gift that will always remind her of the years of history you shared. If the person leaving loves gardening, ask your neighbors who have gardens to put seeds of favorite plants into white paper envelopes. Tuck the envelopes into a card to give your neighbor on the day she moves. Or if she loves quilting, ask others on your street to contribute either a piece of fabric or a quilting square. Present the stack of fabric unassembled so that the person leaving the neighborhood can spend happy hours sewing the pieces together in the way that she wants. The gift of seeds will produce plants, a yearly reminder of how much you all loved and appreciated her. A keepsake quilt will remind her of the sense of belonging and togetherness you all have shared.

STAY IN TOUCH

Buy an address book and fill it with the names, addresses, and phone numbers of everyone in the neighborhood. Don't forget to include e-mail addresses. Include a dozen postcards, already stamped, so your neighbor can touch base with everyone when she arrives at her new home.

"Animals are such agreeable friends: they ask no questions; they pass no criticisms."

—George Eliot

Visit a Pet Store

There's nothing like a pile full of furry animals to make your heart lift. If you have a friend who's been feeling down in the dumps, invite her along for some company while running a few errands and then make a visit to the pet store as part of the day. People can often forget their problems while they're talking about and interacting with animals. You and your friend might find your new pet just begging for your attention.

HELP PETS OUT—TOGETHER

Even if you can't own a pet—or already have one—you and your friend can benefit from interaction with animals by volunteering together.

- Walk the dogs at a shelter together. You can talk and walk at the same time.
- Share the work of fostering a pet. One of you can keep the pet at your house while the other buys the food and cares for it as needed.
- Pet-sit for each other if you each have pets.

"Because time itself is like a spiral, something special happens on your birthday each year: The same energy that God invested in you at birth is present once again."

—Menachem Mendel Schneerson

Celebrate a Happy Birthday!

Birthdays celebrate your entrance into the world. Your birthday is a day to reflect upon how you are sharing the gift of *you* with others traveling alongside you through the journey of life. Talk with your significant other about how you like to celebrate birthdays. While some people love big, flashy affairs, others prefer toned-down versions of fun-filled get-togethers. Perhaps your partner wants a quiet and simple birthday celebration—possibly just the two of you. Whatever you do, make sure not to let the occasion pass unnoticed.

MAKE IT A PARTY JUST FOR TWO

Whether you plan a birthday weekend getaway for two or he orchestrates a blowout surprise party for you that includes family or friends, the important thing is to be thoughtful and considerate of each other's wishes.

1. If your partner prefers marking that special day without all the fanfare, tone down your plans. Forget the party and instead give him a paper crown or birthday hat.
2. Sing the birthday song to him several times throughout the day.
3. Rent a rowboat and enjoy a birthday bash for two.
4. Sip sparkling wine or cider from fluted glasses and dine on tea sandwiches and petit fours.
5. Share memories of your favorite birthdays.
6. Read passages of romantic or erotic poetry.
7. Find a secluded place and sample each other's deliciously sweet kisses. Who needs cake?

"Sometimes it seems your ever-increasing list of things to do can leave you feeling totally undone."

—Susan Mitchell and Catherine Christie

Check in Daily at Dinner

Children are full of boundless energy and excitement. What could possibly be causing them stress? Plenty. Life's gotten busier and more complicated for everyone, including your kids. With a daily dinner check-in, you can keep track of your children's stressors and how they're handling them. Eat dinner together as a family, and encourage each member to share how her day went and anything that bugged her that day. If a child shares a stressor—someone stealing his lunch, a poor math grade—then you'll know how you can best support your child.

UNDERSTAND YOUR CHILDREN'S STRESSORS

Today's child develops more quickly, uses more technology, views more violence, and has a greater chance of losing a parent to divorce than ever before. Learn to see the signs that your kid is crying out for stress relief. The Nemours Foundation's KidsHealth, online at *www.kidshealth.org*, an online resource for children's health, polled junior users about stress and found out the following:

- 36 percent of kids worry about grades and school
- 32 percent find their families a constant source of stress
- 21 percent fret about social relationships, particularly gossip and teasing

The KidsHealth study also explored how kids manage their stress. Two statistics are startling:

- Twenty-five percent of children surveyed practice unhealthy coping mechanisms, such as blaming themselves, hurting themselves, or eating to feel better.
- Seventy-five percent also wished their parents would be more supportive by asking what's wrong, listening to them, and spending time with them.

"You don't have to be noisy to be effective."

—Philip Crosby

Turn Down the Volume

A simple way to improve the restful and relaxing qualities of a room where you and your spouse (and possibly your children) have gathered for the evening is to encourage everyone to use soft "inside" voices. In addition, the television volume can be lowered or turned off. If others are listening to a computer video or music, or playing a computer game, suggest they plug in their headphones.

It's well known that noise interferes with sleep, but it can also trigger antisocial behavior, cause a higher incidence of errors when you are engaged in doing cognitive tasks, and has even been associated with increased levels of stress, high blood pressure, and learning disabilities in children. With the noise volume lowered, you might be able to whisper "I love you" to your mate and have him actually hear it.

TAKE A BREAK FROM NOISE

Ask your spouse (and children) to join you in a daily half-hour noise break, during which you do all activities in silence.

1. While you and your spouse are observing silence, you might catch up on reading magazines, newspapers, or even a chapter of your favorite book.
2. Such quiet time is also conducive for doing homework, and is especially important for the mental concentration kids need.

"The yoga mat is a good place to turn when talk therapy and antidepressants aren't enough."

—Amy Weintraub

Give Yoga a Try

Yoga is an ancient Indian method of exercise designed to "yoke" body and mind. Yoga involves specific postures, breathing exercise, and meditation. Hatha yoga, most popular in the West, consists primarily of the postures and breathing exercises. Go online or to a bookstore and buy a DVD that teaches yoga to beginners. For less than $10, you can try a few poses and see if it might be the perfect fitness and stress management tool for you.

GET THE FACTS

The very word "yoga" seems to rub some people the wrong way, so it's good to get the facts before making any serious decisions about it.

1. Yoga is an excellent fitness activity on its own and also makes the perfect complement to other fitness activities because it increases strength, flexibility, circulation, posture, and over-all body condition. For people who have a hard time slowing down, yoga will teach them how great it feels and how important it is to move your body with slow control. And for people who have a hard time engaging in high-impact or fast-paced exercise, yoga is adaptable to all fitness levels and it's decidedly low impact.

2. Yoga is close to a perfect stress-management exercise. Its original purpose was to gain control over the body and bring it into a state of balance in order to free the mind for spiritual contemplation. This definition can still have implications in your life and in today's world. It can help you to master your body and spirit so that they don't master you.

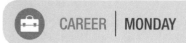

CAREER | MONDAY

"A diplomat is a man who always remembers a woman's birthday but never remembers her age."

—Robert Frost

Celebrate Work Birthdays

Most people in the workplace are flattered and pleased when someone remembers their birthday. This exercise can be as a simple or complicated as you like. Purchase a pocketbook-size calendar and keep track of coworkers' birthdays. You can keep things really simple and buy a box of birthday cards that can be used in a professional environment. When someone's birthday arrives, you can sign the card yourself or circulate the card for everyone to sign. A group card can be particularly meaningful.

The point isn't really that you got them a card or a cake but rather that you and your coworkers took the time to keep track and then to pay homage. In a routine-oriented world where one day often blends into another, a birthday is a wonderful excuse to change things up a bit and make someone smile. Celebrating birthdays creates a more pleasant work environment and gives everyone something to look forward to. It does wonders for office morale. Try it and see for yourself!

WEEK THIRTY-FOUR

VOLUNTEER FOR CAKE DUTY

You don't have to have an elaborate celebration, but if someone in the office is willing to volunteer for birthday cake duty (maybe you?), assign them to be in charge of either baking or purchasing a cake.

1. Have this person bring in plastic forks, paper plates, and a knife as well.
2. Decide on a cake budget and make sure that everyone chips in money toward the cake and any additional items.
3. Rotate responsibilities regularly to avoid overburdening one person.

"You can tell how high a society is by how much of its garbage is recycled."

—Dhyani Ywahoo

Get Back into Recycling

Educating people about recycling and motivating them to participate is especially important in areas where it's not required by law. The benefits can often be greater than we're capable of fully appreciating. Never underestimate your contribution to the cause.

SPREAD THE WORD

As a community, you can discuss the many benefits of recycling, techniques to get things going, ways to seeing your plans through and more. The energy generated by a group discussion could be just the thing everyone needs to finally put a solid plan into action.

1. Hold a meeting in a nearby church basement or at a local school.
2. Create a page on Facebook.
3. Post some attention-grabbing notices on some bulletin boards around town.
4. Organize and host a seminar on creating a unified recycling effort in your community.
5. You might state a lot of things people already know, but it doesn't hurt to remind people of the obvious. You may inspire someone to change or encourage someone else to become part of a group effort.

"One of the first things was these little tape measures. Advertising tape measures that I picked up at a garage sale for a quarter apiece . . . and they brought $22. And that hooked me right there."

—Judy Williams

Visit Yard Sales

Even some of the most rural areas in the country can have as many as four or five garage sales going on over the course of a single Saturday morning. Anyone who lives in a suburban or even metropolitan area can expect that number to be even greater. You can spend the entire day by going to all the garage sales that are typically going on during any given Saturday of the year. You need to find a friend or two to bring along and make it a chance to bond while saving some money.

DO IT RIGHT

Going to a garage sale (or several) with friends is a great exercise in both time and money management.

1. If you're seriously planning to hit as many different ones as possible it would be in your best interest to get together with your friends and nail down a schedule. If you go online, there are websites that can help you plan the entire day.
2. Even so, it might be a good idea to remember that some sales aren't going to be listed online. Another set of eyes can keep a lookout while you're driving from one sale to another. Whoever isn't driving can be the navigator.
3. Help each other remain focused on how much you're willing to spend and even what you're looking for, so you don't wind up buying a bunch of stuff you don't need.

"When you turn to the definition of 'unfaithful' Webster states 'not faithful: not adhering to vows, allegiance, or duty.' Nowhere does it state that unfaithfulness or infidelity is tied to a physical act."

—Dena B. Cashatt

Avoid Internet Relationships that Exclude Your Spouse

It's one thing to log onto the Internet with your husband or wife to talk with friends through video-chat services such as Skype or Paltalk. But it's quite another to slip away from your spouse and log on to surf friendship and dating sites looking for a little titillation. Some people might not view a cyber-relationship as being unfaithful to their spouses because they are not having sex. But regardless of how it is justified by the cheating spouse, the cyber-relationship can be hazardous to the marriage.

BE HONEST—WITH YOURSELF AND YOUR SPOUSE

If you feel more fulfilled surfing the Net and looking at all the possible partners you could hook up with rather than being with the partner you married, ask yourself why.

- The Internet is an easy escape for spouses who want to feel the exhilaration of a cyber-flirtation, sexual attraction, and a pseudo-romantic fling without having to reveal it to their mates or having to make any kind of commitment to their cyber-lover. They just log on when they want a dose of excitement.
- The pseudo-intimacy you get from a cyber-relationship can lead you away from your true spouse. You may think that you are not being unfaithful because you aren't having an affair in the traditional sense, but your husband or wife might see things differently. Instead of spending time online, invest the time in your spouse, working on building a healthy, intimate relationship. Once you do that, cyber-romance won't be as tempting.
- Share your passwords and access questions with your spouse and ask your partner to reciprocate. If your work requires you to remain active in social networking, let your activities be transparent to your spouse.

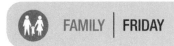
"Jealousy has always been my cross, the weakness and woundedness in me that has most often caused me to feel ugly and unlovable, like the Bad Seed."

—Anne Lamott

Tame the Green-Eyed Monster

Research by North Carolina State University professor Amy Halberstadt published in 2008 found that children jealous of their siblings had four triggers: the other sibling received a special gift, got more of the parent's time, earned the parent's allegiance in a conflict, and got more attention due to a special talent. This child may perceive that a parent favors another child besides himself or gives another child special treatment. This may, in fact, be true if a sibling has learning or developmental disability, is younger, or needs more care for other reasons. Jealousy is also common for older children, who may feel neglected by younger siblings.

MAKE TIME TO BANISH JEALOUSY

Often, a child stressed by jealousy is really just stressed by a lack of attention. Ask a child why he feels that his siblings get special treatment, and make special efforts to give that child attention, maybe even asking a grandmother or other kind adult to specially mentor this child if the parents are bogged down with care for other children. Here are a few tips to deal with jealousy within the family:

- Cherish each child as a unique person. Encourage individual strengths.
- Avoid comparisons.
- Allow children to express their feelings about other family members in a confidential setting.
- Try to practice equal distribution as much as possible. Make certain everyone gets to choose which show to watch on television, which restaurant to eat at, or what to do on a family outing.
- Establish ground rules to create family-friendly boundaries. Rules such as knocking before entering someone's bedroom will promote respect and solidarity.

"A hobby a day keeps the doldrums away."

—Phyllis McGinley

Join the Club

We pursue our hobbies in order to find a balance between our obligations in life and what we like to do when we find some space to breathe. Choose your favorite hobby, if you happen to have several, and join a club related to it. No matter what your hobby is, there's undoubtedly a professional association representing it. Type the name of your hobby into your computer browser and see if it's connected to a professional association.

SHARE YOUR HOBBY

1. Your hobbies are meant to bring you the opportunity to enjoy some time to slow down, reflect, and lose yourself in something you enjoy. Being part of a hobby group allows you to: Share your passion with the rest of the world.
2. Make some new friends.
3. Discover new and interesting things about your favorite pastime.
4. Compete with others.
5. Earn grants or scholarships so that you can learn more about your favorite hobby.

*"The inability to open up to hope is what blocks trust,
and blocked trust is the reason for blighted dreams."*

—Elizabeth Gilbert

Learn to Trust Again

Learning to trust again after being betrayed is one of the most difficult aspects of being human. You feel like a defeated and wounded soldier walking towards your enemy, your arms extended, pleading for a cease-fire. However, you should know that trust is essential for forgiveness and healing. It is essential for you to be able to move on. It is essential for healthy self-esteem.

Trust involves risk, and retrusting involves even greater risk. It means putting yourself "out there" again, sometimes with the same people who betrayed you in the first place. Trust is a self-fulfilling prophecy. If you let others know that you have full faith in them and trust them in earnest, they are less likely to betray that trust. Don't be afraid to say to a person, "I trust you completely. I have faith in you."

RESTORE YOUR TRUST

In order to forgive and make peace with those who have hurt you, you must learn to trust again. The following steps can help you in restoring trust:

- Talk openly and honestly about your pain.
- Ask why the person betrayed your trust.
- Express your intentions to trust again.
- Start with something small and less significant.
- Be a person worthy of trust.
- Establish and communicate the ramifications of future betrayal.

"All work and no play makes Jack a dull boy."

—English proverb

Know the Warning Signs of a Workaholic

You love your job. You work hard . . . okay, maybe *too* hard. One of the many signs of being a workaholic is working more than forty hours a week. However, it is possible that you simply have a strong work ethic and are not a workaholic. The difference is what the workaholic views as a priority.

Having a workaholic spouse can take its toll on a marriage. A workaholic cannot seem to live a life in balance by prioritizing activities and leaving work at work. If either of you is a workaholic, take corrective action before it harms your marriage. Pull your lives back into balance by modifying your schedule so as not to devote a lot of time to things that are not a priority. Seek professional counseling if old patterns of allowing work to fill all your time begin to re-emerge.

WEEK THIRTY-FIVE

RECOGNIZING A WORKAHOLIC

The workaholic cannot seem to differentiate priority—she cannot see certain tasks as less important and some as more important and, instead, sees all tasks as important all the time. In addition:

1. Workaholics often stay at their desks during meals in order to continue working.
2. They think about work when they should be focusing on driving or changing the baby. They believe working long hours is justified if they love the work.
3. They hate being interrupted in their work by family and others who want them to do something else.
4. They permit personal relationships to suffer because of work.
5. They often worry about being laid off or fired even when their present job is secure.

"Blood is that fragile scarlet tree we carry within us."

—Osbert Sitwell

Participate in a Blood Drive

In light of the recent disasters in countries like Japan and within our own country, the importance of available blood has never been more important. The Red Cross has performed admirably and saved countless lives, but the need for donated blood has only increased. Donating blood can benefit your local hospitals, but it can also aid the much larger community that exists beyond your own world. Don't wait for a blood drive to come to you. Check to see if there's a blood bank in your area.

ORGANIZE A BLOOD DRIVE

If you want to do even more, you can organize a blood drive of your own.

- A website such as *www.mybloodyourblood.org* can provide all the information you need. It offers advice on delegating responsibilities, finding a suitable location, delivering the blood after the drive has finished and so much more.
- This may sound like a lot of work, but don't forget that you are making it possible for hospitals and other health care professionals to give the gift of life. How often do you have the opportunity to do that?

*"It is not easy to find happiness in ourselves, and
it is not possible to find it elsewhere."*

—Agnes Repplier

Share Your Happiness

While it is not healthy to rely on others for your sole happiness, others can play a vital and necessary role in your quest for happiness. Isolation from people can be a detriment to your health, and it can be a deterrent to happiness. Family and friends are two of the top factors in guiding happiness into your life. You can bring happiness to other people just by being around, and in turn, you can increase your own happiness by just being with them.

SPEND TIME WITH OTHERS

Here are some simple ways you can bring happiness to others and find happiness in them:

- Go to a movie together.
- Exercise together.
- Make Thursday-night TV watching a weekly appointment.
- Take up a new hobby together.
- Join a social, educational, spiritual, or meditation group together.

If you're feeling good about yourself and about life in general, spread your joy around. Phone a friend and invite him to share one of the activities mentioned above.

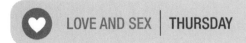

"Love works in miracles every day: such as weakening the strong, and stretching the weak; making fools of the wise, and wise men of fools; favoring the passions, destroying reason, and in a word, turning everything topsy-turvy."

—Marguerite de Valois

Celebrate Daily

Find ways every day to reinforce that special emotional connection you share. Upon awakening, whisper words of love in your lover's ear. Be animated in your greetings to each other, appreciative of your partner's uniqueness, and grateful for the experience of finding that special someone to love.

Do little things to honor and celebrate your love as often as possible. Give a Hershey's kiss, a penny for her thoughts of love, a bouquet, or a single, beautiful flower to symbolize and communicate your feelings.

CREATE A BOUQUET WITH A MESSAGE OF LOVE

One of the most romantic of all the eras was the Victorian, when men and women elevated the writing of a love letter to a high art, using words like *rapturous, inextinguishable*, or *intoxicating* to describe the object of their passion. The Victorians also were obsessed with the hidden meanings of flowers. Take for example, the rose, the queen of flowers, to which the Victorians ascribed the following meanings:

- Orange rose: passionate love
- Pink rose: secret adoration
- Red rose: romantic love
- White rose: innocent love
- Yellow rose: friendship

Create a bouquet containing each color of rose from this list to give to your significant other. Put a note card into the bouquet that describes the meanings the Victorians assigned to each rose color. Let the bouquet express your heartfelt sentiment.

"Stress is the trash of modern life—we all generate it but if you don't dispose of it properly, it will pile up and overtake your life."

—Danzae Pace

Prevent Burnout

The negligent parent stresses out her kids. So does the micromanaging one. Experts agree that parents pushing too hard for a child's success in the classroom, the playing field, or even the social sector are setting up the child for failure.

How do you avoid overwhelming your children's schedules when good grades are connected with college scholarships, and various extracurricular activities are linked to good health and socialization? Moderation. Recognize that being good at one or two things will be better for your child in the long run than being mediocre at five, and that your child is more likely to succeed if given time to think, reflect, play, grow.

UNSCHEDULE YOUR CHILD

1. Sit down with your child and explain that you are going to free up some time in her schedule. Encourage her to choose one or two extracurricular activities she especially enjoys and give her a rare gift in the busy modern world: free time.
2. Creativity, a trademark of childhood, develops out-of-the-box thinking, personal freedom, and autonomy. It's also fun and cheap. As a child learns how to manage certain aspects of her time, she'll learn more about who she is and what she values. These are invaluable tools as she grows into every parent's dream: an adult who knows what she wants and goes for it.
3. Who knows? You may just find some time for yourself to practice your own stress-management skills in the midst of the free time you find from trimming your child's schedule. It's a win-win for everyone involved.

"The consumption society has made us feel that happiness lies in having things, and has failed to teach us the happiness of not having things."

—Elise Boulding

Create a Calming Space

If you and your spouse have ever talked with a real estate agent or home stager, you might have learned that in houses staged for sale, the owners or stagers usually remove excess furniture and position the pieces left in such a way as to allow potential buyers to see 70 percent of walls and floors. That's because potential buyers want to see the home's walls, ceilings, floors, and windows—not furniture, art, and rugs, regardless of how beautiful or tasteful. Likewise, according to feng shui belief, floors and walls should be somewhat open to allow the free flow of life-affirming chi.

CREATE A SPIRITUAL SANCTUARY

1. Clear clutter, especially if it blocks easy navigation through the entry and any other area of the house. Remember the adage "less is more."
2. Freshen and update your home with paint in order to create a warm welcome or suggest serenity, calmness, and peace.
3. Designate a corner, room, or other area of your home as sanctuary. Use a shelf to display sacred art or something else that makes you feel peaceful. The space can be personalized according to you spiritual beliefs. For example, you could hang a cross, an Egyptian ankh, or Native American medicine wheel, an icon, or other symbol or piece of art.

"Meditation is the tongue of the soul and the language of our spirit."

—Jeremy Taylor

Participate in Group Meditation

You might wonder how it's possible to be meditative in the midst of a group of people. Pop psychology gives plenty of attention to forgiveness, releasing anger, bitterness, and dealing with pain and conflict. However, there are few approaches that can be applied to every situation and even fewer that deal with groups. Families, groups of workers, classes of students, clubs, and organizations are all capable of generating problems.

ELIMINATE DISCORD

The Hawaiian ritual of *ho'o ponopono* means "to bring about order." It is a group meditation, a spiritual work to mend interrelationships. A fivefold process is used to return harmony to the group, which takes meditative action at each stage. *Ho'o ponopono* is both simple and complex. There are numerous websites to address the practice in more detail, but a simple way to use the ritual in your own life is to adopt the following four phrases to eliminate discord:

- Thank you.
- Please forgive me.
- I love you.
- I'm sorry that . . .

You can repeat these four phrases in the morning and at bedtime as a form of release. When you recall a past hurt, whisper, "Please forgive me. I love you." When you know someone is hurting say, "I'm sorry you're hurting. I love you." These phrases aren't limited to people you know.

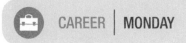

CAREER | MONDAY

> *"Our very lives depend on the ethics of strangers, and*
> *most of us are always strangers to other people."*
>
> —Bill Moyers

WEEK THIRTY-SIX

Resolve to Improve Workplace Ethics

Workplace ethics are codes of conduct concerned with principles and morals. Ethical conduct inspires communication between employees, insists on respect for each person within the organization, and encourages customer relationships based on honesty and integrity. A common misunderstanding is that there is a different set of ethics for the workplace when in fact ethics should be the same whether they are in your office or in your personal life.

Numerous criminal allegations involving high-profile businessmen such as Bernie Madoff have forced many companies to rethink their ethical practices. Some companies are even including ethics in their training. If your company follows a policy of putting profits ahead of ethical practices, possibly even at the expense of exploiting workers or customers, why not seek a review of current company policies with your boss or supervisor?

DO YOUR PART

Such a companywide review of ethical practices and standards of behavior would likely permit discussion of questionable policies. This is where you need to do your homework and be prepared. If you are able, or even encouraged, to challenge practices that you think are unfair, exploitative, or unethical, you must be able to come up with an ethical alternative. When acceptable ethical practices and moral conduct are clearly stated and followed, workplace morale can often improve as well.

"Trust community."

—Eric Young

Start a Neighborhood Watch

A Neighborhood Watch can be one of the most powerful ways to contribute to your community. We trust our local law enforcement to look out for us, but unfortunately, they can only do so much. There are always crimes that go undetected and areas that cannot get the level of protection they might need. This opens the door for everyday citizens to step forward with their own energy and dedication. There are probably other like-minded individuals in your neighborhood, so organizing a group shouldn't be difficult.

TAKE THE RIGHT STEPS

Like any long-term commitment, you need to know what you're getting into and what to expect.

1. Do the research online before making the first step.
2. You will need to determine how much of the area your watch will cover.
3. You will also have to establish a time and place to meet, become familiar with the type of crime you might be dealing with, recruit neighbors, and solicit help from law enforcement.
4. This last requirement is the most important of all. It's worth remembering that you're not replacing your local law enforcement. You're giving them the assistance they need. Working together, you can make your community safer.
5. Attend a neighborhood watch meeting in a nearby community. Be prepared to ask a lot of questions. Learn from another group's successes and failures.

"A friend is someone who knows the song in your heart and can sing it back to you when you have forgotten the words."

—Donna Roberts

Host a Karaoke Night

If you and your friends are in need of a good laugh, there's no better way to do it than to sing along to your favorite songs. Don't worry about whether you're any good at singing—that's not the point. You can have fun whether you're acting silly, doing your best Elvis impersonation, digging deep for heartfelt sentiment—or change it up. Have everyone do one round of songs as perfectly as they can; then do the opposite in the next round.

SET IT UP

You can set up a karaoke night on the spur of the moment, or you can take the time to set up a whole event geared towards singing and celebrating, complete with awards for "Most Tone Deaf" and "Most Likely to Have a No. 1 Hit."

1. You can rent or buy a karaoke machine ahead of time or use specially made CDs. You may also be able to use a karaoke software application on your computer. Or go to a restaurant that has a karaoke night.
2. If appropriate, invite your kids and spouses—more people equals more fun. Plus, you may get to see a side of your kids you didn't know existed.
3. Compete in an *American Idol*–type tournament. Members of the audience vote in different categories.

"Sooner or later, the truth comes to light."

—Dutch Proverb

Reveal Your Sexual Expectations

Physicians, psychologists, and sex therapists agree that the first step to achieving full sexual potential is a no-holds-barred, frank discussion about sexual expectations with your partner. Yet, even though many couples desire deeper intimacy, talking about it often proves to be more difficult than having a root canal.

Even if you don't talk about your expectations, it's a good bet that you and your spouse fantasize about your sexual desires, so why not skip the guesswork and ask the question, "What arouses you?" and "How often do you want to have sex?" Sex talk can be fun. Dirty sex talk can even get you hot. You might start a frank sexual discussion by asking, "Do you want to have sex once a day or several times a week? More? Less?" Talking through the issues, the desires, and the triggers of arousal are all important aspects of a frank sexual discussion.

TALK ABOUT YOUR EXPECTATIONS

Research books, articles, and Internet sites that focus on the sexual aspects to having a thriving marriage.

1. Share what you've learned with your partner. Make information-sharing a regular part of your intimate time together.

2. Marriage and family therapists will tell you that the first step to having a great sex life is finding healthy and positive ways to talk about your partner's and your desires. Use your information gathering as a way to have this talk.

3. Open the conversation with an interesting fact as a point of departure into discussion, or even write out a questionnaire for you and your spouse to complete. Discuss your answers with each other.

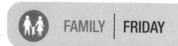

"You've developed the strength of a draft horse while holding onto the delicacy of a daffodil. . . . You are the mother, advocate and protector of a child with a disability."

—Lori Borgman

Support Your Special-Needs Child

Just like any parent, the parent of a child with special needs struggles to make the choices that offer highest quality of life for their child in all areas: medical, educational, recreational, and employment. Parenting a special-needs child takes time, patience, and the wisdom to let go of what's not important and fight for what is. Though others may reject and misunderstand your child, give him the most valuable gift possible: your unconditional love and acceptance. Remember that you and your child are on the same team—both of you working for him to be the best he can be.

MAKE SURE YOU BOTH GET WHAT YOU NEED

Practice the following tips to give both you and your special-needs child what you need:

- Have a plan of care for your child, endorsed by the appropriate profession, which outlines your child's needs and how you are meeting them.
- Know your child's limitations, and do not push, criticize, or ridicule your child for something he is incapable of. Instead, praise what your child does well.
- Encourage your child to explore what excites him. Many children with a learning disability in one area may be exceptionally gifted in another, and all children have talent and passion for something.
- Teach other children in the home, if applicable, to understand the special-needs child's condition and offer support and encouragement where appropriate.
- Don't try to do it all yourself. Compile a list of family, friends, and professional resources that make up your support network.

"Dogs laugh, but they laugh with their tails."

—Max Eastman

Play with Your Dog

If you count your dog as one of your best friends, you're not alone. It's impossible to own a dog without forging a deep bond with your pet. We love our dogs, often because people can be unreliable. Dogs are consistent, and once they love you, they love you for the rest of their lives. It's understandable that you want to do something nice for them. After all, they're your friends, and don't you enjoy doing nice things for your friends? Play an extra game of fetch with your dog, go another lap around the block, or just give him an extra rub and a "good boy!"

MAKE HOMEMADE DOG BISCUITS

Here's a way to spoil your dog and enjoy a relaxing baking opportunity. Instead of buying dog biscuits or other doggie treats, consider making your canine companion some healthy treats.

1. Look for recipes on the Internet (there are dozens) or make up your own, using natural ingredients including wholesome and healthy grains, vegetables, and proteins. Just like humans, dogs like foods that taste good.
2. Remember to avoid chocolate and raw meat as well as artificial ingredients and additives that might cause illness or even death to some dogs. You'll feel better knowing that your dog is healthy and happy. Your dog will thank you with more of that love and possibly a few additional years to show you that love.
3. Take your dog to a local dog park for some fun and obedience training. Use your freshly baked dog treats as incentives and rewards.

"Sleep hath its own world, and a wide realm of wild reality. And dreams in their development have breath, and tears, and tortures, and the touch of joy."

—Lord Byron

Tell Each Other Your Craziest Dreams

Psychologist Carl Jung, who closely correlated dreams with myths and archetypal images, opined that modern people would benefit from relying less on logic and science and more on an appreciation of unconscious realms and spirituality in order to have more balance in their lives.

Try sharing with your spouse a dream that defies unlocking. When you access what Jung referred to as the innermost secret recesses of your soul, you will discover that even crazy dreams are often laden with meaning. People who work with their dreams say that dreams can offer clues to the state of your health, solutions to problems, and sometimes even foreshadow the future. If you haven't given dream work a try, invite your spouse to go on a dream exploration with you.

DETERMINE THE MEANING OF YOUR DREAMS

Buy dream journals for the two of you. Put one on each side of the bed.

1. Write your dreams upon awakening before they quickly disappear, as dreams often do. First, write the narrative of your dream.
2. Then make a list of specific images that appeared in the dream. Use a dream symbol dictionary to extrapolate possible meanings of the symbols, and then rewrite the dream using those meanings.
3. It's been said that only the dreamer can correctly unlock the hidden messages in his or her dream, but analyzing your dreams together can be entertaining.

"Don't walk in front of me; I may not follow. Don't walk behind me; I may not lead. Just walk beside me and be my friend."

—Albert Camus

Make Friends at Work

If you're unhappy at work, maybe you need a friend. A number of interviews conducted by the Gallup polling organization demonstrated that people with one or more friends at work found their job more interesting and satisfying. Research has shown that strong social connections can increase efficiency and have a positive effect on productivity.

If there is someone in the company or on your job site that you trust and who shares your level of integrity and ethics, aligning with him could benefit your professional goals, especially if that person is a supervisor or further along the career ladder than you are. Having someone as a workplace ally means you don't have to feel alone as you navigate through office politics, solve problems, or deal with difficult coworkers. A workplace ally can serve as your sounding board for new ideas, cheer you on when your day is filled with special challenges, and give you a pep talk to lift your heart and hopes when you need it.

FIND A WORKPLACE FRIEND

In order to get the most out of your workplace relationship, you should follow a few simple guidelines.

- Find someone with whom you have a lot in common. For example, if you spend a lot of time dealing with public relations, you might seek out someone doing a similar job.
- Don't be hasty in passing judgment on anyone. Take time to develop your opinion of a potential ally and confidante.
- Look for someone who shares your vision and values.
- Cherish your new friend and nurture the relationship.

"We cannot live only for ourselves. A thousand fibers connect us with our fellow men."

—Attributed to Herman Melville

Maintain Your Neighborhood

In these tough economic times, neighborhoods are facing the problem of blight: vacant lots, foreclosed or abandoned houses. They can become unsightly eyesores that drive down property values even further and make an area seem depressed and neglected. Get together with a few of your friends and spend a few hours doing some cosmetic yard work to maintain your neighborhood. Houses are just like people in some ways. The attention of a few friends can get them back on their feet and ready for new adventures.

HELP A HOMEOWNER

Homes aren't always foreclosed or abandoned when they fall into disrepair. Often, the owners are elderly or have lost their jobs and just can't keep up. Get permission from the owner (or, if you can't locate the owner, the city) before you do any type of work. You don't want someone calling the police on you while you're trying to do a good deed!

1. Find out what the house really needs. This can be a way to connect with a family in your community, too. Maybe a newly single mom is just overwhelmed and some information about local resources or pointers about easy repairs is all she needs to get back on top of maintenance.
2. Create a fundraiser for a local homeowner who needs a new roof.
3. Find out if your community offers any type of grants for housing rehabilitation and help the homeowner apply for one.
4. Spend an afternoon cleaning out a flowerbed.

> *"A family is a unit composed not only of children but of men,*
> *women, an occasional animal, and the common cold."*

—Ogden Nash

Bring Families Together

A joint family outing is a wonderful way to not only spend time with your friends but to bring your families together. Family is often the most valued aspect of our lives. We don't share our families with just anybody. It has to be someone who shares our value and belief system. We have to be able to trust this friend completely. If you're fortunate enough to have a friend who fits that bill, then suggest that your two families get together.

ENRICH YOUR FRIENDSHIPS

Once your friend has agreed to the idea, you can sit down together and sketch out an idea of something you might want to do. It can be as simple as a couple of hours spent going out to dinner or to a movie. Or it can be as involved as a weekend away in the country.

1. Starting with a simple activity might be the best idea, so you can get a sense of whether or not your families will get along.
2. If they do, and chances are they will, you can then take things a step further and decide if you want to try something more elaborate.
3. You will add another dimension to your already-treasured friendship. Members of your different families might really hit it off and create friendships of their own.

"If you don't read the newspaper, you are uninformed. If you do read the newspaper, you are misinformed."

—Attributed to Mark Twain

Snuggle Up and Read the Sunday Paper

For some couples, Sunday just wouldn't be the same without time to leisurely read the Sunday paper. And what could be sweeter than snuggling together on the couch or in a loveseat reading and sharing your favorite sections of the paper? Think of it as a weekly ritual that strengthens your relationship as a couple.

MAKE THE MOST OF IT

1. Work the Sunday crossword puzzle together.
2. Giggle over the funnies.
3. Share tips from a travel article.
4. Resolve to cook a recipe from the food section.
5. Clip sale coupons or use the ads to talk about purchases for your home.
6. If you're thinking about buying a house, take out the real estate section and start dreaming.
7. Read a newspaper that you don't normally pick up to expand your awareness of what's going on beyond the boundaries of your neighborhood, perhaps one from outside of your region or state. Or choose an English-language newspaper from another country, such as the *Sunday Times* of London. It doesn't even have to be the Sunday edition.
8. If all that reading makes you tired, put aside the paper, snuggle closer, and take a nap together.

*"Some of the secret joys of living are not found by rushing from point
A to point B, but by inventing some imaginary letters along the way."*

—Douglas Pagels

Transform Your Children's Stress

If your child has a caring parent or other adult to support him, advise
him, and encourage him to enjoy life and be healthy, he's well on his way
to managing stress for the rest of his life. Teach him the big five tools for
stress resilience: healthy diet, adequate sleep, water, exercise, and fun.
Model them for him, so he knows how important they are. Then:

1. Help him brainstorm healthy stress-busting tools of his own, like
   playing Xbox and practicing karate, and teach him how to practice one when he's feeling stressed. Throw in assertiveness, love,
   and a constant desire to monitor stress and bust it when you see
   it, and you've got a child ready for the stressors of college, marriage, and paying a mortgage.
2. Remember, your child is still a child. Watch how much you push
   him. Be there and care, but also give him freedom and free time
   to explore who he is. Whatever your child's stressors—bullies,
   depression, obesity, or a burning desire to be on *American Idol*—
   he can manage them the same way Mom or Dad does: with
   awareness, action, and a little bit of fun.

ADD A SPECIAL MOMENT

You can reduce your child's stress by adding a special moment
to his day.

- Eat breakfast and dinner together.
- Take the dog for a walk.
- Spend time on a nightly routine that includes laying out tomorrow's clothes, preparing lunch, and sharing a bedtime story. It's
  these little things that your child will remember.

"When you learn to love and let yourself be loved, you come home to the hearth of your own spirit. You are warm and sheltered."

—John O'Donohue

Unwind when You Get Home

You may have a variety of ways to unwind at the end of a busy workday. For example, you may like to have a cup of tea or listen to some classical music. Whatever it is, it's important for you to have a ritual conducive to unwinding. Let it be something you look forward to, but that does not create an additional stress in your life (from trying to pay for it, keep it clean, etc.). Keep it simple but pleasurable.

CREATE AN UNWINDING SPACE

Create a space in your home that draws you to it the minute you enter the house. Let it be an area that beckons you to kick off your shoes, stretch out, and unwind.

1. Maybe you're ready for such a room, but don't know how to carve it out of your existing home. If so, talk with friends who have done it, or watch television shows about gardens and outdoor rooms.
2. Let your fingers do the searching for you on the Internet. Talk with contractors to get their input if necessary.
3. Take a walk in your neighborhood and chat with neighbors who live in a condo, apartment, or house with a floor plan or layout similar to yours. If they have a favorite place in the home to unwind, ask to see it in order to get ideas for your place.
4. Then take the steps necessary to create a place in your house that nurtures your spirit by inviting you to unwind, either alone or together.

"What is this true meditation? It is to make everything: coughing, swallowing, waving the arms, motion, stillness, words, action, the evil and the good, prosperity and shame, gain and loss, right and wrong, into one single koan."

—Hakuin

Engage in Solo Meditation

In many cultures, meditation is practiced for spiritual reasons. The fact that it helps with stress management is a side benefit. Meditation has a profound effect on both the body and the mind. It helps to still the constant chatter in our heads so that we can think more clearly. Meditation teaches us to live in the now. Rather than letting our restless minds, worried thoughts, and anxious feelings carry us away into what might happen next or what we could have done before, meditation teaches us to quiet our mental chaos. It cuts through all our expectations and attitudes. It cultivates mental discipline and, in addition, is exceptionally relaxing. But for today, focus on how meditation can help you connect with your spiritual side.

CULTIVATE A SPIRITUAL MEDITATION PRACTICE

Different meditation traditions offer different guidance for connecting spiritually through meditation. Consider working with a teacher to learn more about this. Whatever your decision, you can make your meditation practice more spiritual by releasing other goals you may have for it, and just sitting in meditation.

1. Practice regularly.
2. Keep your awareness open at all times.
3. Be patient.
4. Continue with the practice even if you don't seem to be getting anywhere or it feels uncomfortable. Let those thoughts drift away.
5. Create an environment that supports your meditation practice.

CAREER | MONDAY

"Know thyself; this is the great object."

—Lucius Annaeus Seneca

Consider a Career Change

Have recent economic events eliminated or jeopardized your career? You may have years of experience and excellent skills, but if you are having trouble finding work in your field, and you've eliminated possible causes like a poor resume or inadequate interview skills, then it may be time for a career change. Changing your career is a big decision and one that you should take very seriously. Take the time to find the best option for you.

WEEK THIRTY-EIGHT

ASSESS YOURSELF

Your first step should be to find the occupations that are suitable for you based on a variety of factors.

- You can learn about these factors—specifically, your personality, values, skills, and interests—while doing a self-assessment.
- You will use a variety of tools to help you learn about these factors. These tools are commonly referred to as career tests, but the word "test" is a misnomer. Tests generally have right and wrong answers. There are no right or wrong answers when you are doing a self-assessment.
- There is just the process of learning about yourself in order to figure out in what occupation you would be happiest and most successful.
- It is important to be as honest as you can when doing a self-assessment. You want your results to reflect your personality, skills, and values. You shouldn't go into it thinking that any answers are bad ones.
- A career-planning professional can administer these self-assessment tests. A simple online search will provide you with other options, many of them available at no charge or for a nominal fee.

Don't sit there wondering and worrying what your next career choice should be. Take a self-assessment test and find out!

"It is the neglect of timely repair that makes rebuilding necessary."

—Richard Whately

Clean Up a Graveyard

It may be a morbid thought, but it's still true that some of our most significant history can be found in our cemeteries. These sacred places can tell a thousand stories from countless points in our history. They are quiet, somber testaments to those who came before us. The shame is that some of these places are crumbling under the weight of neglect. There just isn't enough of a work force to give every single one the care and respect they deserve.

Because the larger cemeteries, such as Bonaventure in Savannah, Georgia, or Arlington National Cemetery in Arlington, Virginia, are popular tourist destinations, they are kept looking neat and tidy. If you're interested in helping to restore an old cemetery, try one of the smaller ones. These are the places that tend to become neglected.

MAINTAIN HISTORY

Check with your historical society to see if they have any workshops on this subject lined up. Visit the website *www.chicora .org* for plenty of information on how to restore a cemetery to its former glory. Pay attention to the important tips on how to clean headstones in order to maintain their patina—and history.

*"There is no trouble so great or grave that cannot
be much diminished by a nice cup of tea."*

—Bernard-Paul Heroux

Invite Friends out for High Tea

A tea party is an opportunity to indulge in an old romantic tradition made famous by the British and French. But you don't have to travel to London or Paris to take afternoon tea with friends. You may be able to find a tea house, hotel, or restaurant that serves a high tea in your own city or town.

PLAN YOUR OWN TEA PARTY

Visit What's Cooking America online at *www.whatscooking america.net* to find out everything you need to know about high tea. You'll find interesting information, lots of recipes, and pictures of mouth-watering food to inspire you.

1. Make it healthier than its traditional counterpart by replacing the white-bread sandwiches with a whole-grain bread choice.
2. Offer sliced fruit and strawberries dipped in dark chocolate and fruit tarts with crusts of ground almonds instead of the more traditional heavily sugared sweet cakes and cookies. Whether you host a tea party or do something altogether different, time spent with friends is an important factor in having a higher level of life satisfaction.

"The Great One produces the two poles (Heaven and Earth), which in turn give rise to the energies of the dark (yin) and the light (yang). These two energies then transform themselves, one rising upwards, and the other descending downwards; they merge again and give rise to form."

—Chinese Classic Text

Discover Yin and Yang

Many Eastern cultures believe that male and female energies run opposite to each other. The Taoists say that man pulls his sexual and life energy (yang) from his feet, up through his penis and then upward into his heart. Woman, on the other hand, takes her energy (yin) from the top, down through her heart and then to her genitals. Hence, the war of the sexes—she needs a heart connection before she has sex; he needs sex before he can have a heart connection. Understanding this is a step towards reducing any conflict. Remember that yin and yang work together to create a whole. While the parts are separate and opposite, together they are one and harmonious.

TRANSFORM YOUR SEX LIFE

Your choice of positions can have a major influence on your yin/yang relationship. Yin is the receptive principle. Yang is the active principle.

1. When a woman opens up her sexual repertoire to include trying positions where she is on top and in control, she becomes the "male" principle or the yang in the sex act at that moment. This empowers her and can give her a growing confidence in taking a more sexually active role.
2. When the male is on the bottom, he can move into his feminine yin side. He can relax. He doesn't have to be in charge and perform.

The simple act of trying a new position can often be transformative for a relationship. Remember the yin/-yang principle during your next lovemaking session and reverse or change positions. See how it can transform sex for you!

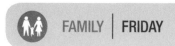

"Your folks are like God because you want to know they're out there and you want them to approve of your life, still you only call them when you're in a crisis and need something."

—Chuck Palahniuk

Communicate about Coming Home Again

Adult children who return home are known as the boomerang generation because many of them left home once for college or a job only to return due to lack of work, financial challenges, or divorce. Especially during tough economic times, adult children head for home. Because parents are often eager to help out, both financially and emotionally, these arrangements usually work out. Be aware that communication is key, both before and during the stay.

NEGOTIATE THE ARRANGEMENTS

No matter how well-intentioned everyone is, problems can arise, so initiate a serious conversation with your adult child and establish the following ground rules.

- Make sure that you and your child have the same expectations about the living arrangement. Identify why your child has decided to live at home and what he hopes to do once the living arrangement has come to an end.
- Talk about your expectations regarding expenses and household chores. Establish ground rules and boundaries concerning your child's social life.
- Discuss a time limit for the arrangement so that there won't be any misunderstandings or resentments later on. You can adjust the time frame later by mutual agreement.
- Charge rent. This may seem counterproductive if your child has returned home due to financial difficulties, but even a nominal amount can help your child prepare for a return to independent living and help you with an increased financial burden.

"Another parable put He forth unto them, saying, The kingdom of heaven is like to a grain of mustard seed, which a man took, and sowed in his field: Which indeed is the least of all seeds: but when it is grown, it is the greatest among herbs, and becometh a tree, so that the birds of the air come and lodge in the branches thereof."

—Matthew 13:31–32

Consume More Herbs

People who cook know that herbs can subtly flavor or intensify the flavors of a dish. You can consume herbs as teas, dried and sprinkled into food, freshly picked from your own garden, or mixed into soups and sauces. Since they are often healthful additions to food, you would benefit from learning how to consume more of them.

1. Whether grown in the wild or cultivated, herbs not only add interest to food, but also have health benefits such as lowering blood pressure, calming anxiety, and relaxing menstrual cramping. For that reason, they have often been used as medicinal aids for the treatment of common ailments. Feverfew, for example, when prepared as a tea, was used in previous centuries for headache and melancholia, whereas sage, comfrey, and horehound were used for respiratory ailments.

2. Today, herbs occupy an important place in alternative medicine modalities. For example, bog bean, white willow, and arnica are herbs useful in relieving muscle pain and inflamed joints associated with acute arthritis.

BUY OR GROW YOUR OWN HERBS

Take a trip to a farmer's market or to a grocery store that has excellent-quality fresh produce. Buy organic herbs, if possible, or better still, grow your own. Find out what you need to know to create your own herb garden at *www.easytogrowherbs.com*.

"The greatest explorer on this earth never takes voyages as long as those of the man who descends to the depth of his heart."

—Julien Green

Renew Your Relationship with Yourself

In order to rediscover yourself, you will need to engage in some self-disclosure, a process by which you will discover the truth about yourself. People with healthy self-esteem have the ability to reveal themselves to themselves, as well as to others.

Take some time now to think about yourself. Do not let any negative thoughts, feelings, or past actions come into play. Think about the good things in your life, your heart, and your actions. Don't stop there. You know yourself better than anyone. Keep on. Think about your life as a joyous story needing to be told. No one needs to be there, so don't be ashamed or afraid—tell it to yourself.

RECORD YOUR STORY

Take some time to reflect on the following questions. Buy a journal to record your answers as part of the journey you are taking to renew your relationship with yourself.

- What is your favorite activity?
- What is your favorite song?
- What is your all-time favorite movie?
- Where is your favorite place?
- What is the best thing you have ever done for yourself?
- What is the best thing you have ever done for another person?
- What is your biggest success?
- Of what are you most proud?

"I tried for modeling work but it was a bit slow and that's when I took a part-time job at McDonald's. It gave me income while I was waiting for my big break and at the very least I could eat."

—Sharon Stone

Try a Temporary Job

When the economy is unstable, job seekers suffer. Consider taking a temporary job until you find something you really want. It can be a wonderful way for a recent college graduate to gain much-needed experience. Those who like variety might find that temping is just what they need. Parents who want flexibility in work hours might also benefit from temporary jobs. You can gain experience without committing to a full-time job, and you can turn down assignments to go on job interviews or to spend more time on your job search.

Another big plus for temporary jobs? Sometimes temporary assignments turn into permanent ones.

TRY THESE TIPS

You can start your temporary job search immediately, and you don't even have to leave the house. Do a search on Google or Yahoo or browse through the listings at one of the popular job sites such as Dice or Monster. The perfect temporary job might just be waiting! Here are a few additional suggestions:

- Update your resume to suit a wide range of job possibilities to make you more appealing to potential employers.
- Investigate seasonal opportunities with local retailers and companies.
- Find a temporary employment agency that specializes in your field such as education, computers, or accounting.
- Connect with old colleagues to let them know you're looking for a temporary job. Network online with other people searching for temporary work.

WEEK THIRTY-NINE

"Education is all a matter of building bridges."

—Ralph Ellison

Attend a School Board Meeting

The continued growth of education in your area is not just the responsibility of teachers and administrators. All of us should strive to play a role in what our schools are doing to prepare the next generation. Even if you don't have children, you should give serious thought to attending your next school board meeting. These meetings often occur with minimal attendance and participation from the community at large, and yet most of us don't hesitate to complain about the state of today's educational system.

GO TO YOUR FIRST MEETING

A school board meeting is the forum in which anyone with concerns about the direction of their schools can step forward, speak openly, and perhaps inspire change. You might even be motivated to run for a seat on the board.

1. At your first meeting, consider the possibility of remaining quiet. Pay attention to the tone and routine of a typical session. This will help you make a more informed contribution the next time you attend.
2. Glean whatever insight may prove useful when trying to persuade others to come with you. You should attempt to bring as many unique and enthusiastic voices as possible.
3. You may not be able to make all the changes you think are needed, but you can still use your right to be heard.

"Culture is the widening of the mind and of the spirit."

—Jawaharlal Nehru

Soak Up Some Culture Together

Choose a cultural event that you and your friend would both enjoy. Present your friend with some culture coupons—IOUs to cultural venues that he can cash in whenever he needs a dose of culture to cure whatever ails him.

Exposure to cultural events can stimulate your minds, engage your senses, and spark interesting conversations. More important, you are enjoying each other's company as you share the experience.

CHOOSE FROM MANY OPTIONS

"Culture" doesn't have to mean a high-brow art film. But don't let preconceived ideas stop you from giving such an event a try. Other ideas for a dose of culture:

- A rock 'n' roll concert
- An opening night at the opera
- An evening at the symphony
- The performance of a work by a local playwright
- An open-mike session of poets at the local coffee shop
- An afternoon at a museum
- A visit to a nearby historical site
- An art gallery showing
- A talk by a local author or artisan

"Among men, sex sometimes results in intimacy; among women, intimacy sometimes results in sex."

—Barbara Cartland

Revive Your Sex Life

There is a lot that one person can do to reawaken sensually and sexually, but ultimately, reviving sexuality in a marriage requires the participation of both partners. If you are the one asking for your partner's involvement in a sexual renewal, be sure to frame your request positively. "I'd like to put more effort in making our sex life better" sounds sweeter and a lot more inviting than "Our sex is so boring; I can't stand it anymore."

If your partner responds either tentatively or negatively, try not to overreact. You may have caught him by surprise. He may still feel stuck in the old stalemate. Give him time to process your request. Be positive. Let him know that your offer stands even if he's not ready to take you up on it just then. Then he can come back to you when he's ready.

If he responds enthusiastically, allow things to unfold without pushing or intellectualizing. The most important thing you can express to him is your real desire to bring back the sexual passion you used to enjoy in your relationship. When you talk, keep touching him. It's amazing how much love can be expressed in a simple stroke.

CONSIDER YOUR PARTNER

Before you interpret your partner's lack of enthusiasm as being a message about you, or your body, consider these questions:

- Is he overtired and stressed out?
- Has he recently experienced a loss?
- Is he just getting over a physical illness?
- Is he worried about his work or job stability?

"Practicing the Golden Rule is not a sacrifice; it is an investment."

—Unknown

Make an Unbreakable Commitment

The Golden Rule, "Do unto others as you would have others do unto you," if practiced, would end all misery and suffering at the hands of other humans. If children are going to have a chance at growing up to be more peaceful adults, the first place this golden rule must be established and taught is by parents in the home. Successful discipline of children requires a strong commitment to a family culture of absolute, inviolable respect for each member's safety and well-being.

This commitment to assuring that everyone in your family gets the same level of physical and emotional safety translates into zero tolerance for verbal or physical assaults made to or from anyone in the family. It can be a difficult balancing act for a parent to play the disciplinarian and still strike a positive tone with children, but always remember that by setting boundaries and keeping to them, you are giving your child an essential life lesson.

MAKE A STRONG COMMITMENT

The unbreakable commitment to respect and safety must first be lived by parents if it is going to be understood and imitated by their children. Read the following questions and answer with a yes or a no.

- Do you maintain your authority?
- Do you refuse to bargain with your child?
- Do you discipline calmly and without anger?
- Do you hide your anxieties and fears when disciplining?
- Do you model vulnerability and an ability to recover from your mistakes?
- Do you set clear limits?
- Do you make simple, clear statements?
- Do you emphasize the positive?

If you answered any of the above questions with a no, then you recognize where you need to make an effort.

"Good battle is healthy and constructive, and brings to a marriage the principle of equal partnership."

—Ann Landers

Avoid Conflicts and Confrontations before Bed

Conflicts at bedtime can come about if one or both of you has not had time to decompress after work or if you have unresolved marital conflict. But when couples argue right before bed, it becomes virtually impossible to relax into restful sleep. Arguing before bed is unlikely to resolve the issue because you are both tired and not thinking as clearly as you will be after you've had a good night's sleep. Find a more appropriate time to have a healthy and constructive conversation about what's bugging you. Save bedtime as the time for love and rest.

MAKE IT THE FAVORITE PART OF YOUR DAY

Bedtime is the time to exchange the cares of the physical world for the peace and restorative benefits of rest. It's a time to allow your body and mind to recuperate from the assaults of the day and to allow the magical imagery of the dream world to emerge in the depths of your consciousness.

1. Make bedtime a special time, perhaps even a favorite part of your day, when you unwind, de-stress, and do those routines that nourish your spirit, restore emotional balance, and nurture your relationship.
2. For example, take a hot shower, share a cup of tea with your mate, do some couples' yoga, give each other a back massage, or read together.

"People take different roads seeking fulfillment and happiness. Just because they're not on your road doesn't mean they've gotten lost."

—H. Jackson Browne, quoting his mother

Feel Ridiculous

Try not to take everything so seriously. Finding and continuing divine maturity doesn't always have to involve the serious or difficult steps in life. We can also find it in the smallest diversions and the most ridiculous momentary distractions. We fear feeling silly or foolish when in fact we should knock down that wall and let new sensations take over and surprise us only as new sensations can.

DO SOMETHING SILLY

Think about something you used to do as a child. Perhaps you enjoyed playing with hula-hoops, jumping rope, or watching your favorite cartoons.

1. Pick something that would make you feel silly if you tried it as an adult, then do it.
2. Let go of your inhibitions. The only person who should care about what you do or how it looks is you. If you think it might bring you some pleasure, then give it a try.
3. When you're done, try something else in a similar vein. Allow yourself to feel ridiculous and celebrate that feeling until it changes from feeling silly to something else.
4. Something entirely new and wonderful such as euphoria or exhilaration. Laugh without being self-conscious about how you sound or how you look.
5. Visit a toy store and buy a toy you remember from your childhood. Allow yourself to revisit the feelings the toy brought you as a child. Use this exercise and others like it to wake up your inner child—a child who believes in a benevolent creator and the inherent goodness of the universe.

"The story of a person overcoming that block to their best self [is] truly inspiring because I think all of us are engaged in that every day."

—Tom Hooper

Cope with Shyness

If you consider yourself shy, you aren't alone. According to a study published by Lynne Henderson and Philip Zimbardo in the *Encyclopedia of Mental Health*, approximately 50 percent of people surveyed considered themselves to be shy. This represented an increase from those who said they were shy in a study published just twenty years before.

Shyness can impact your job search in many ways. While you may be able to deal with it when interacting with people with whom you are familiar, talking to strangers can be very difficult. And what does the job search consist of more often than anything else? Talking to strangers, including interviewers, recruiters, and even receptionists. Take steps to get out of your shell and learn to be more comfortable around others.

THINK POSITIVE

One way to combat your shyness is to keep a positive attitude about yourself.

1. Refrain from negative self-talk, such as "I'm not good enough." Focus on your skills and why they make you a desirable candidate.
2. Practicing for the interview can also be helpful, but don't just practice your answers. You should also rehearse greeting the interviewer and shaking his hand.
3. Become comfortable with making and maintaining eye contact.
4. At first, ask a friend to practice with you. Once you have these skills down, practice them on strangers. Go shopping and talk to salespeople. Talk to the teller at the bank or the clerk in the post office.
5. The more you talk to people and the more often you make eye contact, the more comfortable you will become.

"Public sentiment is everything. With public sentiment, nothing can fail. Without it, nothing can succeed."

—Abraham Lincoln

Check Out a Town Hall Meeting

Few things remind us of our civic responsibility more than a town hall meeting. Most of us are content to read about the results online or in the paper the next day. Sometimes we become extremely irritated by what we read, and we can't understand how certain decisions are reached. Attend a town hall or city council meeting to find out.

Being familiar with the process of a standard meeting can be a powerful tool. You'll become more knowledgeable about the happenings in your town or city, and that knowledge can help others get interested in their potential to effect change. Local politics can be exhilarating and even uplifting. Education through attendance at these meetings beats complaining by a considerable margin, and it's the only way other than voting to initiate change on a larger scale.

GIVE A VOICE TO YOUR CONCERNS

Don't just attend these meetings—speak out! If you're nervous, follow these tips:

1. Write down a question you would ask at a town hall meeting if given the chance.
2. Practice asking your question.
3. Pretend the speaker is responding, and practice your listening skills, paying particular attention to your facial expressions and body language.

275

"Lack of activity destroys the good condition of every human being, while movement and methodical physical exercise save it and preserve it."

—Plato

Walk One Day a Week

If you can't exercise every single day, don't add to your problems by creating more stress over it! For some people, it just isn't possible. Instead, focus on only one day, and convince a friend to come along. You don't have to run five miles or lift heavy weights. Just take a couple of hours to walk in the park with the kind of friend who can make the time fly by. It can be a wonderful way to engage your friend in good conversation, help them incorporate an exercise routine into their own daily life, and a perfect end to the day.

You don't have to use a park, though. What matters is that you're spending quality time with your friend while introducing a positive element into your routine at the same time. You can try walking to work one day a week or using your lunch break to walk to and from where you might be going for lunch. It's just a matter of knowing what would work best for you and the friend you bring along. You might have so much fun that you will have no choice but to add a second or even a third day. Starting with just one is fine.

WALK IN THE RIGHT SHOES

Go shopping at a specialty shoe store and buy yourself a pair of comfortable walking shoes. Any benefits you receive from walking won't mean a lot if you develop blisters or other foot problems from walking in the wrong shoes.

"Do not be too timid and squeamish about your actions. All life is an experiment. The more experiments you make the better."

—Ralph Waldo Emerson

Send Your Spouse a Naughty Text Message

Sending a suggestive sexy text by cell phone has come to be called "sexting." Try sending your spouse short, sexy messages to tease and titillate him. Use your judgment, though; if he's just about to go into an important meeting with the foreign delegation, ask his boss for a raise, direct traffic, or work on a dangerous job site, you might want to hold off transmitting that sexy text.

SAY SOMETHING SEXY

Not quite sure what to say or do? Follow these examples.

1. Tell him:
   - "I'm in the shower, care to join me?"
   - "I'm alone with nothing on . . . want to play?"
   - "Your kisses turn me on."
   - "I'm thinking of you . . . feeling hot and bothered."
   - "You make me want to kiss you all over."
2. You could also send an erotic poem, a joke that has meaning for just the two of you, or a steamy observation about love.
3. See for yourself how sexting can get him through the door faster than pushing "send" on your cell.
4. Think twice before sending a nude photo. You never know when something will end up in cyberspace. If you can't resist sending a digital picture when you are sexting your spouse, choose one that has special significance for both of you and that will evoke a sexy memory that you share.

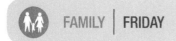

"Eating is not merely a material pleasure. Eating well gives a spectacular joy to life and contributes immensely to goodwill and happy companionship. It is of great importance to the morale."

—Elsa Schiaparelli

Eat Together

It's important that you and your mate be united about your family eating at least one meal together every day, if possible. Busy schedules often mean eating fast food and on the run. Plus, you may find mealtimes with children to be exasperating. Getting kids to eat what's good for them is a common issue that couples face.

Seemingly infinite patience along with the establishment of an unbreakable rule about eating together has its rewards. Nutritionists and food experts suggest that eating meals together not only helps strengthen family bonds, it also is associated with improved diets later in life. A report in *Science Daily* linked the frequency of family meals during adolescence with a better diet when those children grew into adults. They consumed fewer soft drinks, more fruit, and more foods with key nutrients, including dark-green and orange vegetables. Use patience with your children who may be finicky eaters, but put a priority on structured meals to ensure that they eat better as young adults.

PIQUE YOUR PARTNER'S INTEREST

Take out a subscription to a culinary magazine. If your significant other doesn't like cooking, encourage him or her to learn about pairing wine with food. You might even purchase a subscription to a wine magazine for him or her.

"Eventually you will come to understand that love heals everything, and love is all there is."

—Gary Zukav

Soothe Your Spouse's Feverish Brow

When you caress your lover's feverish brow with cool fingertips, the sensation can calm and soothe him. Think of how refreshing it feels to sip a frosty glass of lemonade or a mint julep on a sweltering summer afternoon, occasionally touching your neck or cheek with the cool glass. It's the same kind of momentarily sweet relief your spouse will feel when your cool fingertips trace soft lines across his warm skin.

COOL WITH A TOUCH

1. Wash your hands in cool water and dry them.
2. Scent a bowl of cool water with lavender or citrus. Add some crushed fresh mint leaves. Dip a washcloth into the bowl, then wring the water from the cloth.
3. Gently dab his hot cheeks and temples before folding the cloth and placing it across his forehead. The subtle aroma of the mint and lavender or citrus, coupled with the coolness of the fabric, creates a pleasantly soothing sensation and calms his senses.
4. Suggest to your spouse that he should try to meditate, visualizing himself relaxing in a lush, quiet garden where he receives healing energy through your touch.
5. Then as his breathing becomes regular and slow, indicating a state of relaxation, begin to stroke his forehead very slowly, from side to side. He's bound to feel better, if for no other reason than from your reassuring, loving touch.

"I wish I could show you/When you are lonely or in darkness/The astonishing light of your own being."

—Hafiz

Think Thoughts of Worth

There is an old exercise called "How Much Is It Worth to You?" Imagine that you are approached by a multibillionaire. He has more money than you could ever spend in a lifetime. He approaches you and asks to buy one day of your life, *just one day—twenty-four hours.* The sky is the limit. What would you charge him for one day of your life? What is one day of your life worth?

Common responses range from $10 billion to $10,000 to $100 to nothing. Some people say that they would not sell a day of their life for any price. They give the reason that it may be their last day. (But remember, you can choose the day that you sell.)

TAKE TIME FOR SELF-REFLECTION
Think about these points for a moment:

1. How could $10 million or $100 million change your life? What could you do? How could you help others?
2. All you are giving up is twenty-four hours. Think about this for a while. What would you charge the multibillionaire for a day of your life?
3. If you had trouble answering the question about how much a day of your life is worth to you, perhaps self-reflection will be of assistance to you. Perhaps this is a journal entry for you. Perhaps this is the time to begin spending quality time with yourself to think through questions such as "What is a day of my life worth?" or "What am I worth?" or "How do I value my worth?"

"If you prepare yourself at every point as well as you can . . . you will be able to grasp opportunity for broader experience when it appears."

—Eleanor Roosevelt

Leave Work at Work

Leaving work at work is a challenge for many. With more demands on your time, it may be harder and harder to just say no. In addition, in a tough job market, you don't want to give your boss any reason to let you go. The drive to perform and excel is powerful, yet if you have no life outside of work, then what is the point?

Explore the following questions to increase awareness about this significant work stressor:

- Are you competing with others in your office to keep your job or prove yourself?
- What are you losing when you take work home; what are the effects on your family, spouse, and health?
- Do you schedule time off—weekends when you have plans—and communicate to others you are not to be disturbed during those times to compensate for those times that you take work home with you?
- Do you take work home to avoid other problems in your life—loneliness, depression, or family conflict?

MANAGE YOUR WORK LOAD

Now that you have some awareness about why you take work home, explore some ways to manage it.

- Could you prioritize your time at work to finish the project there?
- Do you really want to pay for your present position with loss of family and relationship bonding?
- Could treatment for depression or grief make you want to live life again, rather than hiding behind work?

> *"Do not go where the path may lead; go instead where there is no path and leave a trail."*

—Ralph Waldo Emerson

Hit a Local Hiking Trail

If you enjoy working up a sweat, especially in nature, go for a hike. If your workday is just too long and there's no way you could do a hike in the evening before dinner, arrange to hike on the weekend. Get out early when the air is still cool and enjoy the fresh beginning of a new day. Plan to hike an hour or two along a local, scenic trail. Take plenty of water with you. If you love to take pictures or make notes about what you see, also slip your camera and a journal into your backpack. That way, if you see some breathtaking scenery or head off the path to explore the woods, you can document special discoveries along the way.

TAKE AN ORGANIZED HIKE

Participate in a hike organized by the Sierra Club or other local organization. Such hikes often have guides who can share insights as well as show you new trails. In addition, you can meet other trailblazers who share your interests in the rugged outdoors.

"The great gift of human beings is that we have the power of empathy."

—Meryl Streep

Empathize When Your Friend Suffers a Setback

Motivational speakers are fond of pointing to men and women of extraordinary accomplishments who also suffered failures on their way to greatness. What is imparted most often in such inspirational stories are lessons learned as a result of the failures or setbacks.

When your friend experiences a setback on his way to achieving her dream and shows it through moodiness or silence, don't downplay what she's feeling. Acknowledge the validity of her feelings and empathize with her emotional response to her difficulties.

LISTEN AND SHARE

When she's ready to talk about it, be a good listener and encourage her to talk at length about the setback.

- Remind her that the two of you are friends, and that includes sharing her dreams. Sometimes two heads really are better than one in trying to figure out why something failed, what went wrong, why it happened, and how to deal with the consequences.
- Misfortune's gift will be to figure out how to ensure that same failure will never happen again.

---

*"If a woman hasn't got a tiny streak of a harlot
in her, she's a dry stick as a rule."*

—D. H. Lawrence

Reverse Your Roles

Falling into habitual patterns of behavior and the same old routine leads to boredom in the bedroom. Try spicing things up in your seduction and lovemaking department by doing role reversals.

Are you the one who waits for your lover to initiate the sex? Or do you usually make the overtures? If the former, become the harlot. Take the position of the initiator. Practice the gentle art of seduction. Offer to rub his back and then permit your hands and fingers to freely roam and explore. If you are usually the aggressor, take a more subdued tack and permit him to have his way with you. Radically changing the way you engage in foreplay can result in both of you becoming bewitched, bothered, and breathless—and loving every minute of it.

GO PUBLIC

Take your role-playing public. Offer to meet him at the neighborhood bistro for a drink. Wear a wig or scarf that conceals your real hair color. Put on your finest little black dress and a pair of dramatic sunglasses and prepare to pick him up.

"Equality consists in the same treatment of similar persons."

—Aristotle

Share the Power

With today's new normal of equal partnerships translating into multiple breadwinners paying the bills, and divvying up housework and child care on an ad-hoc basis, there's a great deal of confusion about how to handle it all. How long should a new mother (or father) stay home with a newborn child? How much "help" with household or parenting should be expected of the person who works outside the home? Who makes sure the bills are paid on time? Who decorates the house? How are buying decisions made?

For better or worse, there are no fixed answers to any of these questions. Your emotional support is the foundation for the discussions and negotiations that will be necessary in order to reach agreement about how to share power as you structure your day-to-day lives together. When you have this unbreakable emotional bond, each of you knows that no matter how difficult your disagreements may be, both of you are committed to seeing the process through.

DIVIDE IT UP

Write a contract for the division of labor in your household. In this contract, make two columns after each chore. One column records who does the task presently. A second column reflects the product of your negotiation: who agrees to take on that task in the future. Beyond the likely tasks such as food shopping, cooking, laundry, cleaning, vacuuming, and dusting, don't forget to list child-care assignments, checkbook balancing, paying bills, dealing with health insurance paperwork, and all the other essential life-management tasks.

"When the breath wanders the mind also is unsteady. But when the breath is calmed the mind too will be still, and the yogi achieves long life. Therefore, one should learn to control the breath."

—Yogi Swami Svatmarama

Breathe from the Belly

We all take breathing for granted, so not everyone realizes the effect it can have on our feelings of well-being. "Belly" breathing is abdominal or diaphragmatic breathing. It relaxes you and reduces many of the symptoms of anxiety and panic. It can be the first step in conquering anxiety attacks and a great start to learning meditation. It can also boost energy and endurance.

When air is taken in, the diaphragm contracts and the abdomen expands; when air is exhaled, the reverse occurs. You can test yourself for abdominal breathing by laying your hand on your belly as you breathe. If it expands as you inhale, you are breathing with the diaphragm. If it flattens, you are breathing with the chest. To practice abdominal breathing, imagine that your inward breath is filling a balloon in your belly. When the balloon is full, exhale until you feel it is completely empty. Just a few of these deep abdominal breaths will bring relief from tension—and pain is one-half tension. By slowing the breath and thought, you experience tranquility and happiness.

PRACTICE BREATHING FROM YOUR BELLY

The goal is to breathe like this all of the time. It will have a very positive effect on your breathing if you practice regularly.

- Try belly breathing when you wake up in the morning and before you go to bed at night.
- In fact, give it a try right now to experience the calming and refreshing benefits.

---

*"Your chances of success in any undertaking can
always be measured by your belief in yourself."*

—Robert Collier

Determine Your Value System

Self-esteem helps determine what you value, and in turn, what you value determines how you act and what you protect. Your value system helps determine how you treat others. If you identify yourself as a kind, caring, compassionate person, this aura will surround you as you interact with others. If you see yourself as cold, calculating, and rude, this aura surrounds you and guides your treatment of others as well.

Closely tied to your value system is your own spirituality. Your self-esteem often plays a role in how you see yourself in the spiritual world. If you suffer from unhealthy self-esteem, you may feel that you do not deserve any rewards that spirituality can offer. But spirituality is about hope, and growing in your spiritual life can help you improve your self-esteem.

Spirituality and religion play vital roles in the way you live. Both have been proved to affect your health by lowering your stress level, lowering your blood pressure, increasing your tolerance of others, increasing your levels of joy and happiness, decreasing your use of controlled substances, and accentuating your wellness in general.

DISCOVER THE BLESSINGS

A strong sense of spirituality can also affect you in the following ways:

- A higher quality of life in general
- A greater sense of peace, purpose, and belonging
- A higher degree of hope and optimism
- A sense of personal empowerment to help others
- A more determined commitment to ethics and morality

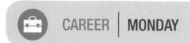

"You don't have to change that much for it to make a great deal of difference. A few simple disciplines can have a major impact on how your life works out in the next 90 days, let alone in the next 12 months or the next 3 years."

—Jim Rohn

Tackle a Career Hiatus

Many people, usually women, make the decision to stay home for a few years while raising their children. Others take time off from work to care for an elderly parent. Most don't take this decision lightly because they know the effect it could have on their careers. Several years out of the work force can mean several more years trying to get your career back up to where it was before you left. If you're mindful of this during your time off, you can mitigate the effects of being out of the work force.

TAKE THE RIGHT STEPS

Follow these tips to keep up with the field they plan to return to someday.

1. You can do this by maintaining membership in professional or trade associations and attend meetings, read relevant periodicals, and keep your network alive.
2. Take continuing education courses. A part-time job in your field will allow you to keep your skills sharp and up-to-date.
3. Join an online professional or trade organization. Visit an online site such as *www.acinet.org*, where you'll find a comprehensive list of professional and trade organizations. You can receive numerous benefits such as tools and resources, continuing education, networking forums, and career advancement opportunities.

*"In America they've forgotten all about [culture and history].
I'm afraid that the American culture is a disaster."*

—Johnny Depp

Appreciate Your Surroundings

Even if you don't live in a cultural mecca, you can still appreciate all that is has to offer. As you go through your ordinary day, stop occasionally and be mindful of what your community offers. Maybe it's a beautiful vista, or friendly neighbors. Maybe it's a thriving writers' community. Say a few words of gratitude—and think about ways to join in and support your community.

BE A TOURIST IN YOUR OWN TOWN

To really get a sense of what your town offers, be a tourist for a day or a weekend.

1. Plan your trip just like you would a visit to any community you don't know well.
2. Visit the website for your city or state with the attitude of a tourist looking for music festivals, art exhibits, and other cultural events.
3. Ask friends and locals what they recommend you see and do. You might be surprised to find all that your community offers that you never knew about.

"The secret of getting ahead is getting started. The secret of getting started is breaking your complex overwhelming tasks into small manageable tasks, and then starting on the first one."

—Mark Twain

Take a Day of Minor Renewal

What happens when you ignore your simple and small to-do list? Before you know it, it becomes something you don't want to deal with. It ceases to be something you could have done with one spare moment or another. It becomes a burden. By then, you're even less motivated to work through some minor accomplishments than ever before.

TACKLE THE LIST

You can either let that list become even more cumbersome, or you can finally do something about it.

1. You have to learn to tackle such a list by starting simple and being realistic. You also need to find a friend to help with those two things.
2. Together, take care of the items on your list—items such as renewing a driver's license, a library card, or perhaps your memberships to the gym or video store. We all have items like that to check off our list.
3. Rather than letting your list get out of control, enjoy the company of a friend while getting through some of those minor, but highly irritating, tasks.

"Venus favors the bold."

—Ovid

Strip Seductively

The sensuous, seductive way that you undress each other can heighten sexual anticipation. Think of the process as foreplay.

1. For women, stand behind him and unbutton his shirt, undo his jean or trouser button and zipper, and slide your hand down his inner thigh, pushing along the fabric of his trousers. Let your fingertips trail over all parts of your lover's body as you inch his pants lower. Lean in close for soft, smoldering kiss against his neck or back.

2. For men, unzip her dress or undo the buttons of her shirt. Pull her close in her half-dressed state and kiss her tenderly. Don't hurry the process. Remove each garment as if each deliberate movement increased your desire and excitement. Don't hurry the process. When she's standing in her undergarments, draw her close and tell her how beautiful she is. Take time to enjoy the tactile sensation of clothing coming off and hands and lips touching each other's flesh. You want a slow sizzle, not a fast burn.

CHOOSE YOUR MUSIC

Put together a playlist of music to set the ambiance for clothing removal. You might choose music that crosses genres or stick to the kind of tunes you and your partner most enjoy. The right music can get you in the mood for prolonging the pleasure.

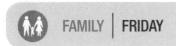

"The ultimate test of a relationship is to disagree but to hold hands."

—Alexandra Penney

Practice Healthy Disagreements

No relationship can be sustained without the occasional disagreement. This is certainly true in today's modern families. All humans are individuals and have different opinions and viewpoints. The best relationships are ones in which you can be supportive of the other person, respect his or her point of view, but also express your individuality, including your opinions and ideas. Differing viewpoints not only stimulate interesting discussions but also provide an alternative lens through which to view life and issues such as politics, sex, and religion.

HAVE HEALTHY ARGUMENTS

See disagreements between you and other members of your family as a place to start a discussion.

1. Agree on how to disagree. It's healthy for you to share divergent viewpoints, talk about them, and grow and evolve together as a result.
2. Clear communication is the key.
3. Practice. Have a lengthy discussion regarding something about which you don't agree. Keep it friendly. Let it get heated, but don't let it get so personal that tempers flare. Then switch positions on the topic. The point is to discover how much fun it is to disagree.

"Dance till the stars come down from the rafters;
Dance, dance, dance till you drop."

—W. H. Auden

Dance in the Moonlight

Dreamy and expressive music reigned supreme during the romantic period of music and dance that extended from the 1800s to the 1900s and from which the great waltzes emerged, along with composers like Strauss, Debussy, and Ravel. You can enjoy that music again and even dance to it in the moonlight. Dance alone or share the moment with your lover or your best friend. The moon rises in the night sky during most of the month, so you have plenty of opportunities to pull your dancing partner out of the house for an impromptu number under the light of the moon and stars.

Grab a portable CD player or iPod speaker so that you can move the instrumental music you need outside. If you can't take music with you, make it yourself. Try humming a favorite tune as you pull someone close for your dreamy "one-two-three" waltz steps around the garden.

SELECT YOUR MOONLIGHT MUSIC

Put together a CD of music for the sexiest dances, among them the super-sexy samba, passionate rumba, flirty cha-cha, and near-erotic Argentinean tango. Imagine you're doing a sultry strip tease for your lover. If you have company and you're feeling bold, go ahead and give someone a real show!

"Motivation is what gets you started. Habit is what keeps you going."

—Jim Ryun

Practice the Habits of Happiness

Happiness is best retained by understanding your spirituality and having a close circle of friends in whom you can confide and disclose important things about your life. Happiness is a habit that can be obtained just as you obtain the habit of having caffeine, or the habit of dessert after a meal, or the habit of saying "bless you" when someone sneezes.

It has been said that if you do something for 21 days without fail, it will become a habit, a ritual in your life. Most people spend time trying to change or break habits. You may not have spent time practicing obtaining a habit, but the habit of happiness is one that is worth practicing.

SPIN THE INFORMATION

Adopt the habit of "spinning." Spinning means that you take the information that you have and make it work for you. Spinning is important to your self-esteem and happiness because it teaches you to take the unpleasant, the bad, the ugly and find good in it.

1. For example, look at the divorce that you just survived and instead of seeing the pain and loneliness of being left, you become thankful that you did not spend one, five, or thirty *more* years *and then* find out that love was not really yours. This is the magic of spin.
2. Think of something troubling you now or something that caused you great distress in the past. Now, put a "spin" on it. Make a decision to do this for 21 days or until it becomes a habit—one that will bring you greater happiness.

*"We should come home from far, from adventures, and perils,
and discoveries every day, with new experience and character."*

—Henry David Thoreau

Overcome Lack of Work Experience

Whether you are new to the job market or new to a particular field, you will have to deal with your lack of experience. You can't create a resume full of jobs in your field if you haven't had any. What you can do is make any experience—work and otherwise—count in your favor.

RELATE YOUR EXPERIENCE

Be ready to let a potential employer know about the things you've done that are related to the skills he wants.

- If one of the requirements of the job for which you are interviewing is the ability to work on a team, talk about sitting on the board of directors of a campus organization, or about working on a team cleaning up your local park.
- If strong organizational skills are needed, discuss the time you were on the committee that planned the high school yearbook.
- Remember that experience doesn't only come from paid employment. Volunteering counts. So do part-time jobs. So if you worked closing shift at a fast-food joint, you were part of a team that was responsible for making sure everything was cleaned up at the end of the day.
- If you don't do so already, start keeping a record—a journal or just a book with jotted notes—of all the experiences you have that relate to your preferred career field.
- The act of cataloging these items will help you remember their details, and you'll always be able to review your notes before an interview to refresh your memory.

WEEK FORTY-THREE

*"Patience is something you admire in the driver
behind you and scorn in the one ahead."*

—Mac McCleary

Be a Better Driver

Being a better driver in your neighborhood or beyond has benefits beyond the obvious ones. It doesn't matter where you live or how large your community is. Accidents can occur on any street at any time. Safe driving begins in your own car. Make a list of relaxation techniques you can use when you find yourself in frustrating driving situations. Methods such as deep breathing and positive visualization can turn a torturous trip into a manageable drive.

PRACTICE MINDFULNESS

All of us have been in a hurry. Perhaps the alarm didn't go off or maybe we have a couple extra errands and precious little time to get everything done.

1. Remember, you're not doing yourself or anyone else on the road any favors by trying to do more than that the speed limit and driving conditions will allow.
2. The next time you feel the desperate need to hurry, take a deep breath, realize what you simply can and can't do with the time allotted, and adjust your driving accordingly.
3. Road rage isn't going to help things either. We would all love to yell at the guy who cut us off or the woman going ten miles under the speed limit. It doesn't accomplish anything except to increase your frustration levels.
4. As soon as you accept your limitations, you can enjoy your drive and help make your community a safer place for everyone.

*"The happiness of life . . . is made up of minute fractions—
the little, soon-forgotten charities of a kiss, a smile, a kind look,
a heartfelt compliment in the disguise of playful raillery, and the
countless other infinitesimals of pleasurable and genial feeling."*

—Samuel Taylor Coleridge

Value Your Friends

Having friends keeps you grounded, reminds you of your hobbies, and offers you support in difficult times. Dig out the phone book, call up a friend who has fallen by the wayside, or join a new activity to make a new one. A variety of healthy friendships is a sign of a healthy, balanced person.

MAKE A LIST OF THE LITTLE THINGS
Surprise a treasured friend with something special.

1. Sit down and write the first ten positive things that come to mind about that friend.
2. After you're finished, put them aside and start a new list. For this one, try to come with ten more positive things about your friend, but if you happen to think of more, write those ones down, too.
3. Think about how easily those first ten things came to mind. They were probably the first things that you always notice when you think about what makes your friend so special.
4. Now, look at the second list—the one that made you think a little harder. Those little parts of your friend's personality, the qualities and traits that usually come to light after years of being in each other's company, are what truly define your friendship. This means your friendship has substance and value.
5. The length of your second list signifies how important your friend is. Show it to your friend, and tell her how much you treasure your friendship with her. Sometimes the best gift we can give is a concrete reminder of our love and appreciation.

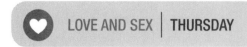

"But pressing with the nails is not a usual thing except with those who are intensely passionate, i.e. full of passion. It is employed, together with biting, by those to whom the practice is agreeable."

—Kama Sutra

Use Your Lips, Tongue, and Teeth

Read the ancient text of the *Kama Sutra* and you'll soon discover that many parts of the body have erogenous zones. It is obvious that the genitals are the first regions to come to mind when you think of erogenous zones. In most people, when even slightly touched, the genitals react immediately with warmth, then a change of color, and then swelling. No other body parts act like that with such little coaxing.

However, do not ignore using your lips to kiss, your teeth to make little love bites, and your tongue to stimulate erogenous areas of your partner's body. Gently rake your fingers through your partner's hair or along the chest area or down the back. Love bites leave the wearer with a remembrance of the erotic activity that produced them. Use your lips and tongue to explore and stimulate his erogenous zones. Allow your tongue to warm and moisten sensitive areas of his body, then blow to cool them. Invite him to reciprocate on your body.

EXPERIENCE A LITTLE PAIN WITH YOUR PLEASURE

Nibbles, bites, and gentle slaps are all a little difficult to comprehend unless you are of a passionate nature and in the moment of pleasure that masks the intensity of the initial mark. Endorphins, chemical substances in your body that are enhanced when you are sexually excited and that cause euphoria, can mask any pain that occurs during receiving the marks. The reminder comes a bit later.

"Accountability breeds response-ability."

—Stephen R. Covey

Hold Children Accountable

When you and your spouse are parenting your children or stepchildren, remember to teach them accountability. The earlier they get that connection in their brains about linking their actions to the consequences, the better. Child psychologists say that it is more difficult to teach accountability to older children who haven't formed that connection in their brain. That's why you need to start teaching your young children that there are always consequences to their actions.

LET NATURE HELP

Let your children experience natural consequences. This helps teach accountability.

1. For example, you've repeatedly told your youngest child not to set his cup so close to the edge of the table because he could spill it.
2. Even though you'll probably have to help him clean it up, notice that if after several warnings (which he ignores) he spills the milk from his cup all over himself, he will immediately understand why you did not want him setting it so close and repeatedly told him not to.
3. When your child does something right, like picks up his room or brushes her teeth before bed without your having to remind or nag, give positive reinforcement. Praise the behavior you want repeated. Or as the late Alex Haley loved to say, "Find the good and praise it."

"The art of living is more like wrestling than dancing."

—Marcus Aurelius

Get Ready to Rumble

Remember rough-housing when you were a kid? If you haven't tried it now that you are all grown up, you might be happy to learn that it's still fun. Wrestling can start simply enough with a challenge, a tickle, or a tease. Regardless of how it starts, that bodily contact of getting physical can get your heart pumping, your mood elevated, and your muscles warmed up. Go ahead, grunt and giggle as you try to wiggle out of the takedown position.

All that maneuvering and laughter provide great health benefits such as lowering blood pressure, strengthening the immune system, increasing pain tolerance, and reducing stress. So let the competitive spirit of your inner child come out and engage that special someone in a wrestling match. Imagine the heat you'll be generating, that skin-to-skin contact, and the release of all that energy and tension.

ENJOY THE HISTORY BEHIND WRESTLING

Do a little research about wrestling's basic moves. Here's a little history to get you started: Three thousand years before Christ, ancient peoples near the Nile drew hieroglyphics in the temple tombs of Beni Hasan, Egypt. Their images depicted wrestlers in many of the positions that are still used today. Share the knowledge and the fun as you practice your maneuvers with your favorite playmate.

"Where words fail, music speaks."

—Hans Christian Andersen

Listen to Spiritual Music

The best music inspires everything that is good within each of us. It promotes dreaming, appreciation for expression, our own creative energy, and our reflection on all kinds of memories. You probably have a song for every emotion and every significant event in your life. You have music for work, exercise, making love, relaxation, sleep, traveling, and everything else.

You may not think you need more music, but it should be clear to you that maintaining an adventurous perspective on the arts can keep you from stagnating and losing your enthusiasm for the pure pleasures of life.

SAMPLE SOME SPIRITUAL MUSIC

Look into music from as many different branches of religion as you would like.

1. Leave your reservations and feelings about the religion itself at the door. Tell yourself that no matter what you personally believe, music with a strong, spiritual intent is that particular faith's idea of speaking to their creator in the most beautiful voice they possess.
2. Learn how different cultures and faiths speak to their creator. Your knowledge and appreciation of these musical devotions will make you a more intelligent, more productive citizen of the world.
3. Go to Amazon.com and listen to some samples of the diverse spiritual music from around the world. If something appeals to you, you can buy it to accompany you on your spiritual journey.

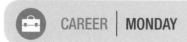

CAREER | MONDAY

"I probably hold the distinction of being one movie star who, by all laws of logic, should never have made it. At each stage of my career, I lacked the experience."

—Audrey Hepburn

Attend Career Fairs

Career fairs are a great, often-overlooked resource for job hunting. At career fairs, you are given the chance to exhibit your skills, enthusiasm, and experience to many companies all in one day at one location. Some of these companies will have specific openings to fill. In addition, a job fair can save you time and money that would have been spent sending out multiple resumes by mail or waiting for advertised openings. Many career fairs are industry-specific. For instance, you can find fairs that specialize in the high-tech, sales and marketing, or health care fields. Others are simply labeled "professional" and consist of representatives from a wide variety of industries.

Upcoming career fairs are often advertised in newspapers. Check out the job and career fairs at websites like *www.nationalcareerfairs .com* and *www.employmentguide.com.* Circle the date on your calendar and attend the next one near you.

> **MAKE THE MOST OF YOUR TRIP TO A CAREER FAIR**
> Here are tips to help you maximize your success at a career fair:
>
> • Dress the part. Dress as you would for a formal job interview.
> • Bring your resume. Make sure you have plenty of copies to pass out to potential employers.
> • Act like a professional. Shake hands with those you meet, stand tall, and speak clearly.
> • Go solo. Traveling with a pack of your friends may distract you from making as many new connections as you can.

WEEK FORTY-FOUR

"Small businesses are the economic drivers of our country, providing the stimulus our communities need."

—Melissa Bean

Patronize Your Local Businesses

Shopping at your local Wal-Mart or other large store is almost essential these days. In a time when counting our pennies is critical, those monster stores can be a good place to put our budget into practice and actually stick to what we plan to spend. Even so, you shouldn't completely disregard those little shops downtown or around the corner. Your local economy can't prosper without you, and the continued health and growth of small businesses is an obvious way to keep the economy thriving.

SHOP LOCALLY

The next time you go out, why not stop at some local stores? You never know what you're going to find, and often, you can find a good deal.

- You can enjoy the intimacy of browsing in a small store. Everything has a personal touch.
- The owner will actually take the time to know your name and treat you like a human being instead of just a wallet with legs.
- By occasionally visiting a family-owned grocery store, non-chain restaurant, or charming bookstore, you're helping the local economy directly and helping the nation get back on its feet in the long run.

"An apology is a good way to have the last word."

—Unknown

Be the First One to Apologize

Some would argue that it's not a real friendship if you and your friend don't have an argument every once in a while. The friendships we have of the greatest, most meaningful substance are not going to be perfect. Sometimes your best friend is going to drive you crazy, and sometimes you'll be the one making her life miserable. Other times, it will simply come down to a case of both of you being wrong.

Most of the time, apologies inevitably follow anything from a minor disagreement to a serious misunderstanding. Sometimes that isn't the case. We can be stubborn and so convinced of our position that we just can't imagine being the one to swallow our pride and admit our wrong-doing. Some friendships are not destined to last, while others are meant to play an important part in the rest of our lives. If you see someone as belonging in the second category, you may want to weigh the value of having that person in your life against the pride of feeling right.

EXPRESS YOUR REGRETS

If you have been in an argument with a close friend, it doesn't matter who was right.

1. You can recognize this by writing to your friend and apologizing for your part in the disagreement.
2. There's no weakness in being the one who admits they were wrong.
3. Long after things have been settled, neither you nor your friend will probably remember who was at fault.

*"Speak when you are angry—and you'll make
the best speech you'll ever regret."*

—Dr. Laurence J. Peter

Remember, Humiliation Hurts

When you feel the urge to lash out in a hurtful way, stop and ask yourself whether humiliating your partner will make the situation better or worse. Humiliation is such a destructive verbal weapon that the only reason a person would use it is to vent pent-up anger or rage.

Why not instead tell your mate exactly what he or she did to upset you and how that action resulted in your feeling hurt, anger, or resentment? Explain that you don't like feeling that way and that it's hurtful and destructive to your relationship. Talk about positive and productive ways to disagree without resorting to insults and personal attacks, which only serve to sabotage a relationship.

TRY SOMETHING DIFFERENT

Shift the paradigm.

1. Choose a behavior different from the pattern of behavior you normally exhibit when you are arguing with your mate.
2. Psychologists say that it only takes one person to shift the paradigm. Only one of you has to make choices that are different from your usual behavior patterns in order for everyone in the paradigm to change their respective behaviors.
3. Give it a try with your spouse and/or your children and see for yourself. It works.

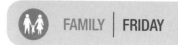

"We are the leaves of one branch, the drops of one sea, the flowers of one garden."

—Jean Baptiste Henri Lacordaire

Beautify Your Community

Take time to beautify your neighborhood with your family working alongside you. The combined sense of purpose will make you feel better about yourselves individually, strengthen your bonds as a family, and give you all a deeper sense of belonging to each other and the community.

WALK YOUR TALK

If you and your significant other feel strongly that something must be done about graffiti in your neighborhood, let your community leaders know. (Alternatively, adopt a section of highway to keep clean.)

1. If a cleanup crew of volunteer workers already exists, join them.
2. If not, get permission to form a group.
3. Ask city leaders to provide a fund for paint and brushes to use on the removal of unsightly graffiti on walls, fences, and overpasses.
4. Form your group by asking members of any service organizations you belong to and asking if members of those groups would like to help your family.
5. All it takes is for one person to feel passionate about the neighborhood to get the ball rolling. When neighbors and small businesses also get involved, a dramatic transformation becomes possible.

"I love that after I spend the day with you, I can still smell your perfume on my clothes. And I love that you are the last person I want to talk to before I go to sleep at night."

—Billy Crystal in *When Harry Met Sally*

Keep Your Date Nights

Couples need to reconnect emotionally and physically on a regular basis. If you both have insanely busy lives, the reconnection is vital. A great way for you and your partner to reconnect and relax at the same time is to establish a date night and honor the commitment to keep it.

Your date night can be as exciting as the much-publicized evening out for President Barack Obama and the First Lady, which included dinner and a Broadway show while their daughters Sasha and Malia remained at the White House, or as quiet as an evening of popcorn, *Masterpiece Mystery!* On PBS, and dessert, which could be just the two of you enjoying the sweetness of a lovemaking session.

SET DATE NIGHTS

Date nights provide respite from the frenzy of hectic schedules and enable couples to romantically reconnect with each other. Whether your date night involves a couples cooking class, a long stroll for a latte and a piece of pie, or a movie you both have wanted to see, make the focus be on the two of you.

1. At the beginning of each month, ask for your partner's input on which nights of that month would be a good date night. Write them into a monthly calendar and tape it onto the refrigerator. Make sure they get recorded in any other planners you use, too.
2. That way, the actual date of your date night will never be in question.

"Character is what a man is in the dark."

—Dwight L. Moody

Understand the Role of Spirituality in Character

Spirituality plays a major role in character development. It is a road map that guides you as you act and move with others in the world. People with strong spiritual beliefs understand and practice the deep convictions of character. It has been said, "Character is who you are when no one is looking."

> **REFLECT ON YOUR CHARACTER**
>
> Character can also be described as how we act when there are no policies and guidelines for behavior. If you were able to treat anyone any way without any culpability or responsibility, how would you respond?
>
> - If you could do what you wanted to do with that person who just cut you off on the interstate, what would you do?
> - If you could say anything to that nasty person at work, what would you say?
> - If you could get your hands on the person who stole your wallet and then your identity, what would you do to them?
>
> Pay close attention to your answers. They will give you some valuable insight into your character. You character is the guiding force for how you act, and your character is a direct product of your spirituality and spiritual nature.

"Your pay raise becomes effective when you do."

—Orrin Woodward

Prepare for a Raise

Before you decide to ask for a higher salary, you must know what number to request. In addition to having a solid argument for why you deserve the raise, you need to figure out how much the raise should be. That puts you in the strongest position. Take the time to find out how much the going rates are in your field to know what a reasonable compensation amount is.

DO YOUR HOMEWORK

1. Read the trade journals for your industry and the online help-wanted ads. If possible, talk to current employees.
2. Remember, salaries vary by geographic region. For example, a teacher in Wisconsin may earn a lower salary than a teacher in California. In addition to finding out what the average earnings are in your field and industry, you must also find out what those jobs pay where you work. There is generally a relationship between the local cost of living, the salary, and the supply of and demand for workers with a specific set of skills.
3. Consult a salary survey. There are many salary surveys available on the Web. Using your favorite search engine, type in the term "salary survey."
4. Use your network to find out how much others are earning at the same level. Talk to alumni of your college or university in similar positions (or employed by the same organization). They may be an excellent source of information. By doing this research, you will get an idea of the salary level you can realistically expect.

"I can no other answer make, but, thanks, and thanks."

—William Shakespeare

Practice Common Courtesy

Do you ever stop and think about the number of people you interact with every day? No doubt, it's a considerable number. Now, think about the people you rely on for various services during an ordinary day. Perhaps the server at the restaurant where you had lunch, your mail deliverer, the guys who pick up your garbage or the salesperson who went out of his way to help you find exactly what had in mind. It's still a pretty impressive number, right? Do you practice common courtesy with all of them, saying "please" and "thank you"? Give it a try. It might make their day, and it will certainly lift your mood.

RECOGNIZE GOOD SERVICE

Just because someone is doing their job doesn't mean they don't deserve some kind of commendation for doing it well. We've all had a bad experience at a restaurant or with a cashier, when we found ourselves wishing for someone who actually knew what they were doing. When we go through something like that, we don't hesitate to devote our energy to complaining.

1. The next time you get superior service at a restaurant, don't be afraid to say so and reflect your feelings in your tip.
2. Why not leave a card in your box for your mail deliverer when the holidays come around? That's the kind of goodwill that can influence the rest of that person's day and how they continue to do their work.
3. Phone the store or restaurant and ask to speak to the manager. Express your appreciation for the excellent service and make sure the manager knows you'll be back to repeat the experience.

*"There are a million ways to lose a work day, but
not even a single way to get one back."*

—Tom DeMarco and Timothy Lister

Play Hooky for Two

When a hectic day (or days, as it sometimes the case) is inevitable, we know that we have little choice but to roll up our sleeves and dive right in. That's a good mindset to have. But sometimes we insist on working ourselves half-to-death even when the situation doesn't call for it. Having a strong work ethic is one thing. Not giving your body and spirit a chance to relax and recharge is another.

Would your job really be in jeopardy if you just took a day off? Would you workplace fall to pieces if you didn't come in that morning? If you can answer yes to this question, and if you can know a friend who's willing to do the same, seize a random day and play hooky.

MAKE IT A DAY TO REMEMBER

Go to the park, grab a nice lunch, and do some wish-list shopping just for fun. Whatever you decide, pick up your phone and call that friend who knows how to take advantage of a day with nothing on the agenda except having a good time.

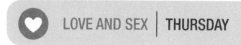

"Marriage, ultimately, is the practice of becoming passionate friends."

—Harville Hendrix

Solve Sex Stress

Sexual imbalances can create stress on a relationship. These occur when one partner wants more sex than the other, or a different type of sex. Each relationship is unique, and there is no set formula to solve all your problems in the bedroom. Brainstorm ideas to decrease sex stress—scheduling two nights a week, using direct commands during lovemaking, getting a toy for the partner with an insatiable appetite—to solve the challenges you face, and put them into practice.

Experiment with different ideas until you've minimized the sources of stress. The health of your sexual life is a direct reflection of the health of your relationship, so keeping life hot is key to relationship bliss.

CREATE A WISH LIST

In an interview with WebMD, sexologist Dr. Ava Cadell recommends creating a wish list of three experiences that would spice up your sex life and sharing them with your partner once a month.

1. As you and your partner exchange lists, you not only learn what the other person desires, but you get your own needs met, too.
2. It is a win/win situation with no room for stress and plenty of room for fun.

> *"A good compromise, a good piece of legislation, is like a good sentence; or a good piece of music. Everybody can recognize it. They say, 'Huh. It works. It makes sense.'"*

—Barack Obama

Seek Compromise

Compromise can work well in families as an effective method for settling disputes. The greatest value of compromise, other than providing a way through a seemingly impassible blockage, is that it can restore household harmony and peace and enable your family dynamic to get back on track.

The next time communication gets sticky or blocked over some issue in your family, figure out an equitable solution in which you and the other party agree to accept something less than what you had originally wanted . . . and move on.

RECOGNIZE AREAS OF CONFLICT

In families, there are four common areas where problems are likely to occur and where growth is possible:

1. Boundaries. Maintain your individual identity as you create an interdependent, not dependent, relationship with your partner and other family members.
2. Money. Create a productive financial partnership with your mate, not using money as an instrument of power but as a foundation for mutual fulfillment.
3. Sex. Restore a fulfilling, respectful sexual union, making sex the basis of an emotional and spiritual connection in your relationship and a foundation for self-growth, rather than allowing it to be a bargaining chip in a relationship power game.
4. Family. Build safety, nurturance, and boundaries for your children, living in community with your extended family, friends, and neighbors.

"A good meal makes a man feel more charitable toward the world than any sermon."

—Arthur Pendenys

Share Sushi

Sushi may be one of the best sources of nutrition available. Technically, the word sushi refers to vinegar rice. Packed with protein and nutrients, and often low in fat, sushi is an excellent source of lean protein and contains very little heart-clogging saturated fat, unlike beef and pork. What little fat it does have is mostly in the form of omega-3 fatty acids. Share some with your buddy, and do both of yourselves a favor.

MAKE CALIFORNIA ROLLS WITH YOUR BUDDIES
Cooking together is a great way to relax and enjoy your friends.

1. Invite your buddies over to make California rolls or other type of sushi. California rolls, one of the easiest and most popular sushi recipes, combines sushi rice with crab meat and bands the moist mound in a paper-thin slice of roasted seaweed.
2. To make California rolls, which includes avocado and crab meat stuffed in the rice, you'll need a bamboo mat (in which to roll the sushi), a cutting board, a sharp knife, a rice paddle or wooden spoon, and some plastic wrap.
3. Lay out the bamboo mat and cover it with a sheet of plastic wrap. Place on the plastic wrap one sheet of nori (dried, roasted seaweed). Spread about 1 cup of cooked Japanese medium-grain rice over the nori, leaving about a 1-inch border at the edges. Straight across the center of the nori, place chopped cucumber, avocado, and crab. Then, taking one side of the mat and plastic wrap, begin to roll up over the sushi. Roll tightly, then unroll the mat and plastic. Moisten the rolled edge of the nori to seal the roll. Slice the long roll, which is like a rolled cookie dough, into 2-inch pieces and serve on a pretty plate along with condiments such as soy sauce, wasabi (Japanese horseradish), and pickled ginger.
4. Serve and enjoy with friends!

"Without continual growth and progress, such words as improvement, achievement, and success have no meaning."

—Benjamin Franklin

Play Spiritual Mad Libs

We all remember the game Mad Libs. Many of us played it to pass the hours on a long car ride or rainy afternoon. The game is simple and can be enjoyed anywhere. It has been a favorite of children and adults for many years.

Take the game into previously uncharted territory. Get a packet of Mad Libs, and by yourself or with like-minded friends, fill in the blanks. But the twist is that you have to use spiritual words to fill in the blanks! Not only is this fun, but it reminds you that the sacred can be playful—and it can be present everywhere.

MAKE YOUR OWN MAD LIBS

1. Sit down someday and write out some sentences while leaving blank spaces where certain words might go. For example: "_____ makes me think of _____ when I can't sleep at night."

2. After you've created a few, put them in a drawer and keep them there for a few days or even a week. The idea is to put some distance between the sentences you've written and the answers you might have thought of as you went along.

3. Read the sentences over and fill in the blanks with the first words that come to mind. Some of them may still be the ones you thought of before, while others may take you by surprise.

4. After you've finished, read the completed sentences, think about why you chose them and take what you learn as an experience geared towards continued growth and improvement. Play this game as often as you like.

"My guiding principles in life are to be honest,
genuine, thoughtful and caring."

—Prince William

Follow Your Guiding Principles

Are you thinking about leaving your current work situation for a position that offers more money? Although it's vital to have a job with a salary that will provide you and your family with a comfortable life, it's also important to remember that monetary benefits alone will not bring happiness in your career. Generally, a high salary doesn't buy job satisfaction. It may seem like the person with the BMW parked in the employee lot has the best job, but she may actually be unhappy at work. You should have a job you'll be happy with, that you'll grow with, and that will allow you to be yourself.

DISCOVER YOUR GUIDING PRINCIPLES

List five principles that you use to guide you in your work or career. For example, do you expect others to demonstrate ethical behavior? Do you believe in being open and transparent? How about being flexible, innovative, efficient, and effective? Do you value diversity in your treatment of all people?

1. Discovering your guiding principles is one way to help you decide if a new job with more money will really give you the fulfillment you need. Your guiding principles are those that reflect your core beliefs and guide not only what you do but why and how you do it.

2. If your guiding principles and those of your current position are in alignment, you should stop and think hard before leaving for a job where these principles might be in conflict.

"I read about eight newspapers in a day. When I'm in a town with only one newspaper, I read it eight times."

—Will Rogers

Buy a Newspaper

These days it seems like there's hardly any need for a newspaper. The Internet and twenty-four-hour news networks provide us with all the information we could ever technically need. Your local paper probably has a website, a Facebook page, and maybe even a Twitter account, too. So, why bother? Because it supports your community.

LOVE YOUR LOCAL NEWS

1. Your local paper could use your support more than ever. The larger papers aren't hurting quite as much, but the smaller, more local papers are quickly losing support in a world that largely depends on the Internet and channels like MSNBC and Fox News to deliver their information.

2. Buying a local paper puts money back into your economy, and it supports the people who still make their living by writing for them. These newspapers won't be around forever. In the meantime, it's not going to break your budget to pick one up once or even twice a week.

3. There's a singular, unique enjoyment to be gained from sitting at the kitchen table and reading a newspaper from start to finish. It's an experience you can't get in any other way. Picking up a paper on your way home from work can let you revisit this old-fashioned pleasure and help keep a few people employed at the same time.

4. If you have an interest in writing and a topic in mind, pay a visit to the editor of your local paper and offer to write a weekly column. You might share your craft ideas or keep the community updated on recent news in the local political scene.

*"Without goals, and plans to reach them, you are like
a ship that has set sail with no destination."*

—Fitzhugh Dodson

Achieve an Achievable Goal

Not every goal or aspiration involves the objective of shooting for the stars. On every inventory of dreams or bucket list, there are always some things that are well within reach. Unfortunately, it often happens to be something we never seem to find the time for. Enlist a friend to help you commit to the goal and achieve it.

SWAP GOALS

The idea is to think of something achievable from both lists and to help the other person make it happen.

1. Find a friend who you can trust to appreciate your need to accomplish something from your list, one who would also be willing to trust you with her dreams.

2. Trusting a friend to help us figure out and accomplish something gives us the ability to do more than we might be able to on our own. It can reinforce the notion of how important it is to trust someone to help us when we need it and how rewarding that can be. It's a feeling that can be realized whether you're helping your friend, or they're helping you.

3. Think of something that you know your friend has always wanted to do. For example, maybe she has always wanted to learn how to speak Spanish or cook authentic Chinese food. Pick up a course catalog from your local community college and ask your friend to join you in signing up for one of the courses that would help her achieve her goal.

"When we seek to discover the best in others, we somehow bring out the best in ourselves."

—William Arthur Ward

Bring Out the Best in Each Other

Healthy relationships are about bringing out the best in each other. You've probably heard that for years, and the idea sounds so simple, but the truth is that it is one of the most important aspects of healthy relationships. At its deepest, it means that every time you are around the other person, you are bringing the best of you, the total sum of you, to that moment.

This doesn't mean that you have to be happy and joyful around that person all the time. What it does mean is that whether you are in complete bliss or complete pain, you bring that emotion in total to your spouse so that he or she can bask in your joy or help you through your pain. It means that you are willing to bring your total self into your relationship and help your partner do the same.

HELP YOUR PARTNER GAIN PERSPECTIVE

If your mate is having self-esteem issues over an ongoing tiff with a manager or boss, help him see everything in a clearer perspective.

- Discuss what makes him unique, what you personally value in him, and what you know his gifts to be.
- Recount past accomplishments, recognition, and awards associated with his career or job.
- Remind him of who he is at his core. That's what counts.

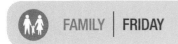

"Each generation goes further than the generation preceding it because it stands on the shoulders of that generation. You will have opportunities beyond anything we've ever known."

—Ronald Reagan

Create a Multigenerational Scrapbook

Are you the keeper of family photos? Why not create a scrapbook with your children and spouse to trace your family's lineage and document births, deaths, marriages, and other important events? During this process, you can teach your children about their ancestry, perhaps inspire one of them to write a report on a famous ancestor, or learn about vital health history.

A scrapbook can contain pages with old letters, documents, deeds, and other keepsake documents. You'll not only have hours of fun working on it and sharing it with relatives on celebratory occasions and holidays, you'll feel a sense of pride and joy at knowing the details of your family's lineage.

MAKE A VIDEO RECORD

Before a parent, grandparent, great-aunt, or great-uncle gets any older, ask him or her to join you for a videotaped chat.

1. Make it informal and begin with easy questions that can serve as points of departure into his story. When were you born? What town, village, or city? What country? Who were your parents? What kind of work did they do?
2. Then ask open-ended questions. Tell me about your earliest memories? What was life like for you growing up in your town?
3. Ask questions about certain periods in his life such as pre-adolescent, teen, young adult, middle age, and golden years, for example.
4. Use the information in your scrapbook, and enjoy the video for years to come.

"If your dog is fat, you're not getting enough exercise."

—Unknown

Start Simple

Exercise does more than strengthen the body and keep you physically healthier; it also helps relieve stress, decreases the potential for depression, and subsequently helps you build healthier self-esteem. If you feel good about your body and your physical appearance, you will see a payoff in other areas of your life as well.

As with so many other things, human beings have a tendency to get carried away, take on too much, become overwhelmed and quit. The answer is to start simple, enjoy the experience rather than focusing on the end result, and build on your success in small increments. Sticking with a simple exercise program—even an uncomplicated, brisk walk down the street—can give you results in just a few weeks.

KEEP THESE SUGGESTIONS IN MIND

When you begin your program, keep the following tips in mind:

- Choose an activity that you like to do.
- Make exercise a daily routine.
- Do simple things like taking the stairs and parking farther from stores than usual.
- Exercise with a group of friends to help time pass more quickly.
- Don't do the same thing every day; vary your workout.
- Join a group at a fitness center (aerobics, kickboxing, tai chi, etc.).
- Work in the yard raking leaves or sweeping the sidewalk.
- Purchase an inexpensive treadmill and weight set for your home.

"Only when inspired to go beyond consciousness by some extraordinary insight does beauty manifest unexpectedly."

—Arthur Erickson

Display an Inspirational Quotation

Take a personal roll call of every inspirational quotation you can think of. Focus your energies on recalling or seeking out the quotations from artists, thinkers, politicians, spiritual leaders, friends, family, and others that have struck you in some deeply personal, emotional, magical way. Write or type out every quotation you find or pull from your wealth of life experiences. Put down as many as you like. Stop only when you feel so inclined. Then, pick one of the quotations that most speaks to you and frame it, put it on a T-shirt, or have it printed on a coffee mug.

CREATE AN INSPIRATIONAL QUOTATION COLLAGE

Don't just throw the collection of quotations away once you've chosen one!

1. Take in this body of inspirational quotations as a whole.
2. Find out which ones are similar, which ones contradict each other, which ones mean the most to you, and which ones incorporate values you either maintain or are struggling to maintain. You probably won't run out of things to think about and valuable moral lessons that can be added to your life's purpose and goals.
3. It will also remind you that our concept of inspiration is rarely a singular thing. It is limitless in its potential, because we ourselves are limitless in our potential.
4. Create a collage of all of these quotations. Write them out in calligraphy, or use letter stickers, or type them using different font styles on your computer. Post them where you can see them and reflect on them.

"No act of kindness, no matter how small, is ever wasted."

—Aesop

Be a Volunteer and Find a Job

You know that volunteering is good for your community and good for you, but did you know that being a volunteer could help you find a job? Volunteering is good for your morale. The stress of a lengthy job search can wear you down. You may have started out with a positive attitude, but if you've been looking for a job for a while, you may no longer be as upbeat. For one thing, rejection can really deflate your ego. Then there's the frustration of plugging away at something that doesn't seem to be moving forward. Sometimes it feels great to just get out of the house and feel useful.

Check out the website *www.volunteermatch.org*. You'll find the perfect opportunity to make a difference—in your community, in yourself, and in your job search.

LET VOLUNTEER WORK HELP YOUR JOB SEARCH

Here are some ways how being a volunteer can help you in your job search:

- Volunteering can help your network to grow. You might just meet the person who helps you find your next job.
- Being a volunteer can help you sharpen your existing skills and learn new ones.
- Volunteering looks good on your resume.
- Your volunteer work might give you inspiration for a new career path. For example, your volunteer efforts at a local hospital might motivate you to investigate a career in the medical field.

"When I was a boy of fourteen, my father was so ignorant I could hardly stand to have the old man around. But when I got to be twenty-one, I was astonished by how much he'd learned in seven years."

—Mark Twain

Take Time for Teens

You may not have teenagers, but you probably remember very clearly what it was like to be one. Teenagers come complete with their own set of needs and problems, and their parents and educators need all the help they can get. When you become involved in the lives of teenagers, you are investing in your own future. These are the individuals who will be running the show, and it's in your best interest to make sure they get a good start.

HELP CREATE A PLACE FOR TEENS

When you think about your community, do you know whether there is a safe place for teens to hang out?

1. If there isn't, think about how you could rally support for one.
2. Creating a teen-designated space starts with one person having the idea and motivation to spearhead the concept.
3. In some communities, teens themselves form a council of representatives from all the schools in an area to raise money, awareness, and a volunteer work force to take the dream to reality.
4. Help teens in your town stay away from gangs, drug and alcohol abuse, and teen pregnancy by creating a place where they can hang out safely and share happy times with friends.

"To listen well, is as powerful a means of influence as to talk well, and is as essential to all true conversation."

—Chinese proverb

Remember to Listen

Our closest friends are the ones with whom we can have any kind of conversation. We can sit around with them over cold drinks and shoot the breeze, but we can also exchange thoughts, feelings, and memories usually reserved for those we trust. We pride ourselves on being as good at listening as we are talking. The next time you're with a friend, be mindful of the importance of listening. Stop worrying about what you're going to say, and be fully present to what he's saying.

LISTEN ONLY

Build your listening skills and give your friend an incredible gift by listening.

1. Offer to sit with your friend for an hour and do nothing except listen.
2. This is an offer your friend has probably never received before. We all know how to have a conversation, but we're so used to the back-and-forth nature of a dialogue that most of us have never been in the position of being able to talk until we've completely satisfied that need.
3. Your friend can use the opportunity to vent, reveal personal troubles, or just ramble. Whatever she chooses, she will certainly be grateful.
4. To show her thanks, she may reciprocate and offer the same opportunity to you.

"I don't know the first real thing about the dating game. I don't know how to talk to a specific person and connect. I just think you have to go to person by person and do the best you can with people in general."

—Jason Schwartzman

Let Your Dating Journey Unfold

You may be surprised to find that your goals and vision change as you go out and meet new people. This is just fine. You may decide that you'd rather not meet anyone for a serious relationship at the moment, or that you would like to have a romantic relationship but want to remain single. You may start dating just to find a supportive friend or no-strings romance, and realize through the dating process that what you really want is a long-term, committed relationship or marriage.

JOURNAL YOUR DATING JOURNEY

Even if you've never kept a journal and don't think you are a talented writer, you'll want to document your feelings, thoughts, and desires on your dating journey.

- You can go low-tech (a spiral, lined notebook and a pen are all you need) or put all your thoughts into a word-processing program or even a complicated database on your computer. Writing down your thoughts, goals, and feelings and then keeping notes on the people you meet is a great way to remember all sorts of reactions and details your brain might not retain.
- Occasionally read through your notes to help gain perspective on your journey. As you read through your journal, you will begin to see significant patterns in the types of people you select and in how you date. For example, are many of the people you've been choosing legally separated but not divorced? Do you have a history of getting past a few dates, then having a blow-out fight that ends the relationship? Documenting your dating journey can also be a great way to relieve stress and frustration. Writing about a particularly funny or gruesome dating experience is a bit like coming home from a bad date and calling your best friend to debrief.

"Train up a child in the way he should go: and
when he is old, he will not depart from it."

—Proverbs 22:6

Instill Spiritual Values in Your Children

Your spiritual values guide your behavior in the world throughout your life, including in business dealings and family relationships. When you impart your spiritual beliefs to your children, you help them understand the moral positions of right and wrong. You give them a code of behavioral conduct to live by and help them understand the place of religion and spirituality in human life. The work of teaching your children about spirituality takes patience and consistency.

REINFORCE YOUR VALUES

By the time children are ready to start school, their moral and ethical values are already ingrained. But that doesn't mean your work as a parent and as your children's primary spiritual adviser ends. As your children grow and become even more inquisitive, you will have the opportunity to reinforce the spiritual values that have guided you.

1. Have family discussions about situations and answer questions that concern your children. Doing this provides a great opportunity to put the discussion in a larger context, because by helping your child grow spiritually and morally, you will be helping them to establish moral families. That's good for society as well.

2. Establish a short list of consequences in the event your child violates the core values held by your family. For example, devise appropriate options for dealing with the discovery that your child has lied to you or stolen something from a friend, the school, or a store.

"What other people may find in poetry or art museums, I find in the flight of a good drive."

—Arnold Palmer

Play a Game of Miniature Golf

Playing a game of miniature golf with your friend or significant other allows you to forget the stresses of life for a while and lifts your hearts into a lighter mood. A miniature golf course doesn't necessarily have to be relegated to the milieu of childhood. As it turns out, the popularity of those courses apparently increases with economic downturns.

Perhaps it's the nostalgia thing—a kinder, gentler time in America when a family would start the weekend with a round or two of miniature golf with the kids, followed by burgers and fries at the local drive-in. Launched in 1938, the culture craze hit its stride in the mid-1980s, with miniature golf courses seemingly popping up everywhere around the country. In fact, it might be easier now than ever to find a course in your neighborhood.

HAVE SOME SPOOKY FUN

Treat yourself to some creepy entertainment at a Monster Mini Golf course (monsterminigolf.com) if there's one near you. You and your friend will feel like kids again as you play eighteen holes through a chills-and-thrills environment that features monster décor and animated props, not to mention creatures with glow-in-the-dark features.

"True religion, like our founding principles, requires that the rights of the disbeliever be equally acknowledged with those of the believer."

—A. Powell Davies

Advocate Religious Freedom

The next time you feel like complaining about the nature of your life, remind yourself quietly of the many things for which you are grateful. Try focusing your appreciation on the religious freedom we enjoy and take for granted every single day.

Your specific opinions on religion do not factor into whether or not you should be grateful. If you believe nothing, then you still have to remember that it is your freedom in this country to be able to do so. People may disagree with you, and the tone of their disagreement can be petty, severe, or even tragic, but you are still protected under law to be able to believe whatever you wish. There are literally millions of people in the world who do not have this gift.

LEARN MORE ABOUT RELIGIOUS FREEDOM

Learn more about the plight of countries whose people do not enjoy religious freedom at *http://religiousfreedom.lib.virginia.edu*. There are resources available in areas such as education and participation (where needed) as a volunteer. Nothing will bring your gratitude alive like getting involved and reaching out to those who do possess the same wonderful endowments that you have.

"The glue that holds all relationships together,
including the relationship between the leader and the
led is trust—and trust is based on integrity."

—Brian Tracy

Safeguard Your Professional Relationships

The old adage about not burning your bridges in case you have to cross them again one day applies to your career. It's not in your best interest to damage or sever professional relationships. You never know when you might meet those individuals again and have to conduct business together. If you are at least on good speaking terms and have shown respect, it will be a lot easier to establish a smooth working relationship. Stay optimistic and do your best to protect and safeguard all professional relationships. That way, you can feel happier and more assured that you are doing something vital to keeping your career or job on track.

IMPROVE YOUR WORK RELATIONSHIPS

Here are some tips to help establish and maintain trusting professional relationships:

- Remember and follow through on your commitments. Keep a diary or some other kind of record to make sure you don't forget your promises and obligations.
- Nurture and build relationships based on trust and loyalty. If appropriate, spend time together away from the professional environment. It's a great way to get to know someone and establish the foundation for a better work relationship.
- Maintain open and honest communication at all times. Misinformation in an office setting can be a risky thing.
- Treat everyone with respect.

*"The role of the writer is not to say what we can
all say but what we are unable to say."*

—Anaïs Nin

Support the Local Arts

If you're familiar with a local artist who could use some exposure, consider holding a showing of his works. Be creative and hold your art show in a neighborhood park so the entire community can enjoy the display.

Buying a book is the easiest way to support a favorite writer. That sentiment is even more significant when it comes to a local writer. There's a good chance you have at least one in your community. Their books can be found in locally owned bookstores, through an online press, or even out of the back of the writer's car. Every sale can be a victory for them. It can encourage their work and keep their dream alive. That's a lot for a price tag that usually doesn't run higher than fifteen dollars.

HOLD A BOOK SIGNING

You can support local authors in an even greater way.

1. Remember that locally owned bookstore? If you know of a local writer and want to do something more than buy their book, call the owner of the bookstore and find out if they might be interested in hosting a book signing.
2. It doesn't have to be limited to a signing either. If the writer is interested, they can offer a reading of their work, too.
3. If there isn't a locally owned bookstore around, check out the possibility of using a coffee shop or small restaurant.

"People who have lost relationships often wonder why they can't just let it be 'water under the bridge.' It is water under the bridge—the trouble is we do not live on the bridge but in the river of life with its many twists and turns."

—Grant Fairley

Help a Friend Get Back in the Dating Game

If a friend has split recently, make a date for a makeover. Spend the day getting your hair styled, your nails done, and picking out a new outfit. Persuade her to splurge a little on a new outfit. Then, take her picture and help her write a compelling, off-beat ad for a reputable online dating site.

ENCOURAGE A FRIEND TO CONSIDER SPEED DATING

When your friend emerges from a longtime romantic relationship, you want to do all you can to help her get back on her feet.

1. When she turns to you for help, consider speed dating. It might sound crazy to her, but speed dating can be a success. It could be the way she meets someone new.

2. Then there's always the entertainment value. If the exercise produces one incompatible prospect after another, then at least you'll have some entertaining conversation for the ride home. Dating disasters have and always will make for some easy laughs. That can have a positive effect on someone just getting back on the dating scene, and you can be right there to be keep them laughing. They might even feel a little better about being single again.

"Those who cannot remember the past are condemned to repeat it."

—George Santayana

Understand Your Key to the Future

Imagine what a timesaver it would be if you could spend just a little time with someone and quickly know if he has what it takes to make a great relationship with you. This might sound impossible, but it's not. You can figure out what makes you desirable to others and, just as importantly, what will make one of them a good match for you. The keys lie in your past relationships. A little time reflecting on them can give you helpful information for the future.

BEGIN AT THE BEGINNING

1. Take a trip down memory lane, starting with your first date. Write down the name of the person who first asked you out. How did you meet? What was this special person like? What initially attracted you to each other? What did you do on your first date? Was it a good experience? Did you see each other again? Why or why not? What things did you particularly like or dislike about this person? How did your relationship end? Why?

2. Now, go through all your past significant romantic relationships, and for each of them write down the answers to the same questions.

3. If you haven't had any significant relationships, write down the names and particulars of people you have dated a few times, had a crush on, or were attracted to, and what happened to your relationship with these people.

4. If you don't consider your past dating history seriously, you may be condemned to repeat it. Be honest about your experiences and learn from them. No one ever needs to know your results, and the only person who can judge you is you.

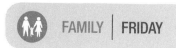
"Celebrate what you want to see more of."

—Tom Peters

Chronicle the Journey

If someone in your family has a long-term goal, put together a scrapbook to detail each step of his journey. Don't forget to include motivational quotationss, inspirational sayings, and photos expressing all phases of his particular objective. Include images and notes about how you celebrated all the milestones he achieved along the way to realizing his dream.

CELEBRATE GOAL ACHIEVEMENTS

Whether it's a major or minor goal that someone in your family has accomplished, think of some appropriate way to mark that special achievement. We all need encouragement—it helps us to stay on course, reinforces our belief in our abilities, and enables us see that our goals and dreams are within reach. The following is a small sampling of ways to express your admiration and offer enthusiastic encouragement.

- Put a note or card with effusive congratulations where he will find it.
- Buy a brightly colored helium balloon displaying the word "Congratulations."
- Hang a banner across the foyer to greet him when he arrives home, or create a congratulatory banner and get family, friends, and neighbors to sign it.
- Prepare his favorite dessert.

"A good laugh and a long sleep are the best cures in the doctor's book."

—Irish proverb

Sleep Like Spoons

Drift off to sleep embracing the one you love. You may find that your sleeping position not only reflects your loving connection with your partner, it is conducive to more restful and restorative sleep. And a good night's sleep benefits both of you.

TRY THE FETAL POSITION

1. The fetal position, many doctors say, is the best choice for a good night's sleep because the position supports the three natural curves in your spine: in the lower back, mid-back, and neck. Curl into the fetal position on your side and snuggle up close to your mate so that your bodies are like teaspoons on their sides in a drawer.

2. With one arm cradling your pillow and the other arm draped over your partner's chest and holding his hand, you both will be in the fetal position for sleep.

3. If your mate is lying behind you, facing your backside, guide his hand over your heart or cup it under your breast and blissfully drift across that threshold between wakefulness and sleep.

4. Try drawing up his knee between your thighs to reduce any space between you. Who needs blankets when you've got each other's body heat for warmth?

*"Harmony is one phase of the Great Law
whose spiritual expression is love."*

—James Allen

Explore Feng Shui

Having a place that promotes solitude and introspection in your home can be a key component in your daily emotional health, but it doesn't have to be limited to just the one room or area. Your entire home can be a tribute to harmony and tranquility. All you have to do is change up your surroundings a bit.

Feng shui is more than just a long-standing decorating style. Many of China's ancient arts have found their way to the West and made a significant impact on modern trends. One of them is feng shui, the art and science of creating a harmonious environment. It is grounded in the Taoist belief in *chi* and its effect on spaces, especially those created and inhabited by human beings.

USE FENG SHUI PRINCIPLES IN YOUR MEDITATION

Meditation aims to create a harmonious environment, and feng shui principles can aid in that process.

- If you learn the basics and acquire the ability to create an aura of peace in your home by changing the underlying message of its layout, you'll be well on your way to creating a meditation oasis that will cover every inch of the walls, floors, and ceiling.
- It will provide a steady flow of aid to your heart and can make you feel once and for all that the home you live in is indeed your home.

"The hardest work in the world is being out of work."

—Whitney Young, Jr.

Decide if a Career-Development Professional Can Help

If you are at a loss as to what to do when your job search is failing, a career-development professional may be able to help. What do you think is holding you back from finding a job? List the main reasons and then decide if you can solve those problems on your own, or if a consultation with a career development professional might be in order.

To be licensed in most states, career counselors must have a master's degree in counseling. Many career counselors belong to the National Career Development Association. The NCDA has a state-by-state list of members on their website, *www.ncda.org.*

Career-planning help can be expensive, but you can get this service at a low cost or even for free. Look into the career services provided by your alma mater. Many colleges offer free career counseling to alumni. Also check with your local college. They may provide these services to the community. Some public libraries even offer career-planning assistance, as do some community agencies.

WEEK FORTY-NINE

"Habitat [for Humanity] gives us an opportunity which is very difficult to find: to reach out and work side by side with those who never have had a decent home—but work with them on a completely equal basis. It's not a big-shot, little-shot relationship. It's a sense of equality."

—Jimmy Carter

Support Habitat for Humanity

Habitat for Humanity brings energy-efficient, affordable housing to the homeless of the world. Their incredible work is well-known, as are their most famous supporters—former President Jimmy Carter and his wife Rosalyn. Habitat is like any other nonprofit organization. They provide for people regardless of race or religion, and the army of volunteers comes from all walks of life. You can help your community by giving money to help build houses for your neighbors.

LIFT A HAMMER FOR HABITAT

Habitat for Humanity works around the world, but they might be working right in your community.

1. Their website, *www.habitat.org,* can let you know if there's one in your area and whether or not they're in need of volunteers.
2. You get the benefits of exercise and helping people to get back on their feet.
3. Sign up online for their informative and interesting e-newsletters. It's the first step to helping someone find a place they can call home.

"Some people go to priests; others to poetry; I to my friends."

—Virginia Woolf

Surprise a Friend at Work

The nature of your own job probably makes you grateful to get some time off at lunch, but even so, that break is a great opportunity to do something nice for a friend. If you have a friend who works nearby or even in the same building, surprise him on your lunch break and take him out to eat. Don't let your friend know you're coming. The element of surprise is what will be the most rewarding aspect not only for them, but for yourself as well. We all like to feel important, and there are few better ways of doing that than to show up unannounced.

Lunch doesn't have to be anything extraordinary. You don't need to take your friend to an expensive restaurant, because the act itself is what will touch their heart. You're not even giving up your own lunch hour. You still get to have your lunch break, but you get to enjoy it with a good friend.

MAKE IT HAPPEN A.S.A.P.

Check your schedule and plan to surprise a friend at work as soon as possible. Decide where you're going to go for lunch and make reservations if needed. Alternately, surprise a friend at home with take-out pizza!

"Be who you are and say what you feel because those who mind don't matter and those who matter don't mind."

—Dr. Seuss

Determine Your Type

Close your eyes, and think about what kind of person you'd most like to be with in a romantic setting. Imagine getting physically close to this person, perhaps holding hands or getting ready to lock lips. Once you have this vision firmly in mind, you can now venture out into the meet market to find your special someone in the places where those types of people are likely to be. Just keep an open mind—and have fun with your adventure.

GET SPECIFIC

Think about who you want to be with. Free association is the best way to make this exercise work, so don't think too much about your answers to the following questions:

- What vision immediately springs to mind?
- What kind of person are you with?
- What does this person look like?
- What images do you see?
- What setting are you in?
- What are you doing in that setting?
- What is the person doing?

"I try to support groups that are about educating people about different races, different religions, different cultures and different situations so that we can break down the barriers of prejudice and bigotry."

—Loretta Sanchez

Introduce Your Child to Other Cultures

Perhaps you enjoy traveling and have already seen and experienced some of the world and have even shared your stories with your child. Take it a step further. On your next family vacation or outing, go some-place where your child can learn about a unique culture. It doesn't have to involve international travel.

For example, you could plan a trip to Pennsylvania to see the Amish country, the Four Corners in southwestern United States where the ancient Pueblo people lived, or to New York or Connecticut—the ancestral home to the Mohegan tribe of Native Americans. Your child will have amazing stories to share with his friends and classmates, and you'll have the happiness that comes from knowing that you've given your little one a gift of a lifetime.

INVITE A FOREIGN CULTURE INTO YOUR HOME

You don't need to leave home to experience another culture. You can open your heart and your home to a student from abroad.

- When you host a high school, college, or graduate-level student in your home for an academic year, you get more than a just a houseguest. You will be gaining priceless exposure to another culture and family through the program.
- Welcoming host families that can provide a safe and support-ive environment for a foreign student are vital for international exchange programs to work. The happy memories during your host year will likely last forever.

"You can discover more about a person in an hour
of play than in a year of conversation."

—Plato

Swim in Oil

You and your lover can relax together and have some fun using warmed olive oil. To play, set the scene and the mood by lighting candles and making sure the room is warm. On the floor, throw some towels or an old rug that you don't mind staining. Also prepare extra towels and something to drink and nibble on, and 2 to 3 cups of olive oil, gently heated in a saucepan. You can add a few drops of a pure essential oil for fragrance, if you wish.

When you are ready to begin, both of you should shower. If you have long hair, you may want to pull it back. Put on your favorite erotic music. As you are sitting on the towels, begin to apply olive oil generously to each other's bodies. Go ahead and really get into it. You're going to get very oily!

TAKE PLEASURE IN TOUCH

As you oil each other, you'll notice an incredible freedom to slip and slide all over each other's bodies. Enjoy this sensual experience to the maximum. You'll feel as though you've never had so much of your body touched and stimulated at one time. Be playful and enjoy yourself to the fullest. If you want to move on to making love, you need to clean off the oil first; salad oil may not be your lubricant of choice.

*"Every child is an artist. The problem is how to
remain an artist once we grow up."*

—Pablo Picasso

Maintain a Child's Innocence

We would all like to maintain that sense of wonder and innocence from our childhood days. It would be a warm gift, indeed, if we could look at the world as they do. If we could subscribe to optimism and fascination that comes so effortlessly to them but becomes more and more of a struggle to realize and hold onto as we get older. We lose so much of that innocence as we age and acquire more experience and insight into the world.

Unfortunately you can't get it back, but you can do the next best thing. If you don't have children yourself, find a niece, nephew, or the child of a close friend and ask them simply if they believe in God. Ask then to explain their answer, and listen intently to what they tell you. A child has no reason to lie about such things. Unlike adults, they have nothing to gain or lose by being honest, and that honesty is still second nature to them at that stage of their lives. You may not get that innocence back for yourself, but hearing it from an unfiltered, uncontaminated source like a child can put you closer to it than when they started. Look within their answers to find your own.

ADOPT THE FAITH OF A CHILD

We can learn a lot from children. Examine these childlike qualities and try to incorporate some of them into your own life.

- They live in the present.
- They have no concerns about money, productivity, or being cool.
- There are few limits to their imagination.
- They play and lose themselves in play.
- They create with abandon.
- They are endlessly curious, and ask questions . . . without end.

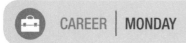
"No man was ever so much deceived by another as by himself."

—Fulke Greville

Take an Inventory

If you are in the process of choosing a career, a self-assessment is in order. Factors such as interests and values help determine which careers you will find most satisfying and in which you will be the most successful.

An online search for "interest inventory" and "value inventory" will present you with some of the options available for a small fee or free of charge. When involved in the self-assessment process, many people elect to work with a career counselor. Although it has been said that you are what you do, think about this phrase reversed: You do what you are. Why don't you use your interests and values to help you find the job of your dreams? Take a self-assessment test today!

UNDERSTANDING INVENTORIES

Interest inventories let you home in on your interests by presenting you with a series of statements and then asking you whether you agree or disagree with each one. The premise of interest inventories is that people with similar interests will be successful in the same type of work. Here are some statements you might find on an interest inventory:

- I enjoy playing golf.
- One of my favorite activities is reading.
- I would rather participate in sports than watch sports.
- I would rather watch sports than participate in sports.

A test that focuses on your values will consider the importance to you of different values. Here are some questions you might find on a values inventory:

- Do you enjoy making a difference in people's lives?
- Is having a prestigious job important to you?
- Do you need to have a lot of leisure time to be happy?

WEEK FIFTY

"The first duty of love is to listen."

—Paul Tillich

Show and Expect Respect

The best way to teach respect is to show respect. During your child's early years, you may be the only teacher he has. If your child knows that you expect respect, he will rise to meet your expectations. Try to provide consistent positive reinforcement for respectful actions and resist the temptation to reinforce negative behaviors.

TEACH YOUR CHILDREN RESPECT

Children who are taught respect at home are more likely to show respect toward others outside of the home.

1. Explain to them why families and societies need rules and authority figures to follow, and enforce those rules.
2. Help them understand how respect is earned.
3. Demonstrate for them how to show respect through listening attentively, valuing others' opinions and ideas, and showing consideration to all.
4. Explain how certain actions, such as pressuring someone to do something they don't want to do, are disrespectful.
5. Teach your children that when you are respectful toward others, the world is a happier, nicer place for everyone. Let them know that when they are respectful, it makes you happy.
6. Watch a television show or movie with your child. When a character displays a lack of respect, engage your child in a discussion. Talk about the behaviors you have just witnessed, paying particular attention to the feelings that may result from a lack of respect.

"In helping others, we shall help ourselves, for whatever good we give out completes the circle and comes back to us."

—Flora Edwards

Support Your Friend's New Business

Starting a new business is never easy. If it happens to be a friend, then you'll likely be exposed to all of those things firsthand. You'll be aware of her struggles and concerns. The first reaction will be to offer a kind word or an anecdote to encourage her. It might be easier than you think to do even more than that. Take into consideration what her business might be and try to think about what they might need in the way of some help. It could be posting a link to their business on Facebook, spreading the word to your other friends, or even helping them balance their books, picking up supplies, or giving them feedback on their product.

HELP YOUR FRIEND

Helping out with the most simple, mundane tasks could make a world of difference if she feels overwhelmed and could do with even the slightest bit of help.

1. It doesn't have to become your second job. Your friend is not going to ask for the world, and you don't have to give it.
2. Anything you have to offer will take off some of the pressure and remind them that they have a support system for anything they might want to do.

"God is closest to those with broken hearts."

—Jewish saying

Get Through the Breakup Blues

When you're trying to find ways to get through a lonely night after a breakup, *never* just lie in bed in the dark and contemplate your situation. Here are some quick-fix ideas to get you through a horrible night, especially if it's romance-related

- Write down your feelings in your dating journal. You'll find that the process is habit-forming, especially when you are feeling down. Think of it this way: Your next entry is guaranteed to be a happier one.
- Wash your hair. It's a cleansing experience, literally and figuratively. Don't like showers? Tubs are another relaxing option. Light some candles. Sit, soak, relax! Push out sad thoughts by thinking of things you love.
- Work it out. If you've got equipment or tapes at home, get moving, no matter how late it is. Exercise produces a chemical reaction in your body that elevates your mood. Or just move your body to whatever music moves you.
- The surf is always up online. Wander through cyberspace surfing for outrageous sites that you can forward to your friends in the morning. Even better, visit some relationship advice sites and resources for singles.

THINK OF SOME LONG-TERM STRATEGIES

Try these pick-me-ups and strategies to feel more positive over the long term.

- Start wearing cheerful, bright colors to lift your mood.
- Sign up to be a volunteer for a worthy cause.
- Reconnect with people or take up favorite hobbies.
- Need tangible proof that good things can happen? Plant some seeds and wait for new growth—in the flower pot and in you.

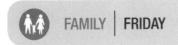
"Buying something on sale is a very special feeling. In fact, the less I pay for something, the more it is worth to me. I have a dress that I paid so little for that I am afraid to wear it. I could spill something on it, and then how would I replace it for that amount of money?"

—Rita Rudner

Hunt for Bargains

Don't keep all the shopping fun to yourself. Invite your family to come along. While you are focusing on that one special bargain, the real treasure will be the time that you carve from your busy schedules to do something fun together. You can also be doing some good! Whenever possible, consider recycled items from consignment shops, church charity thrift stores, and city flea markets.

MAKE IT AN ADVENTURE

Turn your search for a bargain into a treasure-hunting adventure with your family.

1. Explore the yards of the families participating in a block sale.
2. Dig through the contents of cardboard boxes at a garage sale.
3. Paw over tables at a church white elephant sale.
4. Attend a farm auction.
5. Clip coupons and head to the nearest department store to locate that special discounted item.
6. Visit eBay and other Internet sites for the item you seek.
7. Check out *www.freecycle.org*. Freecycle is an organization that focuses on reducing waste that goes into landfills and instead provides the means for people to get recycled products from within their own communities. Membership is free.

*"Whoso neglects learning in his youth, loses
the past and is dead for the future."*

—Euripides

Take an Educational Field Trip

Many colleges, universities, museums, and independent organizations sponsor educational trips with scholars and others who are experts in a particular academic discipline. For example, you could accompany an ornithologist on a trip to the Amazonian rain forest to study birds, a Lewis and Clark expert while you're on a white-water–rafting trip on the Colorado River, or a working archeologist on a dig of ancient ruins in Turkey. Traveling with educational experts and researchers like archeologists, historians, and others working in a wide variety of disciplines can be an enjoyable way to experience and learn about a culture or subject firsthand.

Travel tours offered by Smithsonian Journeys, for example, features experts leading tours to many world heritage sites. A program known as Road Scholar (*www.roadscholar.org*), formerly the nonprofit Elderhostel program, offers 8,000 programs in all fifty U.S. states and more than ninety countries. One of the notable aspects of these programs is the emphasis on lifelong learning. And remember, you can always make the trip with your best friend and lover.

VISUALIZE YOUR DESTINATION

Decide what you would like to learn from a particular destination. Make a poster of that place by gluing a map of it to poster board. Attach pictures of that location that you've clipped from magazines. Add printed recipes and other items that will intensify your desire to make such a trip happen.

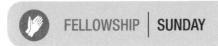

"We are not human beings having a spiritual experience; but spiritual beings having a human experience."

—Pierre Teilhard de Chardin

Try Reiki

Hawayo Takata, who introduced Reiki to the West in the 1970s, explained that the name Reiki comes from two Japanese terms: *rei* is the spiritual wisdom intuitive to each human being known by the religious as God, and *ki*, or life energy, is the nonphysical energy that gives all living things life.

Reiki is another tool to manage body stress. Reiki, or energy healing, is a Japanese healing practice that regulates the body's natural energy flow. The Reiki practitioner will literally lay hands on or above a client's body and regulate his energy flow, smoothing out any blockages and clearing out any negative energy.

UNBLOCK YOUR ENERGY

Reiki is based on the idea that energy flows through all living things, including the human body. A person who is stressed or becomes ill literally has no energy or poor circulation of energy in a particular region or regions of the body.

1. Reiki is designed to free up any energy blockages by stimulating the area of the body where the energy blockage occurs, allowing energy to flow freely once again.

2. Many people experience a sense of peace and hopefulness after a Reiki session. Reiki is a spiritual practice that encourages the participant to tap into his life force energy and seek healing by nurturing the self. Individuals interested in meditation or chakra healing naturally gravitate toward Reiki. If you have chronic pain in a particular part of the body or feel a strong desire to release tension in your body but aren't quite sure how to do it, Reiki may be for you. Be sure to find a Reiki master or healer who is licensed or certified by a credible organization, such as the Reiki License Commission.

"Gluttony is an emotional escape, a sign something is eating us."

—Peter De Vries

Employ Boredom Busters at Work

You could be a major cause of your boredom at work, according to Harvard Business Review blogger Susan Cramm. If you run on autopilot, ignore your energy needs, and just slide by at work, then you are making your life boring! To bust boredom at work, Cramm recommends exercise, a healthy diet, performing daily tasks in new ways, professional goals to achieve, a hobby in your private life, and getting enough sleep.

AVOID EMOTIONAL EATING AT WORK

Work can be boring, as everyone who works can tell you. Whether you stand up for hours at a factory, type documents for hours on a computer, or make tacos all day at a fast food joint, work's monotony can get to you fast. Take comfort, though, that you're not alone.

1. A cup of coffee, chocolate from the vending machine, or other uppers such as a cigarette may be how you manage stress. If you find that you crave unhealthy foods after a stressful event, such as a conversation with an upset boss, you may practice emotional eating at work. Emotional eating is unconsciously choosing a target food to soothe unpleasant feelings of fear, sadness, or unworthiness.

2. Spend some time observing your eating habits at work. Do you eat the healthy foods you would eat at home? What food choices do you make at work that are unhealthy, and why do you choose those foods when you do? Practice substituting other stress-busting tools to manage your stress, such as a walk around the office or a glass of ice water, instead of the bag of potato chips. Your body, and waistline, will thank you.

WEEK FIFTY-ONE

"For those who are disabled, bike riding goes beyond
mere transportation, or therapeutic recreation
for those whose health is often fragile."

—Project Mobility

Support Project Mobility

Bringing joy and life into the days of people less physically fortunate has a lifetime worth of value. Obviously, the people who are unable to help themselves are the people who need our help the most. Project Mobility provides that for anyone who wants to leave a lasting mark on their community. One act can endure for years to come, and there's no better reward than that for giving to your community. You will be blessed by seeing your generosity in action while walking down the street one day.

KNOW THAT LITTLE THINGS COUNT

It's often true that the little things can make the biggest difference in the life of a person. That's even more so for those who suffer from a wide range of serious, physical and mental disabilities.

- Sometimes that little thing can be as simple as a bicycle. Project Mobility believes this and works to bring bicycles and the social programs associated with bicycles into the lives of adults and children who suffer from everything from cerebral palsy to amputation.
- Their website, *www.projectmobility.org,* should give you all the information you need. They provide their background, examples of their brilliant work, their various programs, and ways in which you can get involved.

"Only those who have learned the power of sincere and selfless contribution experience life's deepest joy: true fulfillment."

—Anthony Robbins

Choose to Volunteer in a Community Group

The problems of America's communities are great. The planet is in trouble because collectively we have not been good stewards. The rift between the haves and the have-nots has continued to widen. Wars go on despite popular opinion against them. There are still parts of the world where warlords and thugs commit genocide, where every five seconds a child dies of hunger or a hunger-related disease, and where people are still being forced into forms of slavery.

For these and many other reasons, you and your friends might feel powerless to bring about change, but the truth is that each human being has some power.

CHANGE THE STATUS QUO

When aligned with others, a couple, a community, or a country can change the status quo.

1. Perhaps you start by focusing on ways to become the best you can be and then by volunteering to work with a community group to change your town or city for the better.
2. To shift a paradigm, it only takes one person, one good intention, and one act of generosity at a time. Just imagine what a group, a nation, or an international coalition working together could do.
3. Fight hate in your community. Help the Southern Poverty Law Center teach tolerance and seek justice for victims of hate crimes. To learn how you and your friends can become involved in the movement, go to *www.southernpovertylaw center.org.*

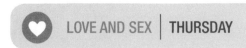

"The greatest compliment that was ever paid me was when one asked me what I thought, and attended to my answer."

—Henry David Thoreau

Check In

A good habit for couples to get into is to have scheduled meetings when they present practical and emotional issues that need to be aired and discussed. Just as a well-functioning business has regular meetings to make certain all the employees work as a team, a good relationship practices the same procedure.

First you need to schedule a regular check-in conversation. Once or twice a month works well, but if you find yourself in disharmony, perhaps once a week is necessary. Once the time is scheduled, it must be viewed as private time where your focus and attention is fully present with no distractions permitted, meaning that children are occupied or attended to and cell phones are off.

The length of time for a regular check-in should probably be forty-five to sixty minutes, no less. Most couples can handle this communication by themselves. But if the tension is too intense and the communication breaks down into rage and anger, an outside mediator may be needed.

Good communication is essential for healthy relationships. Vibrant couples regularly communicate about the agreements they've made to each other.

COMMUNICATE IN DETAIL

Within this period for communication, each of you can state feelings or ask questions while the other listens and then answers. Questions can include:

- What have you not communicated that you want to talk about?
- What haven't you been acknowledged for that you want me to have recognized?
- What's not working? What's working better?

"Worries go down better with soup than without."

—Jewish proverb

Give Chicken Soup and Lots of Love

You know how awful it is to catch the nasty cold that's been going around. So when someone in your family gets sick, consider taking the day off to care for him. When your body is suddenly laid low by an infection, there's nothing better than the warm, fuzzy feeling imparted by the kind words and loving attention of a parent or mate.

It turns out that the advice mothers and grandmothers have been dispensing for generations—actually since roughly the twelfth century—about chicken soup being good for you when you're sick with a cold is true. Research suggests that the soup may actually reduce inflammation associated with the common cold. In addition, the steam can soothe irritated throats and stuffy noses. Finally, soup is a source of fluid for an ailing body fighting infection. So give your spouse a generous helping of love in the form of a steamy bowl of chicken soup the next time allergies, a cold, or the flu takes hold.

MAKE GREAT SOUP

For really great chicken soup, drop a whole chicken (rinsed and patted dry) into a large soup pot along with enough water to cover it. Add chopped carrots, celery, and onions, salt, pepper, and a bit of chopped fresh Italian parsley, and simmer for several hours. The chicken will fall off the bone. The vegetables and chicken will produce a lovely stock and the strained soup will be both fragrant and tasty.

"A driver is a king on a vinyl bucket-seat throne, changing direction with the turn of a wheel, changing the climate with a flick of the button, changing the music with the switch of a dial."

—Andrew H. Malcolm

Test-Drive the Car You've Always Wanted

You don't have to *buy* the car; just take a trip down to the dealership to test-drive the car that you'd love to have. Maybe it's a new hybrid or a hot new roadster. It has an astronomical price tag and your budget can't accommodate that kind of strain, but don't let that stop you. As long as you show interest and are polite, the dealer won't mind.

No one really knows what the future holds. You could come into vast sums of money . . . or not. It's irrelevant, since the test drive costs nothing. And you might have the time of your life.

TAKE A TEST DRIVE IN STYLE

1. Get dressed up for your test drive. Imagine that you are the CEO of a successful business and that your world is one of affluence. For the afternoon of the test drive, imagine that you have all the money you need for that car and more.

2. If the mood strikes you, invite your mate and lavish him with attention. Tell him how positively *GQ* he looks driving that car and that you will be with him on the highways and byways of America or the autobahn in Germany whenever he feels like taking off to a romantic destination.

---

*"I love to cook comfort food. I'll make fish and vegetables
or meat and vegetables and potatoes or rice. The ritual
of it is fun for me, and the creativity of it."*

—Reese Witherspoon

Meditate on Your Everyday Rituals

Can everyday rituals be sacred? Yes, they can be filled with meaning when they are performed meditatively. We can discover why certain actions that we repeat are so meaningful. Here are some examples of ordinary rituals: You always fold your laundry in neat little bundles. When you polish a mirror, you use only one cleaner and work from top to bottom.

These revelations can be sacred because everyday acts can reflect your motives, feelings, and goals in life—in essence, everything that you are. The key to engaging this process is to employ a meditative attitude in all those little rituals. This attitude could reveal the following: You fondly remember a grandparent who polished a mirror the same way. You miss that person a great deal.

MAKE YOUR RITUALS MORE MEANINGFUL

- You can take this attentiveness another step and make these little rituals more meaningful. If you now have plenty of living space, you could make a ritual out of decorating and appreciating it.
- You could honor a beloved relative by creating a home gallery of family pictures for a weekly ritual of remembrance.
- You could make a ritual out of grooming with all your attention focused on yourself.

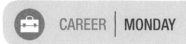
*"I have a lot of stuff I want to talk about and offer up. It
would be odd not to have ideas about something."*

—Ralph Fiennes

Think about Your Attributes

While it's very important to figure out what a job or industry can offer you, it's also important to spend some time thinking about what you can offer an employer. The first thing you bring is the set of skills needed to do the job. But there are other attributes you have that do not necessarily fall under the "skill" category. For example, will your outgoing personality charm clients? Will your ambition and ceaseless energy drive you to work long hours? Compile a comprehensive list of what you have to offer an employer. You'll be more confident in your abilities and more prepared to present them when the time comes.

REASSESS YOUR SKILLS

Throughout your job search and even during employment, periodically reassess the skills you have. Are your skills up to date? Are you willing to get some additional training if they are not up to date?

1. For example, suppose you enjoy writing. If you'd like to become a journalist, there are probably some skills you did not pick up from your high school English courses, such as interviewing and research skills.

2. You might consider taking an adult education course in your local community, or taking some classes at a local college that you could put toward a degree if you wanted to.

3. On a smaller scale, you could speak to the editors of some local newspapers and ask them some questions about what they look for in a journalist. All of these avenues will make you more knowledgeable about the skills you need to enter the field.

"The care of human life and happiness and not their destruction is the first and only legitimate object of good government."

—Thomas Jefferson

Write Your Congressperson

Sometimes we just need to get things off our chest. When we look around the community we live in, we can always find at least one thing we would like to see changed or improved upon. Nothing is perfect. In some cases, the only way we can create the road to change is to take the first step.

Writing to your congressperson has remained a popular way of being involved in local government for decades. The reason for that is because it can, in fact, make a difference. A congressperson is able to focus on the little things that higher levels of government may not be able to see. The very nature of their job is to serve the needs of a small group of people. They read the letters from people like you, and quite often, they respond in some way. Sometimes they even use a letter as the starting point to accomplish something in the community.

PUT IT IN WRITING

The first step is up to you. You'll feel better by letting your voice be heard, and you'll be giving local government the opportunity to do their job.

1. Write the rough draft of your letter.
2. Read it over several times, paying close attention to grammar and punctuation, and then read it again, this time out loud.
3. If you want another opinion, ask your significant other or a good friend for their opinion.
4. Make a final copy and send it.

"Wisdom is knowing what to do next; virtue is doing it."

—David Starr Jordan

Eliminate Unhealthy Behaviors

You may think that your behavior is an innate trait that can't be changed or altered. This is an incorrect assumption. Behavior—all behavior—is learned. You learned your behavior through the environment in which you were raised and the environment in which you continue to live and work. Behavior is changeable, but it takes a great deal of time and effort to change an ingrained behavior. Ask a friend to help. Someone who can hold you accountable is an important ally on the journey to better habits.

TAKE THE RIGHT STEPS

If you are interested in changing some of your negative or unhealthy behaviors, keep the following tips in mind:

- Make a list of the behaviors you wish to change.
- Talk to a close friend about these behaviors.
- Think about why the behavior is unhealthy.
- Make a list of how the behavior can (or has) cost you.
- Make a list of how the behavior has affected others in your life.
- Make a list of alternative behaviors or actions.
- Use one of the alternative behaviors on a daily basis.

"Sex on television can't hurt you unless you fall off."

—Unknown

Change Locations

Having sex on the bed is fun, but don't be afraid to switch it up from time to time. Your house offers plenty of great places to have sex, and changing locations, even within your own home, can add some spice to your sex life. You'll find it hard to repress a smile the next time you're hosting a dinner party and you know what you and your significant other did right where the yams are resting. A few tried-and-true spots to get you started include the kitchen table, the counter, the laundry room (with one person on top of the washer during the spin cycle), the couch (either on it or over the back of it), the floor, and the shower.

CONSIDER GOING PUBLIC

If you've got the guts and you're ready for the glory, consider having public or semi-public sex. The adrenaline rush you'll get from potentially getting caught will add to the passion. Consider having sex in the woods, in the ocean or a lake, at a local park underneath a blanket, in the back of a taxi cab (tip heavily if you do), or in the bathroom of a bar or restaurant. Let your imagination be your guide.

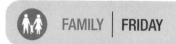

"Drag your thoughts away from your troubles . . . by the ears, by the heels, or any other way, so you can manage it."

—Mark Twain

Bust Stress

When you are fearful or stressed out, your children are, too, but the stress and fear can be magnified because of their vivid imaginations. In addition, children often attribute your suffering to something they did, so they are bearing the burden of guilt for what you are feeling.

If you have a blended family, join a blended family support group and talk about the kinds of stresses your family is going through. Discuss how to help children heal their broken hearts, which can be the result of factors such as the breakup of your or your spouse's previous marriage or the death of a previous spouse, not feeling a sense of belonging in the new family, loss or lack of trust in your new partner, nonbonding with new step-siblings, and the like.

OVERCOME FEARS AND WORRY

Some of the ways you and your spouse can help children overcome fears, worry, and stress include the following:

- Take a break from the negative news—turn off or limit time spent listening to the news from television, radio, and other electronic devices.
- Spend time with your children in nature.
- Meditate and de-stress with your children.
- Pray together to the higher power that your family believes in.
- Encourage your children to talk with you and your spouse about their concerns and fears.
- Read joke books (laughter is a great de-stressor).

"I remember as a child reading or hearing the words 'The Great Divide' and being stunned by the glorious sound, a proper sound for the granite backbone of a continent."

—John Steinbeck

Visit a National Park

Head out to visit a national park and expand your knowledge of American history. Finding a park won't be a problem, since there are literally hundreds of options in America's national park system. Each one has a unique history. For example, if you live in California, you might take a boat out to Alcatraz Island, located in the middle of the San Francisco Bay. Alcatraz was chosen as the site of the first lighthouse as well as the first U.S. fort on the West Coast. On the other side of the country, you could choose to walk a piece of the Appalachian Trail, a scenic footpath that stretches 2,175 miles from Maine to Georgia, crossing through fourteen states. Or, you might visit any number of the national historic sites or battlefields in Pennsylvania. For a really wild adventure, venture down to the Everglades National Park in south Florida to see various endangered species of wildlife indigenous to that subtropical wilderness. For a complete list of America's national parks, go to *www.nationalparks.org*.

VISIT THE NATIONAL PARKS ON TELEVISION

Grab the popcorn and curl up on the couch to watch *The National Parks: America's Best Idea*, a six-segment documentary by Ken Burns. The DVD, book, and CD are all available at *www.shoppbs.org*.

"One way to keep momentum going is to have constantly greater goals."

—Michael Korda

Create Your Own Motivational Poster

We see them everywhere, and if you know your way around the Internet, then you've probably seen a few of the parodies, too. Most of us just ignore them. Motivational posters mean well, and they can provide a smile or glimmer of encouragement to someone, but for most of us, these posters get a passing glance and nothing more.

That shouldn't make you feel guilty. You're not going to be motivated by something streamlined and meant for a mass audience, and you're certainly not going to be stirred to continue your spiritual journey with a positive attitude. To make that happen, you must find something that speaks to you in a way those everyday motivational posters are supposed to.

MAKE A MOTIVATIONAL POSTER

You might just have to do the job yourself. Find your favorite motivational quotation, seek out a photo or take one of your own displaying the most inspiring sight you've ever seen. The quotation and photo don't necessarily have to be related to one another, but they should create an overall harmony when combined and displayed. It will be satisfying to look at that poster and know that it came from you. The best motivation always does.

CONCLUSION

By now, you've probably realized that there is no scientific formula for happiness. There are no exact quantities or precise measurements. But there is a lifestyle you can adopt, one that will nurture and develop a belief that happiness is something that comes from within. By taking a 365-day journey with this book as your guide, you have discovered that lasting happiness comes as the result of living a thoughtful life full of purpose and meaning. Most importantly, you have realized that happiness is the result of giving consideration to all areas of your life and not focusing obsessively on the one thing you believe is the key to your personal bliss.

For an entire year, *Happiest You Ever* has shown you that some of your most pleasurable moments can result from putting the happiness of others above your own and that happiness can come from deceptively simple sources and at the most unexpected moments. You've learned that it's not about beaming like the Cheshire cat all the time or eliminating negativity and sorrow. *Happiest You Ever* has helped you redefine your concept of happiness. Real happiness stays with you, it sustains you, and it has depth. It gives you an enduring sense of contentment and satisfaction. After your journey with *Happiest You Ever,* you know that you don't need to become a different person to be happy, but you do need to look at the world and your life in a very different way.

The truly happy people—and after reading this book, we hope you are among them—will tell you that their joy doesn't come from anything they achieve or obtain. The accomplishments and possessions are great, but real happiness comes from being involved in life, being a part of the world around you, and having the life skills to process both the good and bad things that come your way.

INDEX

Spiritual space, 244. *See also* Sacred space
Spiritual strength, 175, 287
Spiritual symbols, 126
Spiritual teachers, 105
Spiritual walk, 14
Sports, 72, 93, 171
Stress, reducing, 97, 138, 229, 257–58, 312, 350, 362
Studying, 87, 132

Tai chi, 76
Tea-making, 90
Tea parties, 262
Thankfulness, 196
Traditions, creating, 145, 212
Trips/travel, 6, 19, 27, 38, 69, 82, 195, 202, 215, 349
Trust, restoring, 238
Truth, telling, 207, 211

Unbirthday celebrations, 185
Unhealthy behaviors, 360
Unhealthy relationships, 74, 157, 235
Unplugging electronics, 20, 222
Unwinding, 258

Vacation jar, 19
Vacation map, 27
Vacation plans, 215. *See also* Trips/travel
Value system, 28, 84, 287, 327
Visualization, 64, 141, 216, 349. *See also* Meditation
Volunteering, 44, 51, 79, 80, 86, 107, 128, 323, 353